CW00421282

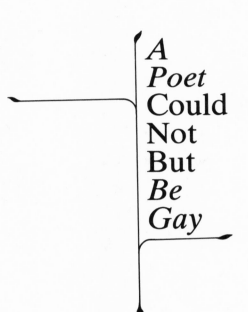

A
Poet
Could
Not
But
Be
Gay

BY THE SAME AUTHOR
Gaijin on the Ginza

James Kirkup

A
Poet
Could
Not
But
Be
Gay

SOME
LEGENDS
OF MY
LOST
YOUTH

PETER OWEN
London and Chester Springs PA

PETER OWEN PUBLISHERS
73 Kenway Road London SW5 0RE

Peter Owen books are distributed in the USA by
Dufour Editions Inc. Chester Springs PA 19425–0449

First published in Great Britain 1991
© James Kirkup 1991

All Rights Reserved.
No part of this publication
may be reproduced in any form or by
any means without the written
permission of the publishers

British Library Cataloguing in Publication Data
Kirkup, James, *1918–*
A poet could not but be gay: some legends of my lost
youth.
1. English Poetry
I. Title
821.912
ISBN 0–7206–0823–6

Printed in Great Britain by Billings of Worcester

In memory of
Nancy and Joe

— • —

A poet could not but be gay,
In such a jocund company . . .

William Wordsworth, 'THE DAFFODILS'

— • —

He who is already a legend need not fear death.

James Kirkup, DENGONBAN MESSAGES – ONE-LINE POEMS

— • —

N'importe où, n'importe qui, n'importe comment . . .

Arthur Rimbaud

Foreword

This book follows in exact chronological sequence my previous volume, *I, of All People: An Autobiography of Youth*. It takes me from Britain to Europe – to France, Spain and the countries of Scandinavia mainly – and stops when I am about to take a major step forward in my life, and go to Japan for the first time.

Because of that Japanese future, and because I have many friends in Japan, I should like to say something about how the Japanese made some great errors of judgement in reading my former book. Most Japanese have a certain sense of humour, though it is quite different from the British. But they were unable to see that some of the things I wrote were written tongue in cheek. To my surprise, they accepted every word I wrote as gospel truth, and overlooked my little warnings at the beginning about the *farceur* in my nature. To be taken so deadly seriously was both a shock and a disappointment. Only my translator, Akiko Takemoto, and one or two others understood the leg-pulls about my 'evil eye' and my immoral conduct, if 'immoral' such patent enjoyment of the good things in life can be called. As for my reference to 'murdering' my professor, it's a common day-dream . . .

In the present volume, therefore, I have tried to appear a little more serious and less 'irresponsible', and to present my peculiar personality more straightforwardly. I hope that not only my Japanese readers of both the original and the translation but all my faithful Western fans will read this book in a different light.

We are all mythomaniacs. Imagination is what distinguishes us from the dead. I remain a *farceur* – it makes life so much more interesting.

J.K.

Contents

SOME DAY MY PRINCE WILL COME   13

BREAKING WITH THE PAST   31

THOSE SPANISH EYES   51

SWEDISH EXERCISES   76

BACKFLASH – INTERLUDE:
'Someone to Watch Over Me'   115

IN A POLICE STATE   143

A FATAL ENCOUNTER   154

TURNING IT ALL TO POETRY   177

WELCOME TO BATH   195

MY DISTRACTED WINTER   201

WINTER'S END   216

AFTERWORD   237

EPILOGUE   239

SOME DAY MY PRINCE WILL COME

The question of freedom was governed by the law of diminishing returns, he said to himself, walking faster. If you went beyond a certain point of intensity in your consciousness of desiring it, you furnished yourself with a guarantee of not achieving it. In any case, he thought, what is freedom in the last analysis, other than the state of being totally, instead of only partially, subject to the tyranny of chance?

Paul Bowles, 'TAPIAMA'

I was beginning to feel that the police must be after me. Was this sheer paranoia, so widespread among gays in the fifties? If so, was it justified paranoia? Was there something wrong with me? Was my behaviour bad, or simply not natural? I was not conscious of behaving wrongly, though I did not behave as most people I knew did, or imagined they did. Or was I simply victim of an over-indulgent super-ego?

Now, in the comparative safety of more tolerant lands, I realize that I had no idea of the effect my appearance and actions were having on other people, least of all on my parents, who suffered my eccentricities in silence, with what I now see as loving tolerance.

It was the way the British police looked at me in the streets and in the pubs that made me feel I was under secret supervision, constant investigation. It was the Cold War made personal in all its Kafkaesque cruelty. Like Gérard de Nerval, whose sonnets I was translating, I kept thinking: 'I have committed some fault, but could not discover what it was.' Was I, too, like Nerval, perhaps going slightly mad, or had I been mad all along?

This was a question I was never able to answer. None of my few friends ever hinted that I was doing wrong; or if I *was* doing wrong, they concealed it from me. It was only the occasional kindness of strangers that sometimes allowed me to feel briefly like a member of the human race. But often such total strangers had the power to make me unhappy, like that very macho bus-conductor on the No. 6 Northern Bus from South Shields to Newcastle, who used to laugh at me openly with his driver and with the passengers, so that I kept my head buried in Proust or Walser or Rilke until that never-ending 'Express' journey brought me to my stop at the 'Chi'. As the bus drove away towards the town centre, I could hear a roar of laughter from the conductor's latest Geordie witticism. No wonder I wanted to get away as soon as possible from that damnable 'Catherine Cookson Country'.

Could it be that my hair was too long for those ultra-sensible times, for what is now Thatcher's miserably puritanical Thingland? Was my make-up less than discreet, my choice of clothes too weird? Was I regarded as a total freak? I began to suspect that I was not human. Not inhuman – just not like other human beings. That was the conclusion to which one of my American lovers came towards the end of our affair, some years later: 'Jim, you're just not human.' I felt relieved to know the truth at last. I'd always sensed that I was a visitor from outer space. In Britain, at least.

On the other hand I was supremely, sublimely unselfconscious. No, that's not quite true: I was *too* self-conscious about not giving a damn what anybody thought or said about me. And in the end, nothing else mattered but my writing, my art, my poetry. They could not take that away from me, whatever happened. My sexual passions were nothing but a sideline, to be got out of the way as often as was necessary to allow me to get on with my real purpose in life, the writing of poetry.

I knew that if I were arrested during one of my many cruising expeditions, I would still be a poet. Even in prison I would create my poems in my head first, as I always do, before entrusting them to the severely rationed lavatory paper, which I would somehow conceal upon my person until I was let out. The one thing that frightened me about this prospect of prison eternally haunting my days and nights was the thought that I should not have access to the books I wanted. I was pretty sure there would be no modern Italian, French and German authors in a British prison library, and the thought of having only English crime fiction and romantic best-sellers to read gave me cold sweats. I had never been able to feel much enthusiasm for English literature.

So I would have to write my own books, for my own pleasure. I could write my secret memoirs of prison experiences and sell them to the *News of the World* for an undisclosed sum that would keep me in comfort for the rest of my Taurean existence.

*   *   *

The police *were* after me. I knew that if I stayed any longer in England they would get me. There were the bobbies on the beat in Chippenham and Bath, and in Corsham itself there was a plain-clothes officer living in the main street just a few doors away from where my parents and I were staying in the Weavers' Cottages, Flemish Buildings. I could not trust some of my colleagues at the Bath Academy of Art, who, though supposedly intellectuals and artists, were more cruel than the villagers, and of as evil a tongue. I knew they wanted me out, and in my place George Barker, a poet who, as Joe Ackerley had reported to me, had announced that 'Kirkup is not a poet', as if that was that. Joe and I used to laugh cheerlessly over the many such attacks made upon me by various writers. He tried to cheer me up by telling me that he had discussed my work with Siegfried Sassoon, who had pronounced me unmistakably a poet.

I could feel an indefinable tension building up all around me. My parents were full of unspoken thoughts, and I realize now that they must have been suffering acutely from my behaviour and my reputation. It was time to get out: I could stay no longer in such an unfriendly and frightening atmosphere. Joe Ackerley agreed that it would perhaps be better for me to leave the country for a while, and offered to write a glowing letter of recommendation when I applied for posts abroad. I think he also had a private chat with my mother and father. I could sense it in their resigned, less distraught silences. Joe left for London after we had attended a student party at Corsham Court, at which a lot of ridiculous parlour games were played, in which Joe joined rather wearily but with great good humour. I was proud of him and happy that he was my friend. But none of the students knew who he was. They seemed to think he was just another pick-up.

The students were a mixed bunch. Some of them were undoubtedly gifted potters, sculptors and painters, but the majority were simply anxious to obtain a teaching diploma in arts and crafts. During my last two years at Corsham, I was saddled with all the duds, those who supposedly would never be much good at anything. They knew they had been singled out for special treatment, and were resentful and morose. I had to try to bring them out of their shells, to encourage them to write and act. It was like working with heavy clay that refused to respond. With the help of Riette Sturge-Moore, who created wonderful costumes and décor, often from the most unpromising materials, we put on some simple dramatic performances: Dylan Thomas's *A Child's Christmas in Wales*, a monologue accompanied by students singing carols; bits of *Under Milk Wood*, anthologies of poems and my short play for children about the Virgin and the Unicorn, in which I am ashamed to say I acted in a dazzlingly camp manner, clad in white tights, and – something I had always wanted – gold sequins on my upper eyelids which created, I was told, an unexpectedly sinister effect 'like the flashes of the evil eye'.

There was a visit by inspectors from the Ministry of Education, which interested me so little that I failed to be present to 'welcome' their arrival in Corsham – it was after all my day off, and I had other things to do. But Rosemary Ellis came dashing round to our cottage at 9 a.m. begging me to put in an appearance. Later in the week I mounted a student performance of poems in which each student made his own costume and with my help produced his poem in a way that fitted into the general production concept, which was anyhow encouragingly vague. Apparently the inspectors were impressed, or at least satisfied. I was amused to see that the hands of one of them was shaking as he ventured to ask me questions about my work and 'how I got on with the students' – perhaps hinting that I got on too well with them. That I should have anything more than an educator's platonic interest in those sometimes supremely unattractive and uninteresting students was something so far from my thoughts and desires that I could not help smiling at such naïvety on the part of a supposedly qualified examiner of art-school teachers. But somehow I managed to play the part required of me in this ordeal. That is the advantage of possessing a multiple personality: it makes one an actor. There is no intent to deceive, and even my insincerity is sincere. Like a good actor, I want to entertain and please whatever audience I may gather. Yet I often take a perverse delight in doing or saying the unexpected when I am apparently well set in the part assigned me at the moment. At Corsham I would give weekly lectures on poetry and on any subject that entered my head five minutes before I faced the assembled Academy, and these 'lectures' – so completely unstuffy I can hardly call them that – mixed serious ideas and mugging, divine poetry and music-hall jokes, all performed in a state of joy and terror, exhilaration and apprehension. I cannot understand how I was able to do this week after week: I must have been possessed or inspired, or just desperate. I remember that before one of these performances I was sitting in the library trying to drum up a little courage for the ordeal, when one of the students, leaning out of a window, called to someone below: 'Are you coming to James's lecture?' And the devastating shouted reply, heard by everyone in the library: 'Not on your fucking life.' The student then closed the window with a smug grin on her face and the others buried their gleeful faces in library books. I walked to the lecture-room in a despondent state, but as soon as I began talking I revived and began to sparkle, and gave one of my best impromptus.

Not all the students were insolent or resentful or unfriendly. There was a small group that used to come and serenade me with hymns or folk-songs outside my window in Flemish Buildings. One New Year's Eve – I had long since given up the custom of seeing in what seemed to me another disastrous year – my parents and I were wakened by students singing carols on the pavement cobbles below our bedroom windows. My father was pleased, for he got up and came to my room, asking me to let them in. But I'd had enough of students, good or bad. I kept my door resolutely closed and all the lights off. My mother, who always liked to celebrate New Year's Eve with a family gathering, broke down and wept. Her tears were caused as much by the students' beautiful singing as by my own perversity and growing hatred of human society.

I knew I was on my usual precarious tightrope, but during my final year at Corsham in 1956 the rope seemed to be fraying and swinging dizzily under my dancing feet, and the drop beneath had grown to the dimensions of the Grand Canyon.

Yet I did nothing to relieve this state of continual neurotic suspense. I felt a morbid compulsion to screw my tensions to the limit, exploiting in order to do so every possible aspect of a personality whose masks were uncountable: masochist, poet, fool, voluptuary, sex maniac, lecturer, lover, son, prima donna, translator, village idiot, hustler, ballerina, Zen adept, music freak, man-hater, woman-lover, shy romantic, caustic cynic, clown, outrageous exhibitionist, shrinking violet, degenerate law-breaker, decadent social outcast, passionate man-lover, party poof, fanatical solitary, religious mystic, devil-worshipper . . . the list was endless. Yet somehow I was able to keep all these divergent destinies moving lightly and effortlessly with a juggler's art, perfecting my various voices with the sinister craft of a ventriloquist. At times, the sheer exuberance of these feats gave me an unholy joy, and I spent day after day in a state of blissful grace and poetic ecstasy – in the world yet not of it. On one of my sexual flings in London, I remember meeting Jon Silkin toting his little magazine, *Stand*, round the Charing Cross Road book-stores. How I admired his tenacity and pragmatism! We chatted for a few moments. 'You're so *complex*, James,' he told me. Despite my multiple lives, I was surprised and even shocked by this statement, for I had always regarded myself as the soul of simplicity and candour, as uncomplicated as a daisy. Yet I was treading a sagging wire across an unfathomable abyss of contradictions and uncertainties.

In the calm before the storm I felt sure was approaching, I clowned and misbehaved with reckless abandon. At the students' fancy-dress party I cobbled up a costume composed of the white tights I had worn as the Sun in my '*Virgin and the Unicorn*' and some paper streamers attached somehow to my torso. From the village shop I bought a dead-white *papier-mâché* pierrot's mask I saw at the last moment lying in front of the window, looking up at me imploringly. On my head I stuck a baby's rattle by way of a cockscomb. When the painter William Scott saw me, he smiled his canny Scots smile and said: 'James, that's so ageless, so classic.' He was a fine painter, and I think he was attracted by the complex simplicity and the almost nude whiteness of the pierrot mask. He was one of the few Corsham artists who defended me, and his death in 1989, after a long and courageous fight against Alzheimer's disease, was so sad. I attended the party with one of my 'dud' students, a shy, introverted girl, Veronica whose heavenly beauty always seemed to me unearthly. For some reason she had fallen in love with me, though I was twice her age. Mainly because she was persecuted by the other teachers and neglected by the other, coarser students, I took her under my wing. I was not in love with her, but I understood her and wanted to help her. She decided to become a nun, but this plan came to nothing; I believe the convent she had applied to refused to consider her vocation. After we left Corsham, we continued to see each other from time to time, and kept up a correspondence, but she developed some kind of mental disorder, something very similar to my own confusions and illusions, and we gradually grew apart. But I have never forgotten her sweetness and gentleness, and the purity that seemed to radiate from deep within her exquisite body and shone from her divine face. I always fall for anyone unpopular, but such a one rarely falls for me.

I was obsessed by public lavatories – 'cottages' or 'tea-rooms' in the gay argot that was so very far from gay. I have wasted half my life standing about in dim-lit, stinking urinals, waiting for the saviour, for the long-longed-for, impossible friend, the *ami amant*. In the old *pissoirs* of Paris, now alas forever swept away by the musical *sanisettes* (one franc a go for what is often *un mauvais quart d'heure*), we used to go by the attractive nickname of *éphémères*, a sobriquet from the nineties. In today's much more utilitarian Paris, we are known with insulting brevity as *pédés*. But the late gay novelist Conrad Detrez coined a witty term for those who stand for hours in the Gare du Nord *toilettes*, where it is often more crowded than in the rush-hour Métro: in *Le dragueur de dieu* he calls us by the precise and elegant name of *faux-pisseurs*, or 'pretend-pissers'.

I roamed the length and breadth of the United Kingdom in search of the perfect 'cottage', but never found it: there was always something wrong – too bright, too out of the way, too central, too appallingly filthy, too near the police station – though the last-named drawback proved a godsend once when I was being beaten up by gay-bashers. A copper just showed his face and they all fled, leaving me torn and bleeding on the piss-sodden floor. I was lucky enough to encounter a sympathetic copper – they *do* exist, though they're a dying race – and he called an ambulance for me.

When we lived in Corsham, the first thing I did was to check the rather limited facilities of the little local village cottage. There were some quite promising graffiti on the ochre-distempered walls, but I sensed at once that it was one of those places where nothing ever happened – a hunch that was borne out on my occasional visits, during one of which I saw written up on the wall: *James is a fairy*. So I had to seek further afield, in disappointing Chippenham, piss-elegant Bath and dangerous Bristol. Pick-ups were rare. Age did not matter to me. In fact I was more interested in the middle-aged and the old than in the local gilded youth, most of whom were on the make anyhow – and I refused to pay for anything.

But one of the most frightening episodes, in retrospect, started in the charmless toilet standing at the top of the main street in Chippenham. Here I picked up an elderly, rubicund gent, and as we stood there weighing each other up and keeping a sharp ear open for a policeman's ominous tread, we exchanged the usual pleasantries: 'Do you come here often?' 'Got anywhere to go?' 'Is this the only cottage in town?' 'Do you do Greek?' ('Ancient or Modern?' was my reply to this never very hopeful query as to whether I accepted anal intercourse – a regretful negative was my answer.) 'Got the time on you?' 'Got a light?' 'What about a bit of French?', etc. etc. These very predictable conversations were of the utmost boredom, like those I usually had years later with the Japanese, though in very different circumstances.

It transpired that my gent had to catch a bus to Bath, the one that passes through Corsham, so we got on the same bus and went upstairs, where there were many empty seats, and indulged in mutual masturbation all the way to my stop. I had an orgasm round about Pickwick, and it was only then that I noticed our local plain-clothes officer was sitting on the opposite side of the bus, a few seats in front of us. We had covered ourselves carefully with coats when the conductor came upstairs to take our fares, and tried to cover our passion with stony faces and nonchalant cigarettes. I was excited by this first experience of sex on the buses, and descended at Corsham post office with a light-hearted step. Now I felt I could turn my mind to the big translation I was working on, a medieval French mystery play later performed on BBC TV, in Bristol Cathedral and many other locations (published as *The True Mistery of the Passion*). But it was not until I'd had a cup of tea and some of my mother's home-baked scones that I got a sickly feeling of nagging anxiety: I was sure that the plain-clothes dick had spotted what my companion and I were up to under our raincoats. Even as I worked at my script in the top-floor attic, I was overcome by waves of nausea and agonies of doubt and fear, and for the next few days I lived in terror of hearing a knock on the door and seeing a detective in our stone porch. It was this incident more than anything else that made me decide I must get out of Britain.

* * *

Why was I so obsessed by 'the Men's'? I remember that when I was a child I used to love to visit public urinals, hoping to catch glimpses of men's cocks, those massive appendages of my favourite males, the pitmen and seamen of Tyneside. In parks and on the prom I would roam from lavatory to lavatory, even in the depths of winter, when they were usually deserted. I rarely saw what I wanted. In those days men used to 'piss elegant' – that is, they would coyly cover their parts with an arched hand, holding the root of the organ between thumb and forefinger in a way that reminded me of how they held their Woodbines, to shelter the frail, glowing ash from our northern gales. When I think now about those days of my childhood, I realize how extraordinary it was that no man ever touched me or noticed that I was watching him perform an intimate physical need. I did not want to touch, just to look out of the corners of my eyes, peeping shyly for a glimpse of foreskin, a tuft of pubic hair. One or two of the places I used to visit in South Shields were, as I later discovered, nightly haunts of homosexual men: the strange open-air one, lit by a street lamp, behind the General Post Office and not far from the police station; and the little underground one, chastely whitewashed, at the bottom of James Mather Terrace, the street where my father was born, at number 22. He must have known all about it, I now realize, because whenever we walked together along Ocean Road he would make us cross over to the other side. That tiny place was unlit, and usually packed at night in wartime. I found it was a good place to take shelter during air raids – if I had to go, I might as well go happy, in the middle of an orgasmic embrace with a total stranger. Today, alas, that little den of pleasure has been prudently bricked in – you can see where the more recent bricks have been laid – and so for me all the romance has gone out of James Mather Terrace. But I often return to it in a recurrent dream. What ensepulchred ghosts stand waiting there hopefully for me to descend again the short flight of stone steps?

Like Joe Ackerley, I loved the basic, down-to-earth humanity of urinals. So did his Alsatian bitch, Queenie, as he describes in his diaries, *My Sister and Myself*. Indeed, I often wrote nostalgically about sitting in toilet cabinets with holes in the partitions, ironically nicknamed 'glory holes'. The only other writer I know to have written on this arcane subject is Mutsuo Takahashi, the contemporary Japanese poet, a good friend and a devout Catholic, whose work I have often translated. Takahashi writes about men in American public toilets – Japanese toilets do not have any 'glory holes'. They were sometimes discreetly yet invitingly, temptingly covered with a square of toilet paper that would flutter a signal when the occupant next door breathed upon it, and one would perhaps respond to the signal by breathing delicately back, until the veil was lifted on one side or the other, often on a disappointment or a vice-squad cop. I was often inspired to write poems during the long waits in out-of-the-way places like that wintry toilet at the Pier Head in South Shields. My inspiration would sometimes come from the long, ill-spelt fantasies scribbled in minuscule script on the woodwork of doors – script so tiny I took to carrying a pearl-handled antique magnifying glass to decipher their often inscrutable messages, and even more inscrutable obsessions. There was a small, primitive urinal of massive, rusticated stone set on the wave-lashed embankment rocks of the pier itself – now vanished, like so many of the traumatic toilets of my adventurous boyhood and youth. Many are the hours I have spent there, in all seasons, waiting for the impossible, gazing out through the narrow slit in the stonework at the distant cliffs of Trow Rocks and the lights of trawlers while the North Sea waves broke over the roof in earth-shaking detonations of thundering spray. I loved the place's isolation and quiet, the briny darkness, the cold that was never warmed by a visiting stranger's sympathetic touch. It seemed the very temple of my loneliness.

In future years I was to write several poems on so-called 'controversial' subjects. The banning of 'The Convenience' by the typists of the BBC I have described in *I, of All People*. But as long as Joe was literary editor of *The Listener* he always tried to introduce poems on unusual themes. 'The Convenience' was admired by many people whose opinion I respect, including E.M. Forster, William Plomer and Norman Jeffares, who, when he took over the English Department at Leeds after Bonamy Dobrée's retirement, asked me for some poems, and one of those I sent him was 'The Convenience', inscribed on a roll of toilet paper. It is still in the Brotherton Library collection of my papers.

Another poem, 'An Indoor Pastoral', was also accepted by Joe Ackerley. I corrected the proof, but it never appeared. When I asked Joe what was wrong, he gave that wonderful wry smile of his and told me the BBC had found it to be 'rather too warm'. Presumably this judgement from on high was handed down to Joe because the poem describes a man and a woman (myself and a friend) copulating on the floor of the flat that Riette Sturge-Moore had rented to me in Adelaide Road. Apparently it was because we were doing it *on the floor* that the poem was deemed reprehensible. But this poem was reprinted without question by the Oxford University Press in *A Spring Journey and Other Poems*.

In later years, other poems were condemned by otherwise enlightened editors. I remember sending my 'Ode to Male Masturbation' to Emma Tennant when she was editing *Bananas* – a title I wanted her to change to 'Banananas' – and as I had not signed it, she telephoned asking if it were really by me. I assured her it was from the series I call 'My Blue Period'. She did not print it, nor did she return the typescript. It has since been published, along with other poems from the same 'blue period', in *Fellow Feelings*. The only other interesting writings I have found about masturbation are the now *introuvable* novel by Bonnetain, *Charlot s'amuse*, and the inimitable Harry Mathews's brilliant *Singular Pleasures*, though Michel Luneau's remarkable *Sexe-Je* runs them close.

*   *   *

Clifford and Rosemary Ellis, who ran the Bath Academy of Art at Corsham Court, were a wonderful couple, full of marvellous creative energy, inspiring to work with, and fine artists in their own right. They had gathered round them as teaching staff some of the very best contemporary artists, sculptors, potters, designers and musicians, but I was the only poet, so I felt a bit lost among all the craftsmen, printers and painters. But I have always preferred artists and musicians to literary people in Britain. I envied artists like Terry Frost, Peter Lanyon, Brian Wynter, Jack Smith (who danced an extraordinary Twist), Kenneth Armitage and William Scott for the physical nature of their creations, and the conviviality of their common activities, while I had to shut myself away in my chilly top attic to compose my poems and write my early autobiographies. I loved the company of artists, and fled from poets as from the plague. In London, dear old Ruskin Spear was a companion in the Hammersmith pubs, along with others I loved and admired like John Minton, Carel Weight and John Bratby (whose 'kitchen sink' period I put into several poems about dustbins and sinks), and later on David Hockney and Kitaj. Painters and sculptors of all kinds have inspired my poems. I preferred art galleries to bookshops, artists' studios to literary circles and the tight little poetic coteries that are still the bane of British literary life.

I was having endless difficulties with my writing – prose, poetry and translations. I lost faith in my ability time and time again, and often announced I had given up writing for good: that I always returned to it was for me a kind of proof that I really was a poet.

Clifford and Rosemary were a great help to me by bringing me out into the open in my dramatic productions and my 'creative writing' classes – usually abysmal failures – and my practical demonstrations of teaching methods with the village schoolchildren during teaching practice. I am by nature a solitary and a hermit, with not much interest in my fellow-men and their preoccupations, but at Corsham I came out of the shell I always had to construct around me in Leeds to protect me from the stupidity of others.

The Ellises had two daughters: the elder, Penelope, known as Nellie, a gifted artist; the younger, Charlotte, an alarming eight-year-old of whom I was in terror. Later in life we became friends, and she told me how impressed she had been when she discovered, at the age of eight, the word 'bum' in one of my poems, 'Medusa' in *A Spring Journey*. I remember the Ellises, and a few of their artists who were not totally antagonistic towards me, with deep affection. I still cannot imagine how they managed to put up with me. Their encouragement enabled me to survive a difficult time, both emotionally and artistically, when I was feeling my way forward blindly, writing by trial and error, never knowing how anything would work out.

But I knew that in the end I should have to leave Britain. I felt sorry to be leaving such a fertile environment, but it had to be done. So while my parents looked after Queenie, Joe and I had a long talk about my future in a pub in Bath next to the Theatre Royal, where we had gone to see a play about the Linleys by Cecil Beaton. Joe felt that I was putting myself in a dangerous situation. The Wolfenden Report was still to take a little of the pressure off consenting homosexual adults. John Gielgud had been arrested by the Vice Squad in circumstances so tragic and so depressingly similar to whatever might be my own fate, and had shown a courage and a dignity I felt I could never have mustered. It was one of the worst witch-hunting times. The next day I talked the matter over with my mother and father, in Joe's presence, and told them I wanted to resign from Corsham and take a post abroad. They were shocked and saddened. I think they had hoped against hope that one day I would change my ways and settle down cosily with them for the rest of their lives. They were still too protective, fearing for me as if I were a handicapped child. They still could not accept me as a prodigal son, an inveterate 'easy rider' over the face of the earth, a kind of Wandering Jew of poetry and absurd sexual mania, a homeless one who never wanted a home of any kind, preferring to live in hotels and bed-sitters and roadmen's caravans. I have always felt that in this life I am just camping out. They who were anxious for us to have a place of our own, 'a nice little bit of property' as they put it, could not understand my gypsy traipsings from town to town, from one anonymous room to another, from one anonymous sex partner to another. But I knew in my heart of hearts that a settled home and a permanent emotional relationship was not for me. (On my father's side, I was a Viking; on my mother's, an Irish gypsy traveller.) Even the unstinted love and admiration of my parents weighed too heavily upon my rootless soul, and I could not bear to think that they considered me incapable of making a living from writing. So I had to get away. After three years I had had enough of Corsham and never wanted to see the damned place again – the sort of reaction whose pattern was to be repeated all my life, in Britain and abroad. I did not know it at the time, but that break with Britain in 1956 was to be virtually the last of England for me.

I wrote a letter of resignation to Clifford Ellis, who at first refused to accept it. But I insisted. I wanted him to write a reference for me, and he did so most unwillingly, thinking that if he went on refusing I might change my mind. In the end he wrote me a perfectly worded tribute, very brief and to the point, which was to stand me in good stead several times during the coming years when I found myself applying for one foreign post after another, usually with total lack of success despite Clifford's glowing words. But they helped me to get my first paying job abroad, as a travelling lecturer in Sweden for the Swedish Ministry of Education. It was the first of what were to be many sudden steps into the unknown, into the vast, eternally beckoning mystery of 'abroad'.

* * *

During all my periods of fear, loneliness and hysteria I was comforted from time to time by letters from total strangers who had read my poems and wanted to meet me. I do not remember ever meeting any of them. I was too nerve-racked, and within all my conflicting personae a lost little boy was crying out for anonymity. The writers were in any case literary – best kept at a distance.

There were letters, too, from poets – a postcard from Lawrence Durrell about *A Correct Compassion*, letters from John Betjeman on *Time and Tide* letter paper; he was the literary editor for a while. There were several letters from Colin MacInnes at 29 Great Portland Street or from his publisher, Davis-Poynter Ltd. With some of these unknown friends I exchanged letters for years. One of them was a fine, now neglected poet, Stanley Snaith, who followed that often poetic avocation of librarian, and who first wrote to me about my poem 'The Submerged Village'. I kept all these letters. Others I was to sell to a dealer in the mid-sixties when I was hard up and at my wit's end, without any prospect of a new job in Japan, and rejected by publishers and editors.

Colin MacInnes's letters to me at this period have been lost or stolen, but I still possess some written in the sixties and seventies. He was always so generous in his praise. After a long silence, during which he seemed to have forgotten he had written to me before, he again sent me a letter on 31 August 1971:

Dear Mr Kirkup,

Each time I have read a book of prose or poetry you've written, I've been on the point of sending you a fan letter – but have desisted, chiefly because, despite the great pleasure your writing has always given me, I've felt you might be obliged to 'reply' – so please don't, to this note I've finally not been able to resist sending to you. The impetus was *Streets of Asia*, in which once again you display the lovely faculty of absolutely hooking the reader, and telling him just the sort of things he hopes to know – instead of those dreadful chunks and lumps of chatty dullness one usually gets from 'travel books'. But your prose is always that of a poet, imaginative, deft and alluring. All kindest thoughts and wishes.

Colin MacIn.

From one of Colin's letters, sent to me while I was living in Nagoya, it appears that I had, most unusually, suggested a meeting during a leave in England:

Dear James,

Best thanks for your kind card and message. I indeed know that you had kindly spoken well of me to your gracious and elegant students, many years back, and was much flattered and honoured.

It would of course be a great pleasure to see you here in Feby 1971. Yet you should surely know that all encounters of writers (whatever their esteem for each other's works) are a disaster: the historical precedents are innumerable, and personal experience is, alas, conclusive on this point. However, provided we speak exclusively of Second Peruvian Serial Rights, and the worthlessness of all our absent colleagues, all will, I hope, be well.

Best,
Colin

His letter expressed my own feelings about meeting writers so well, I decided I could not risk meeting him, even though I had admired his work so much that I had introduced it to my Japanese students in Tokyo and Nagoya, and had written about it in various essays I wrote for Japanese publications. In fact, I think I was the first to introduce Colin to readers in Japan, and when the film of *Absolute Beginners* opened in Tokyo I received a letter from one of those old students reminding me of my talks about MacInnes, and how her notes on what I had said had helped her to understand and enjoy the movie – which was a sad disappointment, however, to me.

Perhaps one of the reasons I decided not to meet Colin was that trendy 'Best' at the end of the letter, which I found off-putting in its determined casualness, like the even more common 'As always' some Americans write – always *what*? I always wonder. It's a sign of mental vacuity or emotional distractedness. I like to end letters with 'Ever sincerely', or, to certain friends, 'Everest'. (It's a joke. . . .)

John Betjeman in his letters to me used to send up the earnestness of Veronica Wedgwood's *Time and Tide* by enlivening the letter heading with comical ejaculations like 'Votes for Women!' In a letter from The Mead, Wantage, Berks, he writes: 'They *will* fill up the paper with stuff about Whither Albania? and Jugoslavia's Next Move? and only put in tiny bits of poetry if there are any inches left over . . . T. and T. I find so unreliable about dates of printing poetry.'

Betjeman liked a rather long poem I sent him about memories of Leeds, 'A City of the North', mainly I think because of its references to some of his favourite architectural Victoriana – Pugin and so on, and the Town Hall with its toothless lions:

> Dear Kirkup,   .XXXI.III. MCMLII.
>   Oh so vivid and good but *length*. I don't think we can take it. It would be *years* before the 'Whither Democracy' end of the paper could find the requisite inches – and have Leeds waiting already. Any shorter ones you have, please do send. And please forgive this measurement view of good poetry.

But somehow he finally managed to persuade Veronica Wedgwood to accept the poem if I could find a suitable artist to illustrate it and make a double-page spread. My former colleague at Leeds, Maurice de Sausmarez, Professor of Fine Art, agreed to do the illustrations, which were strikingly beautiful, and everything was sent off to *Time and Tide*. Yet in the end they could not use it, and Betjeman had the delicate task of explaining why not, which he did very nicely, and arranged for Maurice to receive a modest fee: '. . . As for Mr de Sausmarez, they must pay him – I suggest 6 guineas (1 gn a drawing) rather low – but will he accept? Please explain to him. Send more poems to us. God bless you. I will return the drawings.'

Of course Maurice made no fuss and accepted the fee. I received nothing but I did not mind, for Betjeman had asked his God to bless me. After he left the paper, Veronica continued to print my poems and from time to time commissioned a review. She printed one of my best Christian poems, 'Cena', which I wrote in Austria on a visit to Klosterneuburg. Later, when he was reviewing for the *Daily Telegraph*, Betjeman made a very perceptive remark, that modern poems were becoming more and more like short stories. With the decline of the short story (and the short-story market) in Britain, the poets were taking over the usual domestic-provincial-academic themes of that form, and translating or rather transposing them into verse of the Larkin school, for the most part (unlike some of Larkin's work) extremely dreary, banal and anti-poetic, giving contemporary poetry the bad name from which it has still not recovered and is never likely to recover. Betjeman sent me a cutting of the review he did of my book of poems, *The Descent into the Cave*, with a note saying 'to an obviously un-Telegraph man'. It was a very good review, one of the very few the book received. He also invited me to lunch at Kettner's and to what he called the 'Bertie Woosterish' Wheeler's in Charlotte Street, mainly I think to fish for information about the 'Barone' Seymour Kirkup, the eccentric mediumistic painter and member of the Pisan Circle who discovered Giotto's portrait of Dante. His oddity and his friendship in later life with Swinburne must have attracted Betjeman's passion for unusual Victoriana.

To my knowledge, there is now no literary editor who writes such funny and idiosyncratic letters to his contributors, though John Betjeman was not in the same class as Joe Ackerley, who outdid everyone then and now in that field. Where have they all disappeared to, that race of loving editors? Why has the literary world in Britain and America become so inhuman?

It was Joe who put me in touch with some rare human beings, like the poet R.S. Thomas, who had written to him about some of my poems, but whose letter I have lost or sold. Another was the marvellous, now almost forgotten poet Andrew Young, a writer I had long admired and whose poetry strongly influenced me in the early fifties. Poems like 'Orientations' and 'The Abandoned Harbour' were clearly written under Andrew's spell. He wrote me several letters at a time when I was suffering my periodic doubts about my vocation and wondering if I should stop writing altogether. His are letters I have treasured, and

would never sell to America, however down-and-out I might be. Here is
the first letter he sent me, from The Vicarage, Stonegate, dated 21
December 1951:

> Dear Mr Kirkup,
>   I hope it won't annoy you to receive in your Christmas mail a letter
> from a stranger. Richard Church lent me your book, *The Submerged
> Village*. I opened it doubtfully, but the second poem (the title poem)
> quite took my breath away. I found other lovely poems, above all a
> little masterpiece, 'Orientation'. I detect a strain of mysticism in the
> book, which is very grateful in this 'Waste Land'.
>   With all good wishes,
>
> >   Yours sincerely,
> >   Andrew Young

In October 1952 he wrote me a long letter of appreciation about *A
Correct Compassion* which I had sent him. Here are some extracts from
that letter:

> . . . To give a list of the poems I like would come near copying out
> 'Contents'; but some appealed to me in a special degree. In 'Heroic
> Torso' and 'Reclining Figure' you seem to achieve with words what
> the sculptors did with lines. 'Winter Dusk' and 'London Spring' are
> fine pictures, with something over and above that gives them a mystic
> tone. 'The Caged Bird in Springtime' and 'On a Dead Child' have a
> simplicity and tenderness, singularly absent from modern verse.
> 'Gesture: A Song' is hardly a song: it is just a piece of pure music.
> With what charm and delicacy you express a feeling in 'The Visit'.
> 'To a Painter' is a wonderful achievement: I cannot describe its
> subtlety, but it is perfect from beginning to end. And most of all I
> love 'The Fountain'! . . .

Praise of my work from such a distinguished and perceptive poet was
so unusual, I wept tears of thankfulness. From time to time Andrew
invited me to lunch with him in London at some kind of literary club –
could it have been the Poetry Society? He also invited me to stay with
him and to meet one of his great friends, John Arlott, the cricket writer
and commentator. But as cricket is a game I do not understand and do
not like, I turned down the invitation. Andrew respected my prejudices
about sport and my lack of interest in all games, though I like describing
them in poetry, as in one of my best-known sporting poems, 'Rugby

League Game'. Sport seems to me as bad as war, and should be abolished. In later years I still kept in touch with Andrew, and the poem 'Lammas' was written with him in mind, though he would not allow me to dedicate it to him, saying he was 'unworthy'. He was such a noble, generous and truly charitable Christian, and such an excellent mystical-realist poet. There is no one like him now.

The Convenience

Sharp-smelling, in the working streets
Mingling its sad aromas with the beery gusts
That belch from the stale saloon,
A temple of rotting tin, it meets
With an urbane amenity the needs and lusts
Of weak humanity, an earthly boon.

Its scarred and bitter walls
Contain what could not be contained
In life: – with what passionate relief
Men entered here, and made their scrolls
Of joyous water; with what voluptuous ferocity restrained
Themselves no longer, confessing dreams beyond belief!

Above, the open sky, in rain and sun,
Blesses the roof's grey panes, star-smashed, where stars are seen
At night. By day, a tree-top squirting birds into the air
Casts autumn shade. The waters musically run,
The leaky cistern grumbles and the pipes are green;
The rattling gas-lamp sheds a ghastly glare.

Within the brash saloon, a faded music thumps,
Girls' voices sing, glass chimes, tills ring.
The decent street roars on outside the fretted wall.
– But here is a quiet that gives the heart the jumps,
An elemental peace, a fount of knowledge and a healing spring
Of contemplation and communion understood by all.

A kind of early grave, where all men
Come to conceal, reveal, adjust and find themselves again.

from *The Descent into the Cave and Other Poems*

An Indoor Pastoral

Upon the floor's
Dark blue lawn reclining,
  Behind the high doors
Of leaf-tiled forests leaning,
  Under the ample sun's
  Sheer amber ceiling
  These two simple ones
Investigate love's rustic meaning
  In an urban setting.

Naked they lie
Like two recumbent fountains
  Or distant mountains
Brought nearer but lower by
  The close approximations
  Of kissing smiles
  And hands that hold
In sunny tides their ocean-isles
  Of green and gold.

Upon their love
Draw now the leafy curtain
  Of the city grove.
Let walls of country air contain
  Their bliss from all
  But purest eyes,
  Those of the earth and skies
For whom this indoor pastoral
  Will never change;

For whom no life is strange,
And everything that is, is natural.

from *A Spring Journey and Other Poems*

BREAKING WITH THE PAST

Whatever withdraws us from the power of our senses; whatever makes the past, the distant, or the future, predominate over the present, advances us in the dignity of thinking beings.

Dr Samuel Johnson, JOURNEY TO THE WESTERN ISLANDS

Right into middle age I had this passion for make-up, for the creation of a mask that would reveal yet hide my feelings. I was a dedicated *maquilleur*, and I was attracted to men who made up – the dandies and the *incroyables* of past centuries, the transvestites like Barbette and even the pantomime dames. I was delighted when I learnt that Pierre Loti used to touch up his cheeks with rouge, and, like many an only, lonely child before me, I would experiment with my mother's modest make-up box, consisting just of powder of a neutral shade, a tiny pale-red lipstick and a wee pot of rouge, all of which she used very sparingly, because my father hated women who wore too much make-up. For this reason he disapproved of the women of the Royal Family, particularly the Queen and Princess Elizabeth, whose lipstick excesses often led him to remark that their mouths looked like letter-boxes.

So my mother applied her lipstick very discreetly, almost rubbing it all off after applying it, for fear of offending my father. She would tell me: 'Jim, don't put on too much war-paint, or your father will be furious.' She always gave an excuse for putting on lipstick. In winter it would be 'just to keep my lips from cracking, you know'. And in the heat of summer it would be 'just to moisten my lips'.

As I experimented with her limited resources, I discovered that the corners of my mouth were much paler than the rest of my lips, and that if I touched these paler parts with lipstick it gave my rather small, sulky mouth a sort of smile, by extending and somehow lifting the despondent corners. I should dearly have liked to buy some false eyelashes and some peacock eye-shadow, even if only to practise with them in private. But it was not until I left England for good that I began to show my full make-up occasionally in public, whenever possible in dimly lit dives and gay bars, where I would sit at the counter and gaze at my reflection in the mirrors behind the ranks of exotic bottles. Perhaps that was why no one ever spoke to me. I was too self-absorbed to notice anyone sitting next to me.

Outlining lips with eyebrow pencil, as professional actors, and some non-professionals do – I think that is carrying things too far, especially when people exceed the natural limits of their lips, trying to make them fuller and more sensual with extravagant lipstick extensions. I should never dream of doing that. Anyhow, my lips are full enough already: they need no artificial assistance.

I have always been fascinated by people who dyed or tinted their hair, or who wore wigs. That is why I still find peroxided Jimmy Savile so adorable. Of course I experimented with my own hair, and even went so far as to wear, in Nagoya, what my coiffeur called a 'fun wig' that made me look like Harpo Marx or the boy from *Mad* magazine disguised as Phyllis Diller. My hair is so fine, it falls about in the slightest breeze or with the briefest of movements of my head, so a 'fun wig' was just the thing on windy days. But it was tight and hot, and seemed to obstruct the flow of blood to my brain, so that I had repeated fainting fits in public, which drew a gratifying amount of attention from Japanese ambulance men. So I had to give it up. But with the arrival of the Sony Walkman, I found a way to combine the pleasure of ambulant music and the freedom to forget about my hair, for those early head-sets, with their extensible metal hoops, were perfect for keeping my hair in place, even in a typhoon. And the luxurious plastic foam ear-cushions meant that, in an emergency, the head-set could, with some ingenuity, serve as a truss.

One of my French teachers at Westoe Secondary School used to dye her hair a beautiful chestnut shade, then forget to keep touching up the white hair underneath. She was still quite young and charming, engaged or maybe married to the son of our headmaster, lovable Mr Lawrence-son. Her beautiful bespectacled eyes would open wide in conjecture and innocent surprise every time she told our all-male class: 'Now, boys, get out your Longmans' – we had a French reader, published by that august educational firm, whose editors can hardly have suspected what waves of delicious torment the name provoked in a class of adolescent boys, especially when coming from the lips of that attractive teacher. Sometimes she would change her opening words, and say: 'Now, boys, get your Longmans ready. . . .' We used to play with each other's sexual parts under the desk, and one day the French teacher astonished me and my partner by saying: 'I know what you two are doing, so stop it this minute!' Yes, we had obeyed her command, and got our Longmans out.

Why did she always start the class with those words, which never failed to provoke titters, especially as her gentle request was often followed by mild reproaches: 'Come now, boys – come, come, come, settle down. Try to be more grown-up – you're big boys now, you know.' I began to suspect she knew only too well the thoughts her harmless-sounding words aroused in us. And all her artfully arranged hair, brown on top, white underneath, would softly part and disintegrate upon her slightly flushed cheeks. She was a dear and a darling, and she used to praise me in a way that caused further disturbances in class: 'Albin, you roll your Rs very nicely now.' She had given us all French names, and I secretly wanted to be called Félix, but was clobbered with that awful Albin, which I was later to find was borne by Michel Serrault's *homme/femme* in *La cage aux folles*.

My very blond hair was already blond enough – ash blond my mother used to call it, as, to my intense irritation, she fondly stroked its vaporous, silky moonlight waves and curls. It was the cause of sexual attacks upon my person from earliest childhood by strangers, both men and women, one of whom, an unemployed miner, used to come and visit us after he got out of gaol. I had forgotten completely whatever it was he had tried to do to me, but I sensed there was a mystery connected with him, as my parents exchanged glances and avoided looking at me. I was first 'interfered with' at the age of two, so that perhaps explains a lot, sad to say. Yet even in childhood I enjoyed the power I exercised over a certain kind of man: I could not resist affection, however unlawful.

As I grew older, my hair gradually darkened, as my mother had warned me it would. One day, in my early twenties, I tried to enliven its old-gold glow with an entire bottle of peroxide bought at a chemist's with the delightful name of Darling. 'Stop messing about with all that sissy hair,' my father growled, his pipe grimly clenched between his teeth. 'Why are you always washing and combing and brushing it? You look like a proper Jessie.' I still remember my cheeky reply: 'I don't want to start growing bald like you.'

It was the first and only time I ever spoke to my father in that horrible way. There was a speaking silence. Poor Dad, how I must have hurt and sickened him! But, on the other hand, he had hurt me often enough with his 'nancy-boy' and 'sissy' and 'Mary Anne'. It was a wonder I had not abandoned my usual silence at such attacks and hit back long before then. I am not a vengeful person, but I am in such a vulnerable situation every moment of my life, I sometimes have to use the only decent weapons available, as I cannot use my fists – words and looks. My favourite phrase: 'My dear, I gave him *such* a look. . . .' If I am hurt too much, I can patiently wait for years and years before retaliating – in one case, a humiliation I could never forget was expunged by a few choice words more than thirty years later. It is one of my oriental traits, my Japanese persona.

No, I am not a vengeful person, for vengeance is contrary to my mild and loving nature. But in certain circumstances – for example, cruelty to animals or children, racial bigotry, or wars in all their insanity – I can find myself invested with a power of retaliation that often surprises me, and may shock others. Thus I call down curses upon bullfights and inhuman abattoirs, upon warmongering governments and their parasites, the arms manufacturers, who are the only ones to benefit from armed conflict, and the only ones to escape its tragic and unnecessary consequences. Bullfights are my particular *bête noire*, and when French or Spanish television presents some disgraceful and cruel slaughter of a helpless beast in a gaudy, stupid and pseudo-religious ritual, I switch off. But I do read the Spanish newspapers for accounts of injuries to bullfighters caused by bulls driven to desperation. Such as the recent news story about Carretero, a *torero* seriously wounded in Madrid on 5 August, a Sunday, 1990. I could feel only satisfaction when I learnt that he had received a horn in the pit of his stomach at the very moment when he was stabbing in the *banderillas*, leaving a gash of twenty centimetres. In addition, he got another horn in his scrotum that left a testicle dangling and ripped open the skin of his penis. I hope that will teach him a lesson.

But it was my father who scored in the end, after that confrontation, because after I had rashly drenched my hair in peroxide it nearly all fell out, and it took weeks to grow back, during which time my father chuckled and my mother tut-tutted. I purchased my first velvet beret to hide the bald patches. I even wore it in bed. This headgear further aroused my father's contempt, quite rightly, because I looked 'a proper sight' and 'a real clip' in it, as my mother had to agree, though as my Aunt Lyallie once told me: 'She thinks the sun shines out of your arse.' How conservative and deeply right wing the working classes are in the urban ghettos of the North! It was the first time a man had been seen wearing a beret in South Shields.

How my poor mother must have suffered from my eccentric excesses! And yet she seemed to encourage them, half-unconsciously, as when she had used to dress me in girlish clothes when I was small. I remember her saying: 'Jim, why do you always put yourself in a bad light? People are laughing at you, love. It breaks my heart to see how they misunderstand you. But you give them the wrong idea altogether. You're like another person with them. We know you, we know there's nothing bad in you, you're a good son. So it hurts me when people say things against you – people who don't even know you.' She was Santa Monica to my unworthy Augustine of Hippo.

How was I to explain to my simple, good-hearted mother that I actually relished being misunderstood, that masochistically I revelled in being reviled and spat upon? In a later work, a collection of one-line poems entitled *Dengonban Messages*, I open with this statement: 'I always enjoy creating a wrong impression.'

When I left home and went to stay at Madame Sheba's boarding-house in Tottenham Court Road, I made friends with a West Indian dancer, an amiable and gifted youth with whom I had to share a room for a while as Madame kept rearranging her guests, trying to pack in as many as possible. He taught me the limbo and a lot of other skills. He had a Don Ameche moustache, and his name was Errol. I persuaded him to peroxide his moustache. The effect of that glittering gold bar across his rich brown face, underlined as it was by his dazzling white grin, strawberry tongue and luscious, dark-red lips, was entrancing and irresistible. We were refused entry to the Fitzroy Tavern and the Marquis of Granby. Nothing has given me greater pride – apart from being pronounced *persona non grata* by the British Council.

I even got Errol to peroxide his armpits, then his little tight curls of crotch hair. Naked, he looked like some ancient, barbaric god of a gold-worshipping tribe, and I paid homage often at that rutilant altar. But I was unable to make him peroxide his hair, worn, in true Afro style, like a sooty halo or a dusty black dandelion clock. 'Man, Jimi, ah kin shave off me tash, and no one but you sees the difference inside me pants, but Jimi me head is sacred – nolly me tangerine, they says. I don' want to look like some stain-glass angel.' Madame Sheba, hooting with laughter, hands on her massive hips, would double up until her turbaned head reached her enormous knees at the sight of us – 'the pair of you', as she called us – and, wiping tears from her eyes, would ask when the wedding was going to take place, and 'Who's the missus, and who's the mister in this chicken-roost?'

Now, forty years on, I'm still hanging on to my hair – but only just, so I never go out hatless in a high wind. After that first disaster, I have been through every shade under the hair-drier, and am now back almost to the ash blond of childhood, a pale moonlight grey. But I shall stay natural now – a lavender rinse doesn't go with my dark-blue eyes.

*   *   *

I used to be very self-conscious about a small scar I have in the middle of my upper lip. It was caused by a razor-blade embedded in a potato thrown at me during a pre-war pacifist demonstration against fascists. It is very rare to meet people with a scar in mid-channel of the upper lip. So I was delighted to find in Claude Burgelin's book* on my Oulipien idol, Georges Perec, pictures from his 1974 film *Un homme qui dort* showing the actor Jacques Spiesser, whom Perec chose for the part because on his upper lip he had a scar almost the same as Perec's – 'pure chance, but it was for me the determining factor' as Perec writes in his autobiography *W ou le souvenir d'enfance*, which influenced my own autobiographical writings. There is also a picture of Antonello de Messina's *Le Condottiere* portrait in the Louvre of a Renaissance man with a similar scar of his top lip. Perec often writes about his scar, which was caused during a scuffle with schoolmates. I wish we had met. In my own search for a scar-fellow, I was to find Marcel Jouhandeau and Nureyev. But I sometimes tried to hide it with invisible make-up cream. Now I don't bother: it is one of my prized marks of distinction.

There is a most appealing Pre-Raphaelite painting called *The Last of England*, showing, in a circular frame, a man and a woman sitting under a capacious umbrella and gazing out despondently from the stern of the Channel packet at the receding dingy-white cliffs of Dover. A few years ago, at a time of great economic stress in Britain, I saw a cartoon version of this picture, with the same title, in which the two people were grinning broadly. That broad grin was what I imagined would be on my face when I saw the last of England (almost) in the year of disgrace, 1956. Apart from very brief intervals of almost total misery, I have lived happily enough away from Britain for the last thirty-five years.

I was thankful to be escaping, not only from Britain but from my personal dilemmas. At a time when I was torn between my male and female personae and my homo and heterosexual impulses, I was feeling more than ever without gender. In Virginia Woolf's *A Room of One's Own* I discovered a passage (commenting on Coleridge) that comforted me, though I detested the author: '. . . the androgynous mind is resonant and porous . . . transmits emotion without impediment . . . is naturally creative, incandescent, and undivided. . . . Fortunately, intellect has no gender.' I determined to burn with a pure, incandescent flame – something that could never be accomplished in the England of those days.

All my childhood terror of Britain and the British had grown to panic dimensions. I was living a disordered yet ecstatic sexual existence quite unlike anyone else's, or so I believed, but I couldn't see anything wrong with that. Poe in 'The Black Cat' writes of 'the spirit of perverseness'. Was that what I was suffering from with such enjoyment? He goes on to

---

* *Les Contemporains* (Paris: Editions du Seuil, 1988).

speak of 'this unfathomable longing of the soul *to vex itself* . . . to do wrong for the wrong's sake only'. By so-called 'normal' moral standards I was 'doing wrong', though only to myself. Why couldn't I go on being myself in my own peculiar way? If I stayed in Britain, I knew I should either be arrested for 'indecency' of some more or less gross description, or go raving mad.

Valium was unknown in those days, and in any case I should never have dreamt of seeking medical or psychiatric advice and treatment. When I was a boy, trying to study the deadly boring syllabus for my School Certificate, I was every evening so overcome by the tedium of it all that I used to drift into narcolepsy soon after tea, as soon as I started homework. This worried my mother so much that she went to the local chemist's, Darling, and asked for something to keep me awake. She returned with a little bottle of amphetamine drops – the Benzedrine that was to become one of the Flower Children's favourite tonics. It had the most awful taste, even when absorbed on lumps of sugar. The Benzedrine, combined with the doses of Ephedrine I was taking for my increasingly severe attacks of asthma, induced in me a most peculiar mixture of hysteric exhilaration and depressive melancholia similar to the confused emotional and mental states I found myself in at Corsham.

In the early fifties I became very interested in drugs, prompted by Aldous Huxley's accounts of his experiments in *The Doors of Perception*. In May 1954 (my diary says the 25th) I went to the Burden Neurological Institute in Stoke Lane, Stapleton, Bristol, to meet Dr Grey Walter and to observe his *machina speculatrix*, about which I eventually wrote a poem in *The Descent into the Cave*. I asked him about his researches into LSD, for he was one of the first to explore its clinical possibilities, and begged to be allowed to experiment with it, under his control. It made surprisingly little difference. I had no apocalyptic visions, so perhaps he put me off with a placebo. I concluded that as a poet I must by nature exist in a fairly constant state of euphoria and hallucination. 'Poets are born high,' I informed Dr Grey Walter, and he agreed that there might be some truth in this.

I later met him at a local gliding club, of which he was a prominent member, for we both had an interest in sailplanes, and I made my first flight under his observation. He was not surprised when I produced, almost as if by automatic writing, my poem 'In a Sailplane', which I eventually included in the 1959 volume *The Prodigal Son: Poems 1956–1959*. This poem has proved to be very popular with anthologists of poetry, especially poetry for children and young people.

One week after my first sailplane flight, with members of the Bristol Speleological Society, I went down Stoke Lane Cave – 'twice under sump', my diary says. The day before, I had gone down G.B. Cave at Burrington Combe, and those caving experiences gave me the inspiration and the factual background for my long narrative documentary poem, 'The Descent into the Cave'.

In the same week I went to the Department of Scientific and Industrial Research at Teddington and the National Physical Laboratory, which produced another long narrative poem, 'Journey to a Microsecond'; transcribed as prose, it forms the final chapter of *I, of All People*.

At the same period I was rushing to London to see films at the National Film Theatre of Pavlova, Markova and Ulanova. I marvelled at an exhibition of the drawings of Leonardo da Vinci, whose anatomical notebooks were to have such a decisive influence (via Marcel Jouhandeau's *Journaliers*) on the composition of my poem-sequence 'The Body Servant', in 1970. I saw Fonteyn in *The Sleeping Beauty* at Covent Garden at the 15 May matinée and watched American basketball at Wembley on the 23rd. I had taken my mother and father to see the matinée performance of *Sylvia* at Covent Garden on 17 April. Among the films I saw at the National Film Theatre were my first Japanese revelations, *Tora-no-O* and the unforgettable *Rashomon*.

All this represents but a small part of my unbridled cultural activity and intellectual ferment of those days, and takes no account of all the illicit sexual encounters I was plunging into so recklessly, in defiance of the narks. I must have been in a continual state of what Abraham Maslow has described in the 1950s as 'Peak Experience'.

I felt I had to do something to quieten myself down, and started rereading Jane Austen – a writer my father could not stand. I liked her style and her wit. But I began to comprehend my father's feelings about her when I found that her view of British society would necessarily exclude people like me: she was arousing in me acute feelings of guilt, anxiety and panic. I had to stop reading *Sense and Sensibility*, with its distinct smell of cats, in order to preserve my own sense and sensibility. The narrowness, hypocrisy and censorious conformity of her social spectrum were the very things I was fighting against in my personal life, and hoping to escape from in a more liberal Europe. I found Jane a real balls-breaker.

Like many working-class men, my father was well read. He had a large collection of books on Arctic and Antarctic exploration and of writers like Darwin, Anson and Captain Cook. He enjoyed modern novels, as did my mother, and for Christmas and birthday presents I sometimes gave them books by authors I admired – Elizabeth Taylor, P.G. Wodehouse, Anthony Burgess, Elizabeth Bowen and Barbara

Pym (long before she was 'rediscovered'). Our common dislike of Jane Austen was one of the things that helped to bring my father and me together, to reconcile us before his death.

At one point in the darkness of my soul my bedside reading was reduced to my old Westoe Secondary School hymn-book, *Hymns and Psalms Selected and Arranged for Schools* by J.N. Downes, Second Master at Hornsey County School, with an Introduction by Horace Piggott, MA, Ph.D., New and Enlarged Edition, one of Dent's long-running best-sellers. I took some comfort in the inscription I had made on the inside of the cover, 'Upper Sixth'. Remembering that ghastly school with its sadistic masters made my present plight seem not so bad. But as I read and inwardly sang Bishop Ken's all-too-robust 'Awake, my soul, and with the sun/ Thy daily stage of duty run;/ Shake off dull sloth, and joyful rise/ To pay thy morning sacrifice' I was only too keenly reminded of my anguished feelings at the start of the school day, and of my dread of punishment at the hands of some of the young local rugger toughs who taught us maths, geography and history. 'Paleface', they called me, and mocked my lack of keenness on the football and cricket fields. How different their crude behaviour was from what I expected during their hearty, self-confident singing of those unexceptionable Christian sentiments! 'Thy morning sacrifice' for me was a terrified exposure to lashing sarcasm, insults about my personal appearance and all too often the swish of the bamboo cane upon my palms. My refusal to weep or to show any signs of pain seemed only to intensify their rage against me, and in later life they became associated in my mind with the police and the plain-clothes dicks and coppers' narks who made my life such a misery. I later discovered that one of those masters was hand-in-glove with the South Shields police force members of the Westoe Rugby Club, and had denounced me to them. The Revd J. Keble's 'New every morning is the love . . .' was to me a bitter untruth. This bedside reading became too much for my nerves, which I steadied with long draughts of Proust and Genet.

Joe Ackerley's remedy for anxiety attacks like mine was to read thrillers, of which he received an enormous number for review at *The Listener*. I was surprised to discover that he and his highbrow friends considered the reading of detective stories as an intellectual occupation. I tried to read a few that were passed on to me by Joe, but failed to derive any pleasure from them. Certainly they did not help to allay my acute anxiety attacks. But I remember being interested in Helen Eustis's *The Horizontal Man*, and, much later, by Ira Levin's *A Kiss before Dying*. But when Joe came to stay with me in Japan and I offered him the latter book, he rejected it scornfully. I think he must have grown out of his passion for thrillers and, besides, the title must have cut rather near the bone in his old age. The only thriller writer I could read was Simenon, to whom I had been introduced by André Gide, who admired him immensely. I agree with Gide that Simenon is one of the great modern French prose stylists, and I read his complex psychological novels savouring every word. I am fascinated by his mastery of construction, by how he builds up a character or a scene touch by touch, like an impressionist painter. He sometimes has the pointillist technique of Seurat and his school, used with a poetic realism and a linguistic precision that are classic in their elegance and clarity. But I cannot read too much of Simenon. After finishing one novel, I have to recover my spirits before attempting another, because despite the miraculous prose I find the stories themselves very lowering. Even the much lighter Maigret novels can plunge me into black depression. I enjoy Simenon's accurate descriptions of extremes of weather, especially of the bleakness and cold of Flemish towns, or the exotic heat of Africa and the South Seas, in novels where he surpasses Conrad.

But in the fifties I had very few favourite English novelists, and there were no poets in whom I felt the slightest interest. Yet I loved the novels of Barbara Pym and Elizabeth Taylor long before they became popular, and wrote to them both. Barbara never replied; but I was to have an animated correspondence with Elizabeth Taylor, whose frequent use of the words 'blasphemy' and 'blasphemous' in her early novels greatly amused and intrigued me.

Around the middle of 1955 I had become aware of my multiple personalities as a kind of social system, with myself as governor or benevolent dictator. The poet in me belonged to the upper classes, and tried always to control the disobedient lower orders, both male and female, of which the sexual voluptuary lived in a class beyond the pale, and the teacher and translator of Michaux and Supervielle and Hölderlin occupied the middle ranks. They were always jostling for supremacy, and I had a hard job keeping them all in order, especially at times – every six months or so – when my bisexual nature switched from male to female orientation or vice versa, or refused to do so when I tried consciously to effect the change. Such was the confusing array of personalities I had at my disposal, very often I did not know who or what I was, and experienced somewhat alarming out-of-the-body states, in which the music freak would stand outside observing the frustrated performer, or the dutiful son would be trying to reintegrate with the would-be sexual charmer. I was appalled and horrified, yet also frequently overjoyed and enraptured, by the range of emotional opportunities I kept offering myself. I felt like a supreme puppet master, or a gifted ventriloquist imposing characteristics and qualities on first one then another of my multiplying traits and tendencies. It was like mushing a pack of huskies through constantly changing landscapes, trying to keep the traces from getting entangled, and carefully watching the behaviour of each individual dog as my sledge sped at ever-swifter speeds through nightmare auroras of police batons and searchlights. I was forever 'on stage', making an entrance and at the same time trying to plan an exit from the role in which the moment had cast me. The agonies of indecision could be resolved only by desperate means, by the addictive drug of compulsive sex.

Through my Irish and Scots grandparents I acquired the gift of second sight, and this, too, seemed connected with my multiple selves. I had also inherited mediumship and ESP from my ancestor, Seymour Stocker Kirkup, the 'Barone' who belonged to the Pisan Circle of the Romantics but excused himself from attending Shelley's funeral on the grounds that he had a bad cold. It may be that my gift for foreign languages is just another aspect of multiple personality, taken to the point of multiple nationality. I am not much interested in the spoken word, and conversation soon bores me; I can count on the fingers of one hand the people whose conversation has held my interest for longer than ten minutes. I prefer the endless entertainment of my own thoughts, my own interior monologues and the dialogues between my various selves and non-selves, both male and female. Before I arrived in Japan, I had studied the whole of Japanese grammar and syntax, and acquired a small vocabulary; but I soon realized that most Japanese conversation was not for me. Its predictability and banality repelled me. I was interested in the Japanese, I found, only for very short periods – for sex only: half an hour in bed with a Japanese could be pleasant enough, but that was all I could stand, a hug and a kiss and goodbye, usually for ever. Despite this, I was able to form some long-lasting emotional and intellectual attachments in whatever country I happened to be visiting or working.

But it was the literature of foreign lands that filled every day of my life with inexhaustible discoveries: Marcel Jouhandeau, one of my literary alter egos; Pier Paolo Pasolini, whom I met on my first visit to Italy, when he picked me up at Roma Termini's public lavatory; Vladimir Nabokov, born like me on 23 April, and for whose books and translations I developed a passion that has never abated; the poet Góngora; the heteronymic Fernando Pessoa; the Spanish poet Luis Cernuda, sad homosexual driven from Spain, whom I met during the war in Glasgow and Cambridge; Pasolini's poetic master Sandro Penna; Musil; and finally my other alter ego, the Swiss Robert Walser, to whom

I had been introduced through his strange, deceptively naïve essays and poems by Elias Canetti. In 1956 I went to Switzerland to meet Walser, but found he had just died in a lunatic asylum after a silence of many years.

The French surrealists amused and often stimulated me, but it was the modern classic Paul Valéry whose poetry attracted me most – I found his prose tedious – and I spent many years making a verse translation of his incredibly difficult poems, including his long master-piece *La jeune parque*. When I came to translate Jean Genet's *Un chant d'amour*, I was amazed by the similarity of his style and that of *La jeune parque*. They are both severely classical in tone, and their themes are not unrelated.

But, so often, the writers I should really like to have met were already dead, foremost among them Ronald Firbank. On my first visit to Rome I visited his grave in the Campo Verano near the university – a sadly cracked and weathered slab that I return to every year to scrub with Vim – even before visiting the memorials to Keats and Shelley in the Protestant Cemetery near the Pyramid of Cestius. It is haunted by cats as well as by the spirits of the dead. Ronald lies next to someone for whom he would have felt the utmost horror, and whom he would have satirized in his scintillating novels – Una, Lady Troubridge, the loving companion of Radclyffe Hall. Her grave slab bears the lapidary ex-clamation by Radclyffe Hall (whose name is misspelt in attribution): 'There is no death!'

I wanted to meet Nabokov more than anyone, and I wrote to him several times, but received no answer. His autobiography *Speak, Memory* was one of the revelations of my writer's life. In it he introduces the figure of his 'favourite émigré author, one V. Sirin' who was admired for his 'unusual style, brilliant precision, functional imagery', and for 'the mirror-like angles of his clear but weirdly misleading sentences'. This writer is Nabokov himself, and he emerges as 'the loneliest and most arrogant' of all the young Russian émigré writers of the twenties. It was the loneliness of Nabokov's gift that attracted me: there was no one else like him, so he invented Sirin to companion his solitude. For me, such utter loneliness of talent became a way of life, and I found it reflected in Nabokov's life and in the lives of his characters. In his book on Gogol he writes that 'all reality is a mask'. I saw that the writer's task is to make that reality seem real, to make truth seem true, in both prose and poetry. Loneliness is one way of intensifying that vision of the real and the true.

Nabokov's wit often reminds me of my old university friend David Paul's surreal conversational style, a mixture of the wry, the sardonic and the fantastic, all combined into a poetic scintillation revealing from time to time unexpected depths of feeling and visionary, offbeat observation. David, my constant defender against Professor Girdlestone, whom he loathed as much as I did, was taken ill on a nightmare conducted bus tour in Turkey with his wife Angela in 1984 and his health gradually declined until his death in 1986. All that remains of his genius is an out-of-print masterpiece, *Poison and Vision* (1974), containing his magnificent translations of Baudelaire, Mallarmé and Rimbaud, with a fine introduction, and a number of uncollected essays from *The New Criterion*. It was David who during the war introduced me to Firbank, Ivy Compton-Burnett and Nabokov's *The Real Life of Sebastian Knight*. There will never again be anyone like Nabokov, or like David.

I often used to talk to Joe Ackerley about my literary idols, including Nabokov, but for his part, though willing to listen to my ravings with an indulgent smile, he never admitted any true interest in the writers who then excited me. In this respect, he was very British. The British distrust virtuosity in anything. The only author I can remember Joe suddenly enthusing about was Jonathan Swift – an event that came late in his life. The Gulliver who had enchanted my childhood and whom I rediscovered in Japan, which he calls Zipangu, had somehow escaped Joe's attention. Perhaps he was too busy reading his endless thrillers and crime novels. But I remember he admired greatly the works of the Hammonds, and recommended Steven Runciman's books to me with great enthusiasm: but though I enjoyed reading these authors, they did not thrill me as prose stylists, precisely because they were 'too British'.

Nabokov was an author he said he 'could not get along with'. He thought *Lolita* absurd and unfunny, and I suspect that if that delicious heroine had been a 'faunlet' he would have liked it much better. Because he liked Russian autobiographies, I gave him a copy of *Speak, Memory*, but he 'could not stand all that juvenility and Slav nostalgia'. No comparison with Tolstoy or Aksakov. I pointed out that Nabokov was a writer of a completely different kind, at times equal to his great predecessors, but he refused to countenance this, even when I read him extracts from my favourites, *The Gift* and *The Defence*. Even the fact that Nabokov and I were both Taureans, born in April, left him cold.

I now wish I had asked Joe if he had ever encountered Nabokov, who must have been up at Cambridge at the same time. Had Joe met this brilliant, virile and handsome young Russian, and been smitten by him – only, of course, to be rejected? Joe himself must have been extremely attractive in 1922, when he wrote his poem 'On a Photograph of Myself as a Boy':

How young you look! It was not long ago,
  And yet you seem a child, as fresh and fair
As if the gentle spring itself did flow
  Between your lips, and traceries of care
Could never fret your brow. I did not know
  So beautiful you were. . . .

That is how it starts, and it becomes even more embarrassing in the
other four verses, yet remains very touching. When I showed Joe some
of my translations from Paul Valéry – *La jeune parque* and *Fragments du
Narcisse* – he was immediately reminded of that early, almost forgotten
poem, and gave me a copy, saying: 'I wouldn't dream of showing it to
anyone but you, Jim dear.' Understandably: I could imagine how
William Plomer might have smiled inscrutably on reading it. But the
poem, despite its archaisms and other defects, is not defective in poetic
feeling and emotional sincerity, without which superior technique is
useless. Indeed, before I ever met Joe, I had submitted to him, and he
had published in *The Listener* part of the Valéry poems on the theme of
Narcissus. Joe recognized his own narcissistic nature, the source of some
types of homosexuality, at an early age, and the Valéry poems appealed
to him because the theme had, in my eyes, been hallowed by the touch
of a great poet. He could see himself in the figure of Valéry's Narcissus –
the lovely name that gave us our horrid 'sissy':

. . . how sweet they are, the dangers you and I might run!
To be discovered of oneself, one's self to win!
Our hands would mingle, cares would kiss themselves away,
In silence, each the other's dreamings would enjoy,
The same night's tears be closed in one another's eyes;
Our arms would wrap themselves around the same sad cries,
Enfold the same, for love almost-dissolving heart . . .

  O answer me, and from your solitude depart,
O cruel, lovely boy, beyond the reach of hands,
And bearing all my treasures, that the nymph defends. . . .

This translation did not appear in book form until 1963, in *Refusal to
Conform*. But Joe kept it in a scrap-book of cuttings from *The Listener*
and other journals. The Narcissus legend appealed deeply to me, and I
wrote several versions, including one based on Ovid's

. . . nec duo sunt et forma duplex, nec femina dici
nec puer ut possit, neutrumque et utrumque videntur. . . .

which I called 'Narcissus Hermaphroditus' and collected in *A Correct Compassion*. A Narcissus who was both androgynous and hermaphroditic was a true expression of my confused state in those early fifties. Nabokov was in Cambridge during that year, 1922, when Joe wrote his poem. Could they really have met? I think it is very likely that Joe would have been attracted to that burly young Russian footballer and boyish girl-hunter with literary leanings. (Joe was at Trinity, Nabokov at Magdalen).

Glory is Nabokov's most autobiographical novel, and there is quite a lot about Cambridge in it. Was Joe one of the young male exquisites Nabokov rather slyly teases for their eccentric dress, wearing lounge-suit jackets with flannels or 'Oxford bags' and canary-yellow pullovers on open-necked Aertex shirts? And who is the Archibald Moon of this novel? A homosexual don, 'queer', academic, timid, ugly. Goldsworthy Lowes Dickinson, who, Joe later confessed to me, had fallen in love with him and been rejected in a way that always seemed to fill Joe with sorrow? Could it have been A.S. Gow, the Housman editor, or Harrison?

Nabokov in *Speak, Memory* mentions a mechanical piano in his landlady's digs in Cambridge. He refers to it also in *Glory*, where it is a pianola, just like the one in my landlady Madame Sheba's front room at 77a Tottenham Court Road. In the film of Forster's *Maurice* we see the undergrads in Joey Fetherstonhaugh's rooms fooling around playing a mechanical piano. When I invited Joe and his sister Nancy to visit me at Madame Sheba's, Joe at once noticed her pianola. She put in a roll and began playing it. Later, over a drink in the Fitzroy Tavern, Joe said to me: 'That mechanical piano brought back old times.' I thought he was referring to the past in general, for the roll Madame had put on was 'The Maiden's Prayer'. But now I think he must have been remembering the mechanical piano of his undergraduate days, and possibly the one mentioned by Nabokov and Forster. (Nabokov again refers to a 'mechanical piano' in a late work, *Ada*.)

In my Valéry translations, it was remarkable that Joe should have especially liked the lines:

Mais que ta bouche est belle en ce muet blasphème!
O semblable! . . . Et pourtant plus parfait que moi-même,
Ephémère immortel, si clair devant mes yeux,
Pâles membres de perle, et ces cheveux soyeux. . . .

(But how beautiful your mouth – its silent blasphemy!
O my other self! . . . And yet more perfect than I could ever be,
Ephemeral immortal, mirrored so clearly before my eyes,
Pale limbs of pearl, and all that silken hair. . . .)

They must have reminded him of lines from his own poem:

> What was the love that stirred within your breast,
> And stole in secret wonder from your eyes,
> And moved your lips, and all your limbs caressed,
> And sent its first faint tremor to your thighs. . . .

Incidentally, what a convenient rhyming word was *blasphème* for the French symbolist poets! Baudelaire, Mallarmé and many others found it a suitable echo for other decadent words like *blême*, or *poème* and of course *moi-même*. Mallarmé rhymes it with *suprême*, and – in *L'après-midi d'un faune* – with *j'aime*. It is almost as if this suitably thrill-making word was partly responsible for the decadents' quest for strange sensations and blasphemous passions. It even appears in the libretto of Bizet's *Carmen*.

* * *

The only poets I should have liked to know personally were American – Elizabeth Bishop, Frank O'Hara and Hart Crane. Alas, by the time I got to the United States, Frank had died in a ludicrous accident on Fire Island, Crane had long since been dead, and Elizabeth Bishop was in South America. I was drawn to Americans like O'Hara who understood music (he wrote a magnificent essay on the Noh theatre) and were in touch with international movements in literature, or who lived abroad, like Paul Bowles, another of my great admirations – but he, too, by the time I got to Morocco in the early seventies, was away from Tangier. Today, just about the only poet who interests me and is still alive is W.S. Merwin, as much for his translations as for his highly original poetry. Loneliness is all the more profound when all those one felt were fellow-spirits are dead, with none to take their place. Contemporary poetry in English seems to me to be at a dead end – insular, academic and cosily domestic-provincial – except for the poets of Northern Ireland and the Irish Republic: not, however, Heaney, but rather the late John Hewitt, Patrick Kavanagh, Thomas Kinsella and James Simmons, along with a whole new tribe of younger poets emergent in the eighties whose vitality and originality are a tonic after so much British stuff.

All in all, though, it is the Americans I prefer as novelists: Paul Bowles for his strange intensity and unsettling visions of Arab and South American life, the Blech novels of John Updike, the sheer wit and intelligence of the later Saul Bellow, and a host of new prose writers like

Raymond Carver, Frederick Barthelme, Richard Ford and David Leavitt – the last two better as short-story writers than as novelists. But there is no writer in English whose books I would rush out and buy on publication, as I do with French, German and Italian authors. Even with Bellow, I wait for the paperback editions. And among poets, writing in English, there is none to compare with Paul Celan, Marina Tsvetayeva, George Seferis (the three of them no longer with us), or René Char, Jacques Roubaud, Andréa Zanzotto and the Catalan Agustí Bartra. Not to mention the only great Japanese, Mutsuo Takahashi. . . .

* * *

The season of Christmas was upon us, a time my mother had always disliked. I had come to hate it, too, and in Corsham it seemed more sinister than ever. 'I wonder where we'll all be next Christmas?' my mother asked the air, in her usual unseasonal way, with a neurotic sigh. Both she and my father wanted to get away from the spite and tittle-tattle of Corsham. My mother's excuse to me was that the stone-flagged floors of those ancient buildings were too cold. My father had stopped going to the pub: he was under great stress. But they were to stay there one more year, while I was in Sweden.

There were some massive falls of snow that December, and even Corsham looked beautiful, masked with all that whiteness. This is how I saw it:

Another Season
The panes are furred and feathered over
With frost inlaid as neat and close
As plumes of hens or plots of clover.
Each village cobble is a full-blown rose
That cakes its unshed petals under cover
Of the confected snows.

Under the vaults of tufted yew
That adumbrate a roof of ice
No shadows fall. Only the buried path is true.
The muted light stands still, is shuttered twice
With fronds of glass and buds of bitter dew.
Birds fling down hail from lofts of rice.

Half a snowball crusts each post.
The winter leaf drinks from its own heaped spoon.
A bird-track hints, but like a troubled ghost

Flits in the middle of the paddocked noon
And prints its vanished arrows on a waste
Of time, the earth's compacted moon.

The sultry peacocks cringe, the wild white swans are grey,
The creamy cattle tinge themselves with green,
The milky cat is yellowish: the sheep betray
A dingy brown that once was seen
As golden on a summer's day.
Only the thick-fleeced hedge is clean.

Clear in the flocked woods the trees are bare
But for the snow their candied branches underline.
The green-chapped beech, the ash, the birch all share
The same bleached burden as the pasted pine,
Each knot and twig and elbowed bough a snare
For clumps of stuff slung from the air's white mine.

We step on starch. It mews. The lakeside creaks.
The snow-lagged heads of grass
Are gripped in a pool whose trodden platter squeaks.
The gargoyles on the church have beards of glass,
Ears hung with ice, their noses beaks.
Their blinded eyes look daggers at us as we pass.

The golden light is gone in which love's seeds were sown.
A statue wears the clownish season like a tilted hat.
There will be Spring to pay. Life is not done.
Though black is blackest now, it cannot stay like that.
– Home is illumined like a paper tomb, though not with sun.
Our footprints, like unwanted letters, obliterate the welcome
                                                    mat.

The poem speaks for itself, for the blackness in my frightened life.
Those letters on the welcome mat, had I but known it, were anonymous
poison-pen letters sent to my mother and father, who managed to keep
them secret from me. It was not until my mother's death in Bath that I
discovered them. They were foul and vicious. I must have sensed
something when I wrote 'unwanted letters', though what I referred to
was correspondence from the Income Tax inspector and the National
Health Service. But I also had the sense of something dead at home, our
worn-out welcome in that unfriendly village of bullies and witches.

Our only friends were a lady who lived across the road, who came to
talk to my mother and father from time to time, bringing little presents

of flowers, new-laid eggs, a book, a cake; and a strange, gifted young girl, Helen, a young beauty of boundless vitality and joyful chatter, who wrote poetry. The lady from across the way was a widow who lived all alone with memories of a colonial life in Egypt. She brought us delicate, fragile plates and bowls of Egyptian glass, with the washed-out tints of boiled sweets. I still have some of her delicate gifts. But even more I cherish the way she alone of all the villagers stood by my parents, and by me, and helped them through the coming year while I was away. When we moved from Corsham to Bath, both she and Helen came to see us regularly. No one else from Corsham did, until my father's sudden death, when we had a visit from Isabel, one of the staff at the Academy, to bring condolences from my former employers.

My Christmas present to my father was a bottle of Scotch. I meant it to show I had forgiven him the traumatic shock of his drunkenness at my cousin's wedding so many years ago. But I shall never forget the strange look he gave me as I handed him the bottle, as if he did not know me, and did not wish to know me. After his death I found his work diaries, in which he never once mentions my name, though the names of my mother, my aunt and my grandmother Kirkup appear regularly. It was as if he had begrudged my very existence. He took one sip of the Scotch, and no more. As I dislike whisky, it stayed in the cupboard until his death a couple of years later. My mother was frightened of strong drink and begged me never to take it, as if my father's drinking had horrified her even more than it had me. But at last my father and I were reconciled.

He had stopped going to the local pub for the modest half-pint of bitter he used to enjoy: the cruel country folk and the even crueller teaching staff from the Academy had turned him against the place. My mother shopped in the village once a week, then stayed at home. Or they took the bus for a day in Bath or Chippenham. Joe came with his Alsatian bitch, Queenie, and took my parents to Longleat, where he photographed them while I stayed at home to look after Queenie. Joe and my parents got on wonderfully well together, which surprised me.

During the winter of utter despair I wrote another poem, 'Sick Face in a Frosted Mirror'. Both that poem and 'Another Season' were published by Joe, and opened my next collection of poems, *The Descent into the Cave*.

Another poem I wrote around this time was 'The Kitchen Sink', a poem that happened to be in tune with a passing mood in painting and drama. A *Life* photographer came and took some pictures of me for a picture-essay on the theme. The most successful photograph showed me sitting on the kitchen floor beside the sink, clutching a lavatory brush above my head. That period of my life seems now to have been permeated by a sense of urban squalor and social corruption that was the mark of the art and the literature of the time. I wrote poems on drains, dustbins, old trousers, the convenience, an ashtray and Hiroshima – 'Ghosts, Fire, Water', about the paintings of Iri Maruki and Toshiko Akamatsu, by which I had been deeply moved in a London exhibition. It is one of my best poems, but no British journal would touch it – too disturbing. Now it is often reprinted in anthologies, and has been set to music for unaccompanied choir.

But I also wrote one poem that seemed to give a glimpse of hope, almost of spiritual resurrection, about the figure of a man preserved in peat at Tollund, Denmark, who was discovered in 1950, and the poem was called 'The Resurrected Man'. It was a fitting image for whatever hopes I had left of the future, as was the underlying imagery of the title poem of *The Descent into the Cave*, which was a kind of despairing descent into a personal hell, with no Virgil or Dante to accompany me. Yet at the end of that long poem, a rite of passage, I returned from the depths to the light of day.

As for my poetry, the only thing in the world that meant anything permanent to me, despite my repeated failures to abandon it, I knew that it would continue no matter in what foreign land I found myself, no matter what language I was speaking or what personality was offered by my masks. I was feeling more and more like Nabokov's pseudonym Sirin, who was so original that reviewers and critics were bereft of suitable precedents and comparisons, and so did not know what to make of him.

It was my hope that I should find more understanding abroad, where poetry was less than a merely social activity or a first step on the rungs of the ladder of the British literary mafia, dominated by narrow-minded university cliques. And that hope came to be fulfilled.

THOSE SPANISH EYES

More clearly than anything else at the moment he sensed that this conviction of having entered into a new region of his life was only in the nature of a warning. . . . He could not heed the warning because he could not understand it.

> *Paul Bowles*, 'A THOUSAND DAYS FOR MOKHTAR'

'I hear it's Hebrew in Heaven, sir – Spanish is seldom spoken,' he exclaimed seraphically.

> *Ronald Firbank*, CONCERNING THE ECCENTRICITIES OF
> CARDINAL PIRELLI

The master illusion of Spain is the conviction that the Spaniards are a people different, when they are only a people separate.

> *James Morris*, THE PRESENCE OF SPAIN

My life was becoming more and more complicated in Corsham. It was even more complicated for my mother and father. I regretted having left Riette Sturge-Moore's comfortable London flat in Adelaide Road, where I had worked so well, writing translations of Camara Laye's *The African Child* for the Paris magazine *Réalités*, which paid so well, Kleist's *Prince of Homburg*, Brecht's *Mother Courage* and a large number of modern French, German and Italian poets. One of my fellow-lodgers in Riette's flat had been the theatre director Frank Dunlop, who was about to become famous with his pop productions of Shakespeare at the Edinburgh Festival, whose director he eventually became in the 1980s. I had had terrible problems with my translation of Camara Laye's book, problems that were to pursue me with all his other works. For one thing, when it was finally published in book form, Collins paid me a miserable fee, and there were endless confusions over editing. Sentences, paragraphs and pages were cut without my consent, there was a mix-up with the American publisher, corrections I had made in the proofs were not incorporated into the final text and so on. I loved translating this gifted West African, but it was sheer torture working with Collins, where my editor at that time was the sympathetic Mark

Bonham-Carter, well known for his championing of the underdogs in race relations. It was he who suggested I translate Camara Laye. Later, he offered me Louise de Vilmorin, but such had been my trials with Collins, I turned her down. When I later met this formidable lady in Paris, I was thankful I had done so.

But these professional problems were nothing compared with the horrors of living in a narrow-minded little English village. I had to get out or suffocate. So my parents agreed to stay on one more year while I went abroad to try to sort myself out. When I think now of how I imposed that extra year of torture upon them, I am full of remorse. But at the time, I was in a state of panic: my parents sacrificed their comfort and ease of mind for my temporary well-being.

But 1956 did not start off too badly. My diary records a happy meeting in London with Andrew Young on 7 January: he brought along his friend John Arlott. As I have a fear of being bored to death by sports, and particularly by cricket, I rather dreaded meeting this celebrated BBC cricket commentator, whose books I had not read. But we got along very well, and I began to think that after all cricket could not be quite so tedious if it was immortalized by such a delightful man, who to my great relief hardly mentioned cricket. We talked mainly about writing, and about Andrew's beautiful poems.

I was once more invited to give a reading at the Oxford Union on 17 January – a very disagreeable experience again. The Oxford literary set were a bunch of louts. They all drank beer, which I loathe, and when I asked for some brandy to steady my nerves there were some raised eyebrows. I was made to feel very unwelcome, so I wondered why they had invited me in the first place. I had to do it for the money, as I was chronically hard up. I was treated much more kindly whenever I read at Cambridge: I accepted no more invitations from that other place.

I gave another reading at the Bath Writers' Circle in the Technical College, where the reception was predictably bland – I would rather have had the humiliations of the Oxford toughies. A week later I read at the Royal School, Bath, to an audience of appreciative young ladies and their teachers. I remember my advice to them was never to be mealy-mouthed, which puzzled the young ladies but went down very well with their speech and drama teacher. I was interested to see this educational establishment for the daughters of naval officers, where Nina Hamnett had been 'miss-educated' as she told me once, between double gins, at the Black Horse pub in Rathbone Place.

By this time, the 'Full Inspection' had started at Bath Academy, with 'sherry in the Music Room', where once again I met my inspectors who kept giving me odd looks. Then there was teaching practice, in which I reduced several students to tears with my criticisms of their teaching methods. At last it was the end of term, and I set off the very next day for my first visit to Spain. I had bought a third-class *kilometrico* train ticket, and intended to use it to the full by travelling the length and breadth of Spain for the next month. Through friendship with a Spanish flamenco dancer in London I had become obsessed by Spanish culture, particularly drama and dance. Night after night I used to sit in the galleries of London and provincial theatres drinking in every sound and movement of flamenco artists like Pilar Lopes, Carmen Amaya, Antonio, Luisillo and José Limon. I even took some flamenco lessons, and started learning the classical guitar from an Austrian lady in Swiss Cottage. What impressed me most about these dancers was the accuracy and speed of their evolutions in brilliant technique whose utter mastery left them free to improvise and left room for the angel of inspiration and the demon of passion. That was how I wanted to write poetry. Carmen Amaya was my great favourite, a real demon of flamenco dancing, who often seemed possessed by some private devil. Even the delicious purring of her castanets had something not quite healthy about it, and her furious *zapateado* actually gave me erections. She is the heroine of a marvellous film made in 1963 by Francisco Rovira Belta, when she was past her best, called *Los Tarantos*, in which we can also see another great dancer, the very youthful Antonio Gades in a slow-motion dance later adapted for *Blood Wedding* by Carlos Saura. But it is still Amaya who rivets the attention with her exactly controlled *furia* and her wild but noble gypsy comportment. When I saw this fine film again in January 1990 at a gala projection in the Paris Opéra, all the enthusiasms and passions of my youthful adorations swept over me with almost painful ecstasy and nostalgia.

Dear Agostin at Leeds had introduced me to Portuguese and Spanish literature, and made me promise to visit one of his old haunts in Madrid, the Gran Café de Gijón, once graced by the presence of Lorca, Alberti, Neruda, Hemingway, the bullfighter Ordoñez and Ava Gardner, Truman Capote and Vincent Price.

I stayed a couple of days in Paris, where I watched from the topmost gallery at the Comédie Française a massive production of *Cyrano de Bergerac* which from that distance looked like some abstract theatrical army manoeuvres being performed in a void that had absolutely no connection with the audience. In those days it was easy to get into la Maison de Molière, unlike today, when every kind of obstacle is put in the path of the casual visitor wanting to see a play. Then I took a night train from the Gare d'Austerlitz for the frontier at Irun, where the first sight of Spanish police in capes and black lacquer hats sent a rather cold thrill through my aching body.

But after that initial chill douche, everything went well; I fell deeply in love with Spain and the Spanish people – and with two or three Spaniards that love became a very intimate passion.

Once across the border, I was delighted to find myself in a third-class railway carriage crammed with the gayest, angriest, noisiest and most dramatic people I had ever encountered. There was endless speculation about when the train would start, and even about where it was likely to go. Baskets, live hens, bundles, bottles of wine and lemonade, tortillas, salami sausages and babies were being passed through the lowered window into the compartment. It was a vivid and happy agitation. After the train started, the talk too gathered momentum and questions were frank. Soon everyone knew where I lived in England and where I was going to in Spain: it was a pure and inoffensive curiosity.

After a while we began to eat our picnic lunches. Many were the titbits offered me. This is a formal courtesy in Spain, and in fact one does not accept anything. I in turn offered some teacake, which filled the Spaniards with wonder and was delightedly refused with polite wishes that I might enjoy it myself. After the meal I offered a cigarette to the lady sitting next to me. This was an elementary *faux pas*. A grim-looking priest who had been prowling up and down the corridor shook an admonishing finger and my heart sank. But the lady smilingly refused: she was gracious about my ignorance. In Spain one does not offer cigarettes to respectable women. It was my first insight into another way of life, and it rather frightened me. The priest in his greasy black robes filled me with obscure horror. His presence cast a dark cloud over that happy afternoon. Had the Inquisition returned?

When we arrived in Burgos, my first stop, there were many willing hands to hoist my luggage through the window. (I had brought far too much.) A kind fellow-traveller, a young Englishman who already knew Burgos well, got off the train with me. He took me to the inexpensive *pension* where he seemed to be a familiar guest. We agreed to share a room, two to a bed. I wondered how I should make it through the night, lying next to such an attractive youth. We had dinner, and the food was as good as he had promised it would be. The place housed a large family, kept in order by a fierce old grandmother who took a dislike to me as soon as she saw me. All my life I have had the experience of encountering some stranger for whom the very sight of me is enough to arouse distrust and malice. I was very careful to keep my eyes off the old lady. I think she suspected that I had the evil eye, and was just being wary, as I was.

Dinner had been late, well after ten, but for a Spaniard that means the night is still young. With my English travelling companion I strolled round the animated streets of this sternly beautiful city, which yet has a fairy-tale air, and whose immense cathedral is one of the architectural glories of Spain. I was glad to be out so late, as I wanted to delay as long as possible the awkward moment when we should have to climb into the same double bed. The incessant life of the streets goes on almost until dawn, for this is a society of night. Everywhere there were vendors of hot chestnuts, roasted almonds and melon seeds, waffles, lottery tickets (*para hoy, para hoy* . . .), popcorn, candy, fried squid and shrimps and *tapas*, cheap snacks of all kinds of fiery sausage and briny seafoods. For the *paseo*, the evening stroll, when all the town turns out to take the cooler air of night, girls on one side of the wide promenade, boys on the other, is one of the classic traditions of Mediterranean lands. The street life is for everyone: it costs nothing, and it is the essence of Spanish social ease.

It was in Burgos that I had my first encounter with a shoeblack, only about ten or eleven years old. With dazzling virtuosity in the manipulation of polish, rags and brushes he made my shoes shine like fountains. Spit and polish has rarely reached such an art. He gave the final touch by applying an old nylon stocking, and of course I had to pay extra for this *Americano* highlight of his craft. The shine soon wears off, but it makes a wonderfully relaxing massage for tired, aching feet. In Andalusia the little shoeblacks sometimes run after you in the street, pointing in horror at your shoes, even when they are not very dirty. If you give in, and sit down before the joyous little pests on the folding stool they set up anywhere on the pavement, you may find them tearing off your heels and fixing new ones, or hammering on huge rubber soles.

The people of Spain are warm-hearted hosts to those who come without too many prejudices and preconceived ideas, for Spaniards have, as John Harvey points out in his excellent book *The Cathedrals of Spain*, an 'uncompromising contempt for ways that are not their own'. So the visitor who is always complaining that Spain is not like his own land will soon find himself, as he deserves to be, excluded from any true relationship with this most remarkable country and with its gay, reserved, passionate and severe inhabitants. For theirs is a grave and often sombre morality, but their sense of discrimination gives their land a sharp and profound distinction. And though he may not have much money, a Spaniard knows how to live. This is a lesson that has escaped the hordes of British people who now have turned the Costa Brava and the Costa del Sol into Iberian Blackpools and Margates – to the utter contempt of the natives. But thirty years ago Spain was another country altogether and the Spaniards were a different people. Yet now that the dread shadow of Franco has been lifted from their presence, a new and joyous energy is transforming lives too long oppressed by State and Church.

* * *

At 2 a.m. I could take no more, and told my companion I wanted to return to the *pension*. I was hoping that I would be so worn out that thoughts of love would not cause me to embarrass us both if sex reared its lovely head. But Trevor – such a car-salesmanish name should have warned me – said he would return later, so I went to bed alone. In fact Trev did not return at all – he had left town, I learnt from my astonished hostess, who had assumed he would have told me. I breakfasted well and paid my bill: it was for two. My attractive Englishman had cheated me. Later I discovered that he had made off with a couple of my traveller's cheques, though when I returned to Bath my bank told me he had not been able to cash them. But I was glad these sneaky little crimes had been committed by one of my own countrymen – it was what I had grown to expect from attractive young males who inexplicably attached themselves to me – and not by a Spaniard, the soul of honour, who would disdain to stoop so low for so little.

My next stop was Valladolid. Fortunately Trev had not stolen my *kilometrico* ticket. Train travel in Spain is not an unmixed delight. It did not bother me at the time, but now, travelling on trains that have no non-smoking carriage, or in which the prohibition is cheerfully ignored if they have one, I arrive half kippered at my destination, especially on long trips as from Barcelona to Madrid or Madrid to Lisbon. But this acute discomfort is offset by the incredibly beautiful landscapes passing outside the windows. You travel south through a region of golden-brown plains as carefully plotted and patched as a Spanish workman's trousers; or through wild, rocky landscapes where great worn stones lie half buried in the tired earth like sleeping elephants. Here and there you see a little sand-coloured village, its airy bell-tower bulging with big green bells, or a lonely cluster of stone-pines like toy trees set against snowy sierras. It is a spectacle totally unlike any other – savage, bare, vast, open and mysterious. The slow trains are best. They sometimes stop for so long at small towns, you have time to stroll round the square and have a little cup of thick, black, sweet, boiling-hot coffee. There are patient mules bearing panniers of bread or fruit, or standing resignedly while goods are being delivered to the accompaniment of lengthy conversations. Spanish mules have learnt to ease such long social calls by standing with one neat forefoot crossed over the other while their bonneted ears lazily twitch away the flies. And even the smallest place has its little shoeblack to massage your feet with vigorous brush and cloth. Inside the small local cafés there is the ceaseless click and shuffle of dominoes, the *zapateado* of draughts, the thump of playing-cards. A young soldier sitting next to me in a café makes the whole table shake as he bangs with his big brown fist on the helpless postage stamp he has just licked with long, languorous tongue and affixed crookedly to a cheap, skimpy envelope, inside which he has shoved a small, filthy banknote and a page of ruled paper covered with childish writing. The soldiers are everywhere, looking lost, looking too hot in their clumsy khaki uniforms, their hobnailed boots, their greasy forage-caps with the little tassel dangling over rich black brilliantined hair. They all seem to be country boys, shy and slow, but with beautiful rosy complexions and dazzlingly white teeth. They are adorable, and very approachable, always ready to please for a 'consideration' that means nothing to me but which for them is the equivalent of one month's pay. Many is the local slow train I have allowed to leave without me as I walked along an *arroyo* with one of these rustic, pagan gods. They have the sombre passion of Arabs, and the same instinct to dominate sexually with man or woman. Many of them have Arab blood from ancient times when the Arabs developed their fountain culture all over Spain, where water is often rare, and the sight and feel of it a luxury.

I wanted to be in Valladolid for Easter, for the extraordinary Caritas Procession of hooded penitents and flagellants and polychrome wooden sculptures of religious themes for which the city is famous. In those days, before 'the media' had flooded us with so much unnecessary information, few people travelled, or at least there was not the hysterical mass tourism that blights all advanced countries today. So I found a moderately priced hotel room quite easily in the centre of town. The streets were full of gypsies and horse-dealers, farmers; and señoritas in traditional flounced costume rode side-saddle on the backs of their booted and spurred gallants' steeds jingling with silvery bells and ornaments. Though the next day would be Good Friday, there was an air of festivity for the long, painful and very moving procession, which was especially impressive at night, under the flames of the torches shining on sweating faces of penitents. It was all deadly serious, and to me it seemed very gruesome, though the ecstatic coloured statues and tableaux were quite agonizingly impressive, especially the one of a bleeding, naked Christ with his crown of thorns, carrying his cross. There is a famous museum of these figures which I later visited in Valladolid, and the churches in the city are full of them. One of the most horrifyingly beautiful examples is of a very lifelike, bleeding Christ –

Cristo yacente – in the Iglesia de San Miguel. The streams of blood on his face, chest and shoulders are depicted with amazing and rather disgusting verisimilitude: the blood streaming from his eyes is particularly grisly. But the people of Valladolid worship these tremendously moving examples of the local sculptors' craft, now dying out. Most of the best sculptures are centuries old and have been carefully preserved. But for me the experience of the Caritas Procession was overwhelmingly sexual. I found it stirred my sexuality to the roots, and I sensed a certain sexual indulgence in all that simulated agony and contorted nakedness.

I was trembling with unnamed desires and longings, and I thought I was about to faint, so I escaped to the comparative calm of my hotel bar for a cooling drink while I tried to put my emotions in order, unsuccessfully. At the bar were a young American couple who were obviously exchanging catty remarks about my appearance. I flashed a look at them, and the young man whispered: 'He's watching us.' They soon left. I had dinner and retired to my room, but the noise in the streets kept me from reading or even thinking. Sleep would obviously be impossible that night.

So I went out into the night, with all its theatrical threats and promises. Passing a pavement café, I heard a slow handclap and wondered if someone were 'sending me up'. (I did not, of course, look round, and one of the first rules of self-preservation for intermediates like me is never to turn round if someone shouts one's name, or some humiliating *maricone* with an inverted exclamation mark at the 'm' and a right-way-up one at the 'e.') However, by squeezing my eyes into their long-lashed corners, I realized that the slow handclap was from someone calling for a waiter.

Just opposite the Hotel Moderno – I was staying in a room with a marvellous view of the main street crossing – is a sort of park, with a stand of bosky trees, unlighted. Partly to escape from the stupendous noise, partly to investigate this enticingly dusky Arden in case there were any cocks in town, I crossed the road into its kindly shadows, and almost at once fell headlong into romance. As I entered a little grove of trees, I saw a figure standing half concealed by a tree-trunk. I approached slowly and nervously, for there was no one else in sight, and I thought it might be a thief. But as I drew near, a dazzling smile broke the darkness, and a deep male voice greeted me with '*Buenas tardes, señor.*' I paused, smiled and returned the greeting. The rest of our encounter was wordless, for I felt the breath expelled from my chest by a sudden ardent embrace, and a warm kiss full on the mouth prevented me from taking another for some time. It was one of the most surprising and charming encounters I had ever known, and after the sordidness of my pranks in Britain it seemed full of unexpected affection, sweetness, innocence. I felt like a boy of six again, when I had my first such overwhelming sexual encounter behind a telegraph-pole in the dark back lane behind Ada Street in South Shields – something that was to haunt me all my life. Now I felt the same boyish rush of fresh passion for my new friend with his fine, dark Spanish eyes sparkling among their thick, furry eyelashes. When we had taken our fill of one another, in a simple, childlike manner, we just stood together for a long while beneath the tree, holding hands, intermingling fingers, giving here a hug, there a kiss as the festivities roared on a few yards away. It was an enchanted hour. And I knew I had found a friendship that would last longer than one brief encounter.

He was called Jordi – a Catalan name. He was a working man, a farm labourer, though on his own small stretch of ungrateful land. He told me how hard it was to make a living, how he had to fight corrupt officials just to get enough water to irrigate his field. That evening he had left home in a fury after being refused the water from some nearby American swimming-bath belonging to the US Army. He was sad and frustrated, and so he had come to this rendezvous with the unknown. I knew only too well that desperate reaction in times of trouble or anger or sorrow, when the simple longing just for the touch of a human hand is more than one can bear, and one goes out to find it somewhere – anywhere, anyhow – 'N'importe où, n'importe qui, n'importe comment', as Rimbaud said.

Jordi could not come to my hotel. To do so would have exposed him to humiliating inquiries in that police state, where one still has to surrender one's passport as soon as one arrives at an hotel. Nor could we go to his home, where he lived with a sister and an invalid mother. We left the main streets, where Jordi was afraid of meeting someone he knew, not because he was ashamed of me, but, as I sensed only too well, because it would have created an embarrassing situation for him, a workman, in a plain white shirt and worn black corduroy trousers, seen walking with a foreigner with blond hair wearing smart sports clothes – unthinkable! So we walked arm in arm, something acceptable between males in Spain, along back streets, and came to a small, empty café near the outskirts of the town. We were both tired with walking, and Jordi was hungry – he had rushed out of the house refusing to eat dinner, so urgent was his need, so ardent his longing. We had some wine, then soup, a wretched concoction of warm water, rancid olive oil and chunks of stale bread – *sopa de los pobres*, poor men's soup, as Jordi called it – and then a greasy omelette filled with chopped potato and onion, followed by some dried-up fish and the *flan* which is Spain's omnipresent dessert. Then a cup of coffee, Bisontes cigarettes, a cognac or two, another carafe of the rough red wine. We kept trying to avoid each other's eyes, but it was impossible. From time to time, when the elderly proprietress was not looking, we squeezed hands or knees under the table. After we finished eating, we did not talk much, just looked at one another. My heart felt as if it were choked and overflowing with bliss, and I was sure that Jordi felt the same. He walked me back to the centre, after refusing to let me pay for the meal. He left me a few blocks from the Hotel Moderno. We arranged to meet again next evening, and parted with a lingering handshake to seal the promise of tomorrow's Good Friday love.

From my window, before I got into bed, I looked out and saw at the end of the street the enormous illuminated figure of Christ the Redeemer on top of the cathedral tower. I thought how Christ and the Roman Catholic Church dominate the lives of most of the Spanish people. Yet Jordi had been bitter in his attacks on the clergy, and about the money wasted on statues and golden tiaras for the Virgin when the poor and crippled of Spain were starving in the streets.

I slept the dreamless sleep of the utterly happy.

* * *

I was wakened early by a bedlam of bells calling to early Mass, and by the noise of traffic, people shouting morning greetings, car horns honking, children laughing and screaming in the street below my window. The noise all day (and nearly all night) is almost unendurable at times. But it is also curiously invigorating, full of heat and Spanish pride and energy, an aural extension of that outrageous vitality which does not content itself with the minimum but always goes to extremes, with the maximum of volume and gesture.

After breakfast, I strolled round the town. The sun seemed much more immediate than in stuffy England's lukewarm springtime, though it feels no hotter. One senses that its greater intimacy with the body has a more direct effect upon one's health. I can feel it benevolently toasting my pale Nordic skin and drenching my hair with its strong and equal bleach. Of course we are only in March and still in the northern part of the Iberian Peninsula. In general, I dislike strong sunshine and its accompanying coarse heat, so already I am viewing with dismay the prospect of life in southern Spain during April. But for the moment my new-found love makes everything seem endurable – 'All for love, and the world well lost. . . .'

As I wander round the animated and increasingly noisy Good Friday streets, I have a sense of liberation. Here I am unknown and I feel the release for the mind and spirit of not having to encounter preconceived and mistaken ideas about what I am and what I write. All the problems of identity and character dislocation related to my multiple personality and to my ambiguous sexual nature seem to have been partly resolved. Until, that is, I hear a passing peasant woman laugh and turn round to look at me as I pass, crying: 'Is it a man or a woman?' At this remark other passers-by cast fleeting glances of surprise or *goguenard* relish upon an appearance which for me seemed conservative enough: a pale fawn duffle-coat with scarlet lining bought at Gieves in Bath, a pair of lemon-yellow gloves, with matching socks and string necktie along with a lapis lazuli azure shirt with black pearl buttons, and on my dancing feet a pair of dark brown suede pumps with oxblood heels. In honour of Good Friday I was carrying a small bunch of violets and primroses, their sweet-scented posy enshrined in a silver doily. After only one day in the Spanish sun, my longish hair, I must admit, had taken on an almost platinum tint, but I had kept my make-up very, very restrained – a real sacrifice for a dedicated *maquilleur*: no more than the airiest brushing of 'invisible' shaving talc, which had a tendency to extend beyond the shaving areas to the hairline; just a touch of Cherry Blossom black boot polish on my long but rather colourless eyelashes, and the merest hint of crimson on my lips derived from the Gordon Moore special brand of 'cosmetic' toothpaste I employed to provide more definition in the play of contrasts between my modestly pink gums and my sparkling white teeth, whose artificial-seeming regularity enjoyed an inbuilt guarantee of authenticity in the genuine, natural gap between my two front teeth in the upper range – a sign both of my Viking descent and, I felt proudly convinced, a living symbol of my divided self.

Perhaps it was the brilliance of the strong Spanish sun that had so exposed me to those beautiful big dark Spanish eyes? As I proceeded towards the cathedral for my devotions, I caught a few unobtrusive winks from male passers-by – and how that smart Spanish tailoring sets off a Spaniard's usually immoderate sexual assets! I could hardly tear my eyes away from some of them, both young and old. However, the boys' shorts often seemed very inelegant after the abbreviated ones of French schoolboys, which so perfectly mould their thighs and bottoms. It was almost like being back in puritan England to see those rivals of Bermuda shorts coming well down to the dimpled knee. Is this an example of Spanish prudishness? I notice that even small girls have Easter dresses almost down to their ankles – even two- and three-year-olds. And the number of very stout children is very noticeable, as they parade between their stout parents in fiesta finery among the more soberly clad matrons and *caballeros* in funereal black, that depressing all-over blackness which Spanish widows don upon the death of a husband is somehow medieval in its grim awfulness.

To my surprise, in this anticlerical region the cathedral was packed, and I had to stand at the back to observe the moppings and mowings of the clergy and choir and the genuflections and curtsies of the congregation. But the singing was superb, ethereal boy voices seeming to float high above the choking clouds of incense. A man standing next to me took my hand at the end of the service, but it was only to shake it as a sign of brotherly love united in Christ.

The comedy of the street crossings absorbs my attention as I sit at a pavement café sipping a dark, sinful coffee and a curious violet liqueur whose name I do not know – I obtained it from a toreador-like waiter by indicating it with my long cigarette-holder on the table of a nearby *grande dame*. She gave me a scandalized look and whispered something to her husband, whose flabby jowls, black glasses and thin, dyed moustache proclaimed him an ardent nationalist and Franquisto. He just grunted and returned to the moderately enlightened pages of his *ABC*.

The traffic police, too, wore black glasses and toothbrush moustaches. Otherwise their flabby faces were unshaven, and some were smoking small, thin cigars or cigarettes as they directed the traffic with many a salute for important local personages and the utmost contempt for pedestrians. One of them is wearing a dented white helmet and he is implacable when a Spanish matron, all in black, with a black mantilla cast over her iron-grey bun and family-heirloom tortoise-shell comb, gesticulates furiously and passionately because he makes her go back to the pavement when she tries to cross before reaching the *paseo de pietones*. However, when a pretty young girl attempts the unauthorized crossing, the cop bows and offers her his arm as he escorts her across the busy street. I shudder at such blatant sexism and ageism. Then he dictatorially sends an ugly, fat peasant back to the kerb.

Many Spaniards seem to be incapable of submitting themselves to this elementary discipline, so how can they stand the Franco regime? Well, there are fortunately many who cannot. Perhaps the proud Spanish individuality resents any small intrusion upon their arrogant sense of personhood. Many seem not to understand that they cannot traverse the pedestrian crossing itself even when there is no traffic approaching it but the red light is showing. There are many arguments which give the Spaniards a great opportunity to indulge in their favourite sport, shouted conversations bristling with picturesque invective. The policemen are absolutely just and strict, most of the time, in the performance of what must be one of the least popular duties in a

Spanish city. But sometimes the strictness verges on the absurd, for every Spaniard relishes a display of authority. It seems odd to see a cop make an old lady cross a street full of traffic *twice* because she has started to cross the zebra stripes when the lights are red: she is more than half-way across when, to her white-faced fury, he blows his whistle at her and with a commanding gesture almost operatic in its absurdity forces her to retreat among the cars that have suddenly surged forward, hooting angrily, across her path. During *ferias* there seems to be more difficulty than usual in persuading pedestrians to use the crossings and use them at the right time, perhaps on account of the numerous country visitors and *gitanos*, who are accustomed to being laws unto themselves, even under Franco. It is also rather odd that people are allowed to walk on the road, provided they go parallel to, and not far from, the pavement edge. The accident rate in Spain is extremely high and warrants such rigid methods of control, but so far, though my room looks on one of the most important crossings in Valladolid, I have seen no serious accidents.

I was one of the few, like the pretty young girl, to get away with crossing the street at an unauthorized point. I had decided to test the reactions of an unusually good-looking traffic policeman. He whistled automatically as I stepped off the kerb, then smiled and strode towards me, and with an elaborate show of courtesy offered me his arm, bowed and escorted me through the blaring traffic to the safety of the other side, to the great amusement of all the spectators of this little macho scene. 'Hasta la vista!' he whispered as I took a dignified leave of him and his for once admiring public. But I realized, as I made my way back to the Hotel Moderno, that I should have to tone down my appearance somewhat. Fortunately I had my all-black velvet outfit with me, and black patent-leather boots with Cuban heels of the kind favoured by many Iberian males. However, I would refuse to parade with my over-coat slung over my shoulders, as is the 'smart' male Spanish fashion: in England it would be considered the height of camp.

So I was all in black that night, with a virginal white shirt and a dark-red tie, when I had my second meeting with Jordi – a romantic assignation under the very umbrella pine where we had met the night before. Jordi longed to spend a whole night with me, but this was out of the question in provincial, uptight Valladolid. So, as I would soon be leaving anyhow for Madrid, he decided to take a couple of days off from his back-breaking field labour and spend them with me in a cheap hotel in the capital.

We left the following day, by night train. It left about 4 a.m. It was a strange experience for both of us, travelling in a crowded compartment, happy to be with one another yet not daring even to hold hands. There were two other couples in the compartment, and I envied the way they were able to sleep with their heads on each other's shoulders in the chaste abandonment of acceptable heterosexual embraces. Their faces in the dim blue light were so moving in their vulnerability and innocence, their gentleness and concern for one another expressed with such perfect openness. Half-way through that long night, when all were asleep, Jordi drew my head down in his lap, where I fitfully dozed. Medina del Campo . . . Avila . . . Madrid Chamartin just after 8 a.m. and straight to bed in a small, cheap hotel near the station. There we alternately slept and made love until afternoon, when we went out for lunch. Then Jordi took me to the bullring, where the apprentice bull-fighters were putting on a *novillada*. All my instincts revolted against the barbarity and cruelty of this national sport. But Jordi so much wanted to let me see it, I accepted his invitation. He was full of excitement at being back in Madrid: he had been a member of the Blue Brigade in his late teens and had gone to Russia with them. During the Civil War he had fought on the side of the Republican Loyalists and had been in the siege of Madrid. Now he looked with deep emotion at the snowy Guadarrama. He had been in the rout of the Italian Fascists at Guadalajara: he was full of contempt for the cowardly Italian troops, but spoke with admiration of the Germans, even though they were Nazis – at least they fought well. He took me to look at the Prado de San Isidro, on the other bank of the Manzanares, where the vague outlines of wartime trenches could still be seen, and he wept as we stood at the grave of Goya in the nearby cemetery. He had lost an adolescent lover at San Isidro. . . . I could only squeeze his hand, and, drawing him into the shadow of a tomb, embraced him with all the love I could summon from my sex-racked heart. Leandro Fernández de Moratín is also buried in that cemetery, and down in San Justo there are the tombs of Larra and Bécquer among other well-known writers. It was like reopening my history of Spanish literature.

A bottle of wine and some *tapas* cheered and warmed us: this Easter Sunday in Madrid was sunny, but with a chilly wind. Then we were off for an afternoon of *corridas* at the bullring. My heart sank in the taxi from the Gran Via.

When I was living in France before the war, I read a book on bullfighting by a surrealist writer I much admired, Michel Leiris, entitled *Miroir de la tauromachie* (1938), written under the influence of his friends Picasso and André Masson. Like Montherlant in *Les bestiaires*, Leiris saw the sexual drama in bullfighting. To him, the various stages of the encounter were preludes to a symbolic copulation, with the passes of the red cape stiffened by the *muleta* as theatrical foreplay, revealing increasing sexual impatience for the final thrust, the kill of bloody orgasm that could be associated with the erotic imagery of St John of the Cross. The final bursts of applause and the rain of roses, fans and programmes from the crowd were seen as the release of a copious ejaculation.

From Jordi I had learnt quite a lot of Spanish slang, and I knew that the word *corrida* came from the verb *correr*, to run. When we were reaching climax, Jordi would cry *¡corremos, corremos!* meaning 'let's come together now!' At the bullring, I learnt that the verb *acoplarse* (to couple, to 'make the beast with two backs') was in common usage among *toreros* and *aficionados* to signify that the *torero* was completely involved with his bull and in the *faena* as a whole. So the *festa brava* for Leiris is a mixture of savagery, sex and erotic mysticism that is uniquely Spanish. There is a passionate beauty for him in all that artistic brutality, in which the matador appears as the delivering angel, releasing us from guilt and sin in a Baudelairian geometry of spectacular action that ends in castration – the cutting off of the dead bull's ears and tail.

Arena is the word for sand. We climb, high in the graded stands of the bullring's perfect crater, a temple open to sun and shade, a theatre like no other, its arcaded galleries a sandy rose. The amphitheatre sparkles like a loosely packed mosaic with paper hats, black suits, white fans. The sun slants down, and cuts with a curve as definite as a sombrero's tilted brim the arena's tawny dial. A giant bottle, advertising Anis, waltzes slowly out of shadow into the noisy sun, and into dark again. A brass band plays a faded *paso doble*, indifferently, as if by a far-off shore.

The trumpets' voices seem to break with eager strains. Two riders demonstrate upon the well-raked sand the artifices of the *haute école*, acknowledge the impatient crowd's half-grudged applause with noble smiles. The six tight-breeched matadors enter the spanking sun. The slaughtered light capers round their spangled shoulders, and their sequined suits of lights in smart lime-green and azure, rose and lemon, seem to flower to the passion of applause within the desert of their setting.

Flourishing red and yellow plumes, the *capas* stride in, black, white-ruffed. The funeral horses, three abreast, prance in, escorted by lesser men in workmen's clothes – a humble and magnificent procession that investigates the ring, the temper of the day, and silently retires to the stables, to the *burladeros* of this most formal circus. Attendants in these slips beside the ring are running with buckets, swords and brooms, and capes of shocking pink are draped along the barricades.

The ring is empty now, the necessary preludes done. The crowd fizzes, the band plays on. Flexing their tight, pink calves, the matadors, like women getting the hang of a new dress, try out the swing of their capes. A pause. The pale-faced young fighters retire to the *burladeros*. Sudden as the crowd's roar, the young black bull trots out of cold and dazzling dark into the stunning liberty of day.

He stops short, and turns to look at the cool tunnel he has issued from; it is shut now. The crowd seethes with comment. The blaze of the shimmering ring plays upon him like a burning glass. He starts to run, daintily, picking up neat and supple hoofs, making the tour of a barren field that has no corners and no quiet shade.

One by one, like figures in a country dance, the black-capped matadors advance upon him, making play for a moment only with their capes of acid pink lined with a sullen yellow. The bull follows the moving arm, attempts to plunge right through the screen of red that bathes his vision, and finds himself alone outside a barricade of wood, the *burladero*. He digs it with a frustrate horn, while the crowd hoots and whistles.

A single matador advances now upon the waiting bull, which elegantly paws the ground, then runs with lowering head into the crimson veil his twisting horn catches and rends, but which vanishes in air, while the matador discreetly turns from the waist – *Olé!* – as the bull's hot flank brushes his tinselled thighs.

The matador advances once again, with little sideways steps, and shakes invitingly the well-cut cape. The bull seems bored, but suddenly dives through a hoop of air, and turns, with rolling head, and dives again – *Olé!* – returns, and yet again – *Olé!* – batters the flourished flag – *Olé* – as the fighter turns on himself, with indrawn breath, tight stomach, heels together, towering on tiptoe with arms outstretched – *Olé!* – turning his back at last on the turning bull – *Olé!* – ends with his cape wrapped like a skirt about his thin disdain. The bull pauses. His adversary strolls away, applause like a great fan beating his grave and lifted face, his grateful hands.

Enter the clumsy picadors like two bullying buffoons on blindfold, padded nags, obedient, trustful, calm. One man digs his lance into the bull's deep back, and holds it there, while the bull bellows and pushes, tosses in vain his simple horns against the horse's armour. A grotesque, ungainly struggle which the second picador repeats. He is unlucky, falls to the sand where he lies dead still. The bull runs over him, but the thundering hoofs avoid his body. The man rises and staggers from the ring while the crowd applauds and boos. The great shadow slowly shifts across the sand. We are in the shade.

Now the *banderillero*, poised like a hypnotist with upraised arms, holds high the decorated darts, watches his chance, makes his run with desperate precision right up to the bull's black head, and plants two azure *banderillas* in his shoulders. Two more are yellow, and another two are pink. The bull bellows to the crowd's approval, runs and shakes his head from side to side, but cannot loose these coloured barbs that clatter on his back and dangle round his shoulders like a foolish ruff.

He is tiring. He does not run so well, or on such easy hoofs. The shadow deepens, lengthens on the stands. He pauses, and we see the great belly panting, the muzzle white with froth. The blood, like house-paint, yokes his shoulders with a broad red band that fumes and glisters in the sun. Intent, he plays for time, which will destroy him.

Now the grand torero with vermilion *muleta* strides to deliver him: he makes an entry like a *danseur noble*, and the crowd roars with a fiercer zest. The torero flings down his cap, walks to the moment that the bull, too, anticipates. He goes through a swirl of scarlet passes, *ayudados*, *naturales*, *derechazos*, dream-slow *veronicas*. He stands both rigid and flexible, wary yet disdainful. The bull labours and lunges round him, unattainable as a mosquito.

Cool in his pastel suit of lights, the fighter draws the final blade from red concealment and holds it straight before him. The bull, unwilling but entranced by the scarlet pall, which twitches on a field of blood and sand, plunges, and the blade too plunges, back into red, into the sheath of flesh that dims the bull's red gaze. The creature sinks to his knees, lays like an offering his huge head on the scuffed sand at his persecutor's feet, then slowly founders. The legs kick convulsively. He tries to raise his head again. It drops back like a rock.

Three by three and gaily plumed the funeral horses come. The torero retrieves his hat and walks in a rain of coins and roses round the ring, while the dead bull is swiftly hauled away into the pits of dark, leaving in the blood-stained sand a question mark.

*   *   *

Jordi looked with concern at my face, which had gone white. I felt the blood draining from my head, as if I had been that stricken creature. The bull appeared to me as the very image of myself, of my own life pursued by relentless attackers, before whose intentness all my efforts to escape or to subdue were helpless and vain. I felt such a fellowship with the bull. I had longed for one of those tormentors to be gored, to be shaken like a rag doll on the bull's horns and trampled to death. I saw all my art, my poetry, my love of life in the bull's confident yet doubting steps in a desert filled with enemies, with the shadow of death growing insistently minute by minute. I wept for the bull.

We left after that one fight. I could take no more, though Jordi was eager to stay and see the rest of the kills. I was sorry to be depriving him of his pleasure – he had generously paid for the tickets in the shade, the most expensive kind. At a nearby café he bought me a restorative brandy.

That evening we attended a wonderful performance by my favourite dancers, Rosario and Antonio, with his famous *zapateado*. I had often gone with Federico to watch them dance in London, where Antonio had thrilled me as no other male dancer had ever done. But in Madrid he was simply overwhelming – that lithe, muscular body in its tight black silks seemed to be dancing the story of our love, a love such as I had never expected to know again after the death of my drowned sailor, my childhood friend who was never my lover, who indeed laughed my adoration to scorn.

All night we lay in each other's arms, making plans for the future. In the morning Jordi had to return to Valladolid. I was going on south, to Aranjuez, Toledo, Cordoba, Seville, Granada, and slowly back to France by way of Alicante, Valencia, Tarragona, Barcelona and Gerona. We made a solemn promise to meet again the following year, but our parting nearly broke my heart, and the rest of my travels round Spain often seemed meaningless without Jordi. As always in my loneliness I took refuge in writing, in scribbling impressions and poems in my notebook.

In Toledo I fell in with a young American professor from I forget which university in the United States. He was an experienced European traveller, and gave me the addresses of some gay bars in Amsterdam, the sort of places I should never dream of entering, for I distrust any kind of ghetto, be it Tyneside or transvestite taverns. We shared a room, but one with two beds, for there was something about him I could not like. Once when we were walking round Toledo he took offence because I went walking ahead of him, for he walked too slowly for my liking. I always prefer to travel alone, so now I cannot imagine what possessed me to take the train with him to beautiful Aranjuez and then to Alcazar and Cordoba. I cannot remember where it was that we were walking in the centre of a southern city, and during the *paseo* a small group of young men passed us going in the opposite direction. One of them, who had obviously lived in the United States, boldly announced to his grinning companions that we were a pair of *maricones*, then loudly in heavily accented American 'They're getting everywhere these days!' as the group walked on, leaving my companion and myself rather breathless with the unexpectedness of that English language attack. It

was just another of those incidents so common in the lives of intermediates, a salutary and in some ways not unwelcome shock that brings
us to our senses for a while, out of the world of illusion we spin for
ourselves.

We parted company soon after that, to my great relief. We had met
in the Prado in Madrid and recognized one another at once by unmistakable signs, then run into one another in Toledo. Those signs we had
thought secret were obviously no secret to certain persons of ill will.

I had brought very few books with me, and only two Spanish ones:
the *Soledades* of my favourite classic poet, Góngora, and the poems of
Federico Garcia Lorca. My only English book was one I had discovered
in a second-hand bookshop in Bath, not long before leaving for Spain. It
was Gerald Brennan's *The Face of Spain*, in its rather battered original
edition of 1950, published by the Turnstile Press. I read this wonderful
account of Spain almost at a sitting. It had nothing about the north, but
it fired my enthusiasm to see as much as possible of Andalusia. With
Brennan as the best possible literary guide, I was to discover things in
Cordoba I might well have missed, the city of Seneca and Góngora, but
also one of the most beautifully preserved examples of medieval
Hispano-Arabic culture, typified by the great mosque, which the Arabs
began to build rather haphazardly but with a sure eye for architectural
originality as early as AD 785. It still stands as a beacon of beauty and
devoutness from the Dark Ages of Spain, and, for me, as a symbol of
the unity of all religions.

Brennan also introduced me to the fourteenth-century synagogue, near
the Plaza Maimonides, named after the great Jewish philosopher and
poet who was another of the literary glories of Cordoba. The old houses
in the Jewish quarter are entrancing in their loveliness, with their little
fountained patios luxuriant with big pots of flowers and ferns and palms.

Brennan has a most disturbing chapter on the murder of Lorca: he
tries to locate Lorca's grave on a barren hillside outside Granada, but
fails to find any sign beyond a charnel-pit, open to the sky, where the
bodies of those slain by the Falangists in the Civil War still lie mouldering. I made my way as Brennan had done to the small village of Viznar
but failed to find anything in the sinister *barranco* where Lorca was shot.
In his *The Assassination of Federico Garcia Lorca* (dedicated to Brennan) Ian Gibson says the poet was not buried in Viznar but interred by
mourning gypsies on the slopes of the Cerro del Aceituno behind the
Albaicín. However, I visited Góngora's house near the Plaza Maimonides in Cordoba, though I was unable to find the country cottage where
he retired to write his exquisite and profoundly original poetry of the
Soledades.

This is a land that murders and imprisons its poets. Everywhere I go in Spain there are memories of St John of the Cross. His fellow-writer, St Teresa of Avila, whose mysticism reformed a hidebound religion bogged down in antiquated dogma and cruel un-Christian formalism by the powerful and cruel Inquisition, lived in her little Carmelite convent in grim, rocky, monkish Toledo. She read the great visionaries: their eclectic, rhapsodic ejaculations had been placed on the Index by hostile and unimaginative inquisitors, who humiliated and disgraced St John of the Cross by throwing him into prison.

Toledo felt cold-hearted and relentless still. I remembered that one of my early long poems, *The Creation*, written while I still had my fellowship at Leeds University, and which gave a very unconventional account of a Creation that was not even *ab nihilo*, because I first had to create *nothing*, had been placed on the Index. 'Nothing will come of nothing. . . .' But in Lorca's flowering Granada, St John of the Cross had written his mystic-erotic poems of passion for the love of Christ. In honour of his memory I bought a copy of his poems and translated some. Brennan again guided me: 'Just beyond the Washington Irving Hotel, at the entrance to the wooded region of the Alhambra, lies the drive to the Carmen de los Mártires. . . .'

Flame of Living Love

O flame of living love
That tenderly brands me,
Pierces to the centre of my soul!
Now that you no more escape me
Let it be done at last
And rend the veil upon our sweet encounters.

O gentle burning!
O delicious wounding!
O blessed hand! O delicate touch
Whose savour tells us of life eternal
And pays all debts I owe!
Killing me, you turn my death to life!

O you lamps of fire!
In your resplendent illuminations
The profound caverns of sensation,
Once blind and dark,
Now with their strange gifts
Lend the lover both light and heat!

How calmly and lovingly
Within my breast you waken,
Where you alone may secretly abide!
And your rich-scented sighs,
Overflowing so with glory and with bliss –
How delicately now he brands me with his love!

Gerald Brennan – by now I was thinking of him affectionately as 'Don Geraldo' – is especially good in his descriptions of Aranjuez, the Spanish attempt to rival Versailles. It is a pleasant, leisurely sort of little town with broad streets and squares framed by rows of neat servants' quarters and the residences of the attendant nobility, all in classic eighteenth-century style, severe without dullness, simple without vacuity. The great palace contains scores of rooms, some decorated in extravagantly exotic style – chinoiseries, *Arabian Nights* capriccios, fanciful turqueries. There are huge mirrors everywhere, and the ones hung on opposite walls provide those tunnel reflections that are an image of unprobable infinity. For a dedicated narcissist like myself, they are agonizing in their relentless repetition of ungraspable desires and unfulfillable yearnings for that impossible He. 'Das Ewig-männliche zieht uns heran . . .' as Goethe almost said, losing a point of wit by substituting 'Ewig-weibliche', which is far too banal. At Aranjuez I felt I was in a Ronald Firbank setting, something like my favourite *The Artificial Princess*. Aranjuez is caught precisely in: ' "It is two o'clock," remarked the Princess. "All the town is at siesta; it is an hour more secret than midnight," and she slightly shivered.' But I suspect that Firbank used Aranjuez in more than one bizarre description of decadent, faded, self-absorbed little courts athrill with petty scandals. Brennan writes well of the extraordinarily tall planes and elms, of a noble grandeur unusual in Spain, where he says trees are hated, as in China – a rather too sweeping generalization for so fine a writer.

He never exaggerates when he praises the enslaving glamour of Spanish eyes, those passionate, eloquent, mischievous, soulful, disdainful globes: '. . . those large brilliant eyes with their clear whites which can throw a signal as far as one can throw a tennis ball. . . .' I had already fallen under the spell of so many of those ardent, melting gazes framed in their long, rich lashes, their slightly discoloured lids hinting at unmentionable depravities and smouldering lusts. Brennan talks of how Spaniards like to converse looking straight into each other's eyes, to relish to the full the various effects of their resounding rhetoric: '*Mal d'occhio*, evil eye, is thought to be a Mediterranean rather than a northern superstition, but really it is the English who suffer from

collective fear of it: it is an instinctive belief of theirs that the human
glance is dangerous.'

As I possess this 'evil power', I know that only too well. I find that
even Spaniards and Italians, particularly Sicilians, cannot look me in the
eye. It makes them very uncomfortable. Some even cross themselves,
and men scratch the crotch – supposed to be a universal remedy against
the 'Eye'. So I often turn it upon better-looking younger men, for the
sheef pleasure of watching them fingering their fly.

For the rest of my journey, thankfully I travelled alone. Being alone
always intensifies impressions of distant places: there is no one to
distract our attention from ourselves, from our relationship with new
scenes, new climates. So I wrote a number of poems, like this one, so far
unpublished, that I wrote in the gardens of the Generalife in Granada,
Cerro del Sol:

> Always the strumming waters run
> on the hill of the sun in the ordered gardens.
> Deep in the drenching cypress shade
> erected fountains ceaselessly
> lifting, ceaselessly lapsing, brilliantly
> juggle with handfuls of shaggy fans.
>
> Always the strumming waters run
> on the hill of the sun in the ordered gardens.
> The fountains clothed in their own abstractions
> toss on the arch of air their flowers and massive doves.
> Always their sun-combed cascadings run
> on the hill of the sun in the ordered gardens.
>
> Deep in the dark, arcaded grove
> light from a marble basin channels
> watertracks to a courtyard's hanging
> cistern of sky, and down the azure tiles of air
> always the strumming waters run
> on the hill of the sun in the ordered gardens.

In the Alhambra, in the gardens leading to the Arab baths, the
honeymoon couples snap each other, and the American family doing all
of Spain gets in the Lion Court a souvenir of Ma with a hand laid on a
water-nozzle as confidently as on a canasta table in Larchmont. Two big
New Zealand girls take snaps of each other leaning on a balustrade, with
an out-of-focus backdrop of the Sacromonte district. And there a British
rosebud, in front of an eternal doorway, puts on film her Mister Right,

who stands lopsided in dacron suiting, the sun in his Midwest eyes, a
look of puzzlement or fright balding his scholarly temples, sensing like a
coming headache an uneasy vista of married bliss against a very un-
American background of complete British assurance.

Water is the eternal Arab heritage in Spain, so I was writing about
tanks and fountains and pools all the time, as at La Granja, Segovia:

> At the end of the dark glade
> light on awkward wings
> suddenly springs into a dwarf
> fountain shuffling like a spook
> that bobs and beckons, but never budges,
> a stooping figure that hops and trudges
> up to the neck in chilling shade,
> yet stands, deep in the book
> of its own wet leaves
> held on an arm that nothing sleeves;
> and dies, like a small cloud thinned
> on a wet sky, by a darkling wind.

I loved Cordoba for its mosque, another enduring Arab relic, like the
heart of the great cathedral in Seville. Cordoba was all narrow lanes,
deep, secret courtyards filled with the scent of flowers and running
water, the walls a moonlight whiteness guarded by black wrought-iron
grilles on the hidden windows. Sometimes a sad lover could be seen
clinging to these grilles, whispering to some unknown *enamorata* within,
who never showed her face. Or a band of strolling musicians with
mandolines would serenade the fair one with the dark Spanish smouldering eyes, whose only reward, if any, would be a thrown carnation:

> Under the noon's white walls
> where steep shadow piles its shade
> a dry guitar
> sprinkles the courtyard air
> with a complaint that love has made,
> the steady hunger
> of the long unsatisfied,
> the lonely lover
> clinging to the bars of pride.

In springtime I walked through drifts of orange and lilac blossom in
the fragrant streets and squares of Andalusia, my heart aching as I

watched the señoritas in their tall mantillas and flounced frocks riding side-saddle behind their handsome cavaliers. I longed for both the ravishingly pretty girls and the utterly male escorts, for the shoeshine boys and the flower-sellers and gypsy fortune-tellers with their brilliant, inward eyes moving from table to table in the cafés throbbing with flamenco music and clapping hands. But always the face of Jordi would come between us, his earthy simplicity more lovely than any fandango couple in their elaborate costumes and with their haughty stances. I was disappointed by the very tidy gypsy caves of Granada, with their whitewashed walls, heavy Victorian furniture and almost every mod con. But the young gypsy girl whose worn palm I crossed with a shabby hundred peseta note assured me that my life would be filled with love and money, though not without its dark disappointments and some approaching heavy sorrows.

The rest of Spain passed as in a dream, symbolized for me by the weird beauty of Gaudi's Parque Güell in Barcelona, from whose fantastic structures I could see in the distance the strange towers of his incomplete masterpiece, the Sagrada Familia.

After one month in Spain it was something of a relief to enter the cooler climates of France and the Low Countries on my way home. As I rode the train from Gerona to Port Bou, I saw in the distance the snowy peaks of Andorra which I wanted to visit at the first opportunity; in fact it came the following year. But at that time I had no idea that the little principality was such a unique realm. I gazed upon those Magritte-like peaks with dreamlike longing to know their savagery and noble severity. They reminded me of Magritte's *Le domaine d'Arnheim*.

In the meantime, I made up my mind that as soon as possible I would try to find a post at a Spanish university, so as to be near Jordi. The following summer I had arranged, through my old friend in the Portuguese Department at Leeds University, Agostin de Irizar, to teach English language and literature at the ancient university of Salamanca.

But before then I had to resign from the Bath Academy of Art and look for a temporary post. I searched every week the overseas positions column of *The Times Educational Supplement*. What I eventually succeeded in getting was what I thought would be an interesting post as travelling lecturer for the Swedish Ministry of Education, through the British Centre in Strandvägen, Stockholm, which was all that remained of the defunct British Council there, an organization with which I was later to have some unpleasant experiences.

As soon as I got to Corsham, I sat down to write a long letter to Jordi and posted it. The next day there was one from him. Our correspondence continued regularly until our next meeting, in the summer of 1957, when I had for the first time passed through Andorra on my way to Salamanca.

SWEDISH EXERCISES

. . . Ancestral heroes, gods of the epic north, whose tongue
Lingers among the stillnesses, and cannot die.

James Kirkup, 'THE DEAD FALLS AT RAGUNDA'

I now realize that I was before my time. I should have been born either in
the 1870s or in the 1970s. By the time the sort of clothes and make-up I was
wearing were the accepted attributes of even straight males, I was already
too old – or at least supposed to be too old – to wear them: alas, so
conventional ageism has it. I should love to wear the punk hair-styles and
rainbow garments or crummy, lopsided rags some of the young sport so
confidently today, or the outrageously pseudo-traditional Giorgio Armani
or Issey Miyake get-ups one sees paraded by those scowling, fake-macho
models with their black lipstick and bruised-looking, eye-shadow effects,
their stick-on, artificial fingernails that look as if they'd been jammed in a
carelessly slammed BMW door. I should love to flaunt myself in
pachydermatous pants and funfair-funfur fablousons aswag with heavy-
metal chains and badges and whole packets of outsize safety-pins. I long to
dress up in this way, if only in the strict privacy of my boudoir. Yet given the
right occasion, I should boldly sally forth in the most catastrophic clobber,
male or female. I would swish into grand hotels and government offices,
submitting to the most thoroughgoing of body-searches and identity
checks – no, dear, that's *not* a pistol in my pants – and after a suitable
interval to freshen my blueberry lipstick and avail myself of the amenities I
would simply sweep out again, leaving a trail of broken hearts and
bewildered bruisers agape at my camp effrontery. Why shouldn't the old be
bold? I want to be my age with a vengeance!

In my considered opinion, one is never too old for the glad rags.
Never, ever! From time to time I still enjoy putting on the slap and the
gay glitter of bicycle-slut cross-dressers. If ever I were to let my beard
grow, it would be to set off my tinkling tiara set with sinister second-
hand trinkets. And I should decorate it (the rufous-pearly beard) with
little highly tinted velvet bows, like a home-grown pet or poodle. I'm
sorry that muffs are no longer fashionable, like the one belonging to
Queen Marie of Romania that I wore throughout the darker days of the
Cold War, when I found myself in Sweden.

Yes, my spate of job applications to 'overseas vacancies' in the dear old *Times Educational Supplement* eventually paid off. I had written for posts in Mali, in Egypt, in Turkey, in Taiwan and even in the United States, all to no avail. I remember being interviewed in London for a British Council post in Egypt, and the lady in charge of the investigating committee, after her first shock, recovered enough to ask her first, and last, question: 'What do you consider the aim of education to be?' To which I replied airily: 'I haven't the faintest idea, but I'd know it if I saw it.' There were some interviews to which I had been invited, I now see, simply for the entertainment of the interviewing committee, something I was to have to endure years later when I was applying for fellowships in 'creative writing' at British universities, where all creative writers are regarded with the utmost suspicion and resentment by the academic staff. I shall not soon forget the sneers and the condescension when I applied for something or other that was in any case hardly worth it, considering the pittance offered, at the University of Norwich, or the alarmed giggles at the University of Sheffield when I appeared wearing my rings outside my black kid gloves, to conceal a touch of eczema and my very first liver spot, cautiously concealed beneath a black sequin Restoration patch, in case I should be requested to remove my rings and my gloves. (I got that fellowship, which meant a year of utter torture: I just wanted to be a little nearer my dying mother, but she died before the job started, and so I had to go through with it.) But more of all that peculiarly British balls-up later. . . .

I got the position in Sweden, I am sure, because no one else had applied for it. It was all rather mysterious, for I had to meet someone at a secret rendezvous in London, somewhere in the Temple. Almost as soon as I entered the door the gentleman in charge offered me the job and no questions asked. I had the vague feeling that one of my dearest ambitions might be going to be realized – to be approached by 'a foreign power' and enlisted as a double agent. But what on earth, I wondered, could I tell them? What dread secrets could I reveal, what plans could I snap with my micro-camera hidden in my cornflower buttonhole? I could see that I should have to put my already considerably overworked imagination on overtime. Could I even disguise myself as an exotic female temptress, *à la* Marlene Dietrich 'underneath the lamplight by the barracks square' ready to seduce the first likely looking officer to cross my vicious path? I should see what I should see, I hoped. . . .

But it all turned out to be perfectly pedestrian. The British Council in a fit of extravagant economy had closed their Stockholm offices and had them replaced by what I took to be leftover or recycled staff, both British and Swedish. As in all British Council operations, the staff were

shining examples of sheer incompetence begot upon pedantic preten-
sion. Fortunately they were now only agents for the Swedish Ministry of
Education – and I am always surprised how foreign governments put
their complete trust in the recommendations of the British Council. So
after an initial chat and the routine cup of tea with the Britisher left in
charge of what was now known as the British Centre, I was passed on to
the wonderfully friendly, unprejudiced and efficient Swedes. I took to
them at once, and perhaps they recognized in me a fellow-Viking, for
there was never a cross word between us, and I loved every moment of
my multifarious activities they dreamt up for me – and many they did
not dream up, of course. It was the first flush of my love affair with
Sweden, and like all love affairs it later turned sour.

My 1956 Letts Diary tells me I left Corsham on Wednesday, 15
August ('Princess Anne born, 1950 – Dep. Liv. Station') on the boat-
train for Rotterdam, since I intended to take in as much of Dutch and
Flemish and German and Danish culture as possible en route to Malmö
and Stockholm. At my hotel in Rotterdam a glum waiter told me:
'There's nothing doing in Rotterdam – all the gay life is in Amsterdam.'
He had weighed me up on sight as he served the evening soup. But I
only wanted to see the Boymans Museum – such a suggestive name! –
because of my passion for Dutch primitives, of which I also had my fill in
Delft, the Hague (the Vermeers – Bergotte's 'little patch of yellow wall'
is very elusive) and Amsterdam. I spent some days there, visiting
museums, picking up impressions and whatever else came my way. I
soon learnt to avoid Rembrandt's megalomaniac masterpiece *The Night
Watch* – surely overvalued? – by dashing straight up the stairs as soon as
the doors opened at 10 a.m. to the strains of the first four notes of
'Daisy, Daisy, give me your answer, do!' and right on to the Flemish
Primitives that I could have all to myself before the ignorant hordes of
Rembrandt lovers – those portraits, all nose and good nature! – caught
up with me. Besides, they're mostly fakes or part-works.

There is also a heavenly oriental collection, nearly always deserted,
where I found a very sexy and enterprising uniformed attendant: almost
anything was possible behind the Ming vases or the Japanese screens,
because I was always the only visitor. He was still there a few years ago,
but now seems to have been retired, or moved on to more fertile fields.
We used to acknowledge one another with a weary smile of unwilling
recognition; but time had left its mark, and we went no further than a
passing grope, for old times' sake, as I proceeded towards the giant
Korean gongs and bells. It all reminded me of the time in St Peter's,
Rome, when I had attached myself to an American tour group to enjoy
the benefit of a free lecture from the scholarly guide, and I was 'felt up'

by a Vatican prelate, the spitting image of Firbank's Cardinal Pirelli, who had paused to check the accuracy of the historical data, the orthodoxy of the theological dogma and any convenient cock.

One day of intermittent rain I took a guided tour on the multilingual bus of Amsterdam and her great port. It is always a good way of getting a quick grasp of a new city's layout. (Or, if one can't speak the language, buy a packet of picture postcards and show them to a taxi-driver.) One rarely meets anyone interesting on such tours, but there are always the vivid, enthusiastic Americans to perk up one's spirits, for they are keenly interested in everything they see, determined not to lose a cent's worth of 'talking points' on their European package.

'Hiram! Did you get that?'

'Did I get what, sugar?'

'Washing hanging over leafy waters of historic canal?'

'It's in the can, dear.'

'Washing hanging anywhere abroad is always very picturesque.'

'So it is, Elma. Real authentic.'

'Like those stepped gables, Hiram, reflected in antiquated canal waters.'

'OK, Elma dear, don't fuss me now.'

'I always tell him, when we get back Stateside, he wouldn't have a thing if it hadn't been for me.'

'You're dead right, sweetie.'

'Hiram, did you get that there?'

'Get what, Elma?'

'Like what the guide said, that glimpse of Rembrandt's house above bicycles ranked on hump-backed bridge?'

'Oh my goodness yes, dear.'

'We just reverence anything old like that.'

And so it goes on, a never-ending stream of inconsequential chat, often on a playfully childish note, with some baby-talk. There is something soothing in the continual contented drone. The Americans seem more alive than the natives to the fascinating world around them.

I love those big, bosomy, good-tempered Dutch girls, their perfect complexions never touched by anything but nature's hand. Even the painted ones in the windows of the red-light district look appetizing. And those sporty Dutch boys, with their hair of butter!

The Americans are a great improvement on the Japanese tour groups lolling in their air-conditioned coaches, some of them sound asleep, or glumly jet-lagged, or girlishly hysterical. They are still back in Japan. Moving around in compact groups led by a fellow-countryman guide waving a white and purple flag so that no one will get lost, they are totally insulated from all the entrancing foreign life around them. When a large group invaded my hotel (the pleasant Victoria, opposite the station), they seemed to do everything by numbers, including the taking of baths: at least a hundred started taking a bath all at the same time before dinner, resulting in a complete lack of hot water for my evening shower.

The bookstores in Amsterdam were a revelation after Charing Cross Road, for they were so international in spirit, with works by many rather obscure foreign authors translated into Dutch and also into English. There were many books from small presses in America and France, publishing authors rarely to be found in the staid shelves of British bookshops. The Dutch also found room for all kinds of exotic erotica in books, comics, newsletters, guide-books and magazines. Gay guides to Amsterdam, Europe and the entire world were prominently on display at Bruno's: the Spartacus Guide was selling like hotcakes. The guides to Amsterdam's gay life were especially informative and accurate, as was only to be expected, though the action was mainly centred on small hotels and on the bars whose addresses that American in Spain had given me. I tried one, and was disappointed by its stuffy chauvinism – a row of Dutch guys sitting on bar-stools at a long counter. In later years the scene was to become much more open and adventurous; but I never got over my dislike of 'special places for special people', for I wanted to be accepted on my own terms, without compromise, everywhere, and by everyone. I much preferred ordinary pubs and cafés and their customers to selected gay joints where one was always conscious of eyes looking over shoulders to check on the latest arrival, weigh him up and put him down. Those who did not like me could direct their attention elsewhere: they could either like me or lump me, and no skin off anyone's nose. This conviction that I had to be liked 'just as myself, without one plea' was one to which I have held all my life. I did not expect justice or even understanding. My parents knew by heart the great speech, which they taught me when I was still very small:

> . . . Therefore, Jew,
> Though justice be thy plea, consider this,
> That, in the course of justice, none of us
> Should see salvation: we do pray for mercy;
> And that same prayer doth teach us all to render
> The deeds of mercy.

and: 'To do a great right, do a little wrong.'

My favourite bookshop in Amsterdam was always that most eclectic of establishments, the Boekhandel Allert de Lange on the Damrak at No. 62 since 1880, with its wide and up-to-date selections of French, Dutch, English and American books, both popular and scholarly, and always room for specialist presses and *curiosa*. And there is the Athenaeum not far from the university, as well as a host of similar well-stocked, broad-minded bookshops, always packed with eager readers and buyers. Would that British bookshops were like that!

* * *

From Amsterdam I took the train to Hamburg, a seething port of sex and sailors on floating feet, where I stayed five days. On the way there I met a German countess. Ilona was a woman of great wit and intellect, past her first youth but still beautiful, with an aristocratic sharpness of eye and speech. Once we started talking, we could not stop. She was one of those rare people to whom one suddenly feels able to say everything, and it was one of those lightning-struck friendships in which we sense that we have somehow known each other all our lives. In no time we had told one another our life stories, and cynical Ilona was moved to tears when I related my pacifist experiences: she had had to endure the Hitler regime and the Allied bombing of Dresden. For a moment I wondered if she might be the beautiful spy I was fully expecting to contact me, but as we talked I realized that such a suspicion was ridiculous. It was love at first sight for us both. But she had to go on to Warsaw. We got off the train at Hamburg, hastily sought an hotel at the station accommodation bureau, and spent a few hours together before she had to leave. With heavy heart I took the ferry on 25 August to Copenhagen, a city I came to admire for its civilized restraint that yet allowed every freedom, one that looked upon my intermediate state as perfectly natural, without surprise or comment. I spent happy hours in Tivoli and in the cobbled streets and quaysides of the port, and promised the Little Mermaid that I would return – I was to do so again and again, charmed by the light, the cool climate, the ungloomy Danes, the human elegance of the native architecture in Elsinore and Arhus and Odense, birthplace of one of my favourite authors, Hans Christian Andersen, with whose Ugly Duckling I felt a very special affinity. On a hired bicycle I went on to Fredericia, Esbjerg and all the way up that crab-claw peninsula to Thisted, Hirthals, Alborg – all memorable places, with many lovely small villages on completely unspoilt beaches along the way.

During my time in Sweden I was to roam all over Denmark on bicycle. From Hamburg I cycled to the awe-inspiring Emil Nolde

Museum at Seebüll near Flensburg with its magnificent collection of the artist's lithographs, water-colours and a whole room devoted to his great paintings of the life of Christ, completely convincing in their total lack of religiosity, and projecting a vital, crude, visionary passion. I grew fond of all the Scandinavian lands, where I knew my real roots belonged. That optimistic 'up' at the end of my name was echoed in so many other place-names and family names, and wherever I went I was mistaken for a local inhabitant. I felt I had lived somewhere between northern Friesland and Trondheim or Esbjerg in a long-lost former existence, a feeling I was not to experience again until I set foot in Japan three years later.

But Sweden was calling. So I took one of my favourite routes from Copenhagen, through Helsingborg on its sparkling straits with a grand view of Elsinore, and through a series of late-summer landscapes lit by the luminosity of lakes and sea, for in those angelic lands the sea is never far away: it illuminates the whole sky.

In Stockholm arrangements had been made for me to stay a few days in a private home with a young married couple. Their modern, airy apartment was my first introduction to the superiority of Scandinavian taste and design, and to the warm-heartedness and sheer human good-ness of the Swedes, so often considered cold and proud by ill-informed southerners. In later years I was to become friends with a fine young Swedish artist and print-maker, Birgit Sköld, with whom I created books of poetry and photo-etchings. We worked together on those books – Zen Gardens, Scenes from Sesshu, The Tao of Water – and many other unfinished projects with the sort of understanding that exists only between people with the same roots, until her tragically early death in 1980. She was one of the true loves of my life. I learnt so much from her that I have never forgotten, about art, poetry and the mysterious practical craft that can unite them to create new dimensions of vision. To work together intimately with an artist, an actor, a film-maker, a theatre director, is for me the utmost in the artistic experience.

As soon as I got to the British Centre in Strandvägen, I received a message from my mysterious German countess: she wanted to throw everything aside and come and join me in Sweden. But it was not possible: I was being briefed for a year-long series of wanderings all over Sweden between Stockholm and almost every city, town and village in the land. I would be constantly on the move, staying at most three or four nights in each place. I was to teach English to every kind of student, from kindergarten to university graduates, to members of the Swedish Air Force, the police, the naval training schools. For the next year my home was to be the almost identical Stadhotellets, usually next to the railway station, found all over Sweden as far north as Kiruna in the Arctic Circle.

So I sent a telegram to Ilona, asking her to wait for me at our hotel in Hamburg in a year's time. As I was to discover, 'Too long a sacrifice can make a stone of the heart.'

* * *

Sweden – a country without preconceived notions of what I am supposed to be. In this life, few people have ever met me; in Sweden, until now, none at all. This immensely varied land to which I feel so irresistibly drawn is for me a clean slate, a new page in the constantly turned pages, turned and turned and turning still in the wind of my days and nights on earth. But one day, I suspect, I may run out of new countries in which to start all over again. Then I might even have to return to Britain, to Tyneside, that most Scandinavian of regions. My life is an endless recommencement, a putting-all-behind of a dissident waif and stray living by his wits, which often get him into scrapes.

But here in Stockholm and in all the other places I shall visit in my perambulant instructorship, can I face these clear-eyed paragons of correctness and social conformity with sufficient sang-froid to disentangle my most suitable self from all my contradictory yet complementary manifestations? Perhaps my multiple personalities can be put to use to entertain, to hold the brief attention-spans of my auditors by a continuous quick-change act? Sending myself up, my favourite hobby – will they at least perceive that it is a sick joke against my true self? If even my fellow-countrymen cannot see it, how can foreigners? Can their different point of view, unclouded by prejudice, pierce the maskings that are also genuine aspects of my true self? Can I manage to be both an exquisite and a brute, both a sensualist and a saint, or to keep them apart whenever necessary? Meeting a new land presents problems for me that few other people encounter.

I tried to defuse some of my minor terrors by composing some introductory limericks, which I call Jimericks, in a parody of Lord Eliot the Righteous:

'Is it pleasant to know Mr Kirkup?'
The answer can only be 'Ump'.
   For sometimes he's charming
   And sometimes alarming –
You never know how he will jump.

> There was an old morphy named Sparrow
> Had a prick like an old withered marrow.
> He was gaga as shit
> So they cut off his clit
> And wheeled his fat arse on a barrow.

I had long ago discovered that once you start writing limericks, it is very difficult to stop. Would I, perhaps, be able to stem this flood of comic pornography in squeaky-clean Sweden? I doubted it, for I had heard tales of the Swedes' voracious sexual appetites and their open-mindedness towards every form of erotic expression. It was in Sweden that I began writing one-line poems, hoping to find them useful in teaching my students English composition, for the practice of poetry is by far the best training for the writing of good prose. But all my one-line poems seemed to have a tinge of naughtiness in them: 'I played the lead in *A Penis too Frequent*', 'Sex always makes my nose run', and so on. . . . Could I adapt my new form to the stylistic requirements of adolescent foreigners?

There was a period of grace, three days, to allow me to acculturate myself – something I have never found difficult, except in the United States. So I walked and walked all over Stockholm, and as if by instinct sniffed out those places I most needed: the Opera and the State Theatre, the parks, the rare *pissoirs*, the splendid galleries and museums, in particular the Östasiatiska Museet or Museum of Oriental Antiquities, and an intimate little *kino* called the Bio, which has long since vanished in Stockholm's successive waves of rebuilding – not always to the best effect. The Bio, like the Biograph in London, was conveniently dark, and the male customers shifted their seats in an unselfconscious way that would have got them either arrested or thrown out in our Victorian and dangerous Biograph. In Sweden there was never that sense of danger: on the one occassion when my nose got punched for attempting too forward a fondling, my attacker picked me up, apologized, then offered me delights I was too groggy to appreciate properly. Afterwards we went for a coffee and cognac. This occurred in the far north, in a park in Gävle, which Swedes always warn you not to pronounce 'Djävle', which means 'devil'. But it was a delightful town, and I found it was not devilish at all.

I went to a magnificent symphony concert in the great hall decorated by immense sculptures. It was a concert of the works of the Danish composer Carl Nielsen, to which the Professor of Music at Newcastle, the exuberant Sydney Newman, had introduced me. Nielsen was the exact contemporary of Sibelius: both were born in 1865. I was passionately fond of Sibelius at a time when he was out of favour with moderns like Britten and Tippett, whose music then meant nothing to me. The wonderful Danish Radio Symphony Orchestra played Nielsen's Fifth Symphony at the Edinburgh Festival in 1950, twenty years after his death. In Stockholm I heard his 'Sinfonia espansiva', his third symphony, which totally enraptured me.

Perhaps one of the reasons why I love Nielsen's music so much is that he was a peasant from the island of Fyn, which is Hans Andersen country, over which I had cycled on my way to Sweden. His roots were there, as I had sensed were my own ancestral roots. And in the programme there was a photograph of the composer at the age of sixty, and I was struck at once by his resemblance to my father – the broad brow, the level eyes, the sweet smile with its touch of grim humour, the firm chin, the well-set ears, a really manly face. That resemblance persuaded me as much as anything of my family's Viking origins. Nielsen's 'Springtime on Fyn' is a delightful work, a folk cantata written for a local choral society near his birthplace about the same time as his magnificent Fifth Symphony. He also wrote operas, which I have not heard except for the enchanting comedy *Maskerade*, which some friend taped for me from the BBC Third Programme.

One of the simple, sexless pleasures I often enjoyed in Stockholm was a ride to the top of the Katarina Lift, and I wrote one of my first poems about Sweden describing this experience at night:

> The ground drops, the street lamps fall away
> With the speed of divers slowly hurtling through
> The sluices of the deep, flyover dark.
> Gradually, with a decent readiness,
> The city like a bride unfolds herself,
> Her willingness made modest by the night
> That yet more fervently reveals her fire,
> Those radiating centres of desire,
> The clustered lights of crossings,
> The jewelled veins of squares and parks,
> The looped ropes of doubled radiance down the lakes
> On which the golden ferries burn
> And move like hands intelligently down
> The swan-clouded currents in the knocking ice
> Whose opening and closing estuaries finally reflect
> A distant fall of houses, every window bright.
>
> Now, at the tower's top, and in the hanging

Gondola of stars we stand astride
The city of our admiration, she who lies
Profuse, and naked, passionate yet calm,
Inscrutably collected, in a brilliant pause
Before the swoop of love, the fall without a cause.

I can almost hear Sibelius and Nielsen in that poem, hastily scribbled at
the top of the towering lift before I descended for that night's park-
prowling, for 'the swoop of love' and 'the fall without a cause'. But
going the rounds of the dimly lit parks rarely produced any satisfactory
convergence of souls. When it did, there was no love in it, just physical
delight, reason enough to seek 'the fall without the cause' – the cause
being love, which, despite many disillusionments, I still believed
existed. I never found it in Sweden, though I found something better –
an affection for her land and people that persists, despite my disillusionments.

I was to return to Stockholm several times: first in November, when
my records tell me I taught at the Högre allmänna läroverket för gossar
a Norrmalm; then in the winter vacation, when the city became even
more beautiful under deep snow. I remember meeting a sympathetic
German businessman one night in the depths of a snowy park where we
were the only wanderers and seekers. It was so icy cold, even the
Swedish homos had been discouraged, and their occasional hooligan
attackers. The Herr Doktor was from Stuttgart Nort, and with him I had
my only extended relationship at this period, from which some fragments of an unfinished poem exists: 'Together, treading the whispered
dark, the snow-sheeted dark, where every window hangs upon a ledge
of snow, with snowballs in our hands we go. . . .' The poem, 'A
Midwinter Night's Dream', like our friendship, never came to anything.
In November, I was staying at the Hotel Hellman in Bryggargatan, and
one evening as I stepped out of the front door I bumped into two
medical students I had known in Leeds, always inseparables, but they
had both been my lovers. This meeting was one of the few coincidences
in my life. Another concerns a beautiful girl I met who was singing in a
Stockholm night-club – straight, unpretentious, classic jazz standards
done very well indeed. Some years later we met again in Manila when
we found we had both engaged the same taxi for a ride into the country
to the volcanic crater of Taal Lake, described in my book about the
Philippines, *Filipinescas* (1966).

But it was also a time of Cold War, of refugees seeking asylum in the
'free' countries of the West. Theirs was a political asylum, mine was a
cultural asylum, the one as important as the other, but not necessarily

linked, as I tried to express in a poem, published by Joe Ackerley in *The Listener*, and which also appeared in the Swedish magazine *Moderna Språk*:

The Winter of the World
In the dark streets of earth the children run
Far from the father and mother of them all.
In all the cities of the world they die,
In all the places where violence can drop
Its cliff of stars upon each separated heart.

This is a vision of the winter of the world.
The child's face will not be lifted again;
He looks deep into the iron earth
And his eyes are sharper than the eyes of men.
He sees the world's death, a still and monstrous birth.

Joe Ackerley also printed another uncollected poem which I wrote later in Göteborg, and in which I tried to link the Hungarian refugees pouring into Sweden, homeless and hopeless, with my own case; a sexual as well as cultural refugee:

The Refugees
Winter is hard for these homeless lovers,
They who must hunt and hide
Their private passion in a public park
Whose trees are bare – scant covers
From the searching wind, and from the secret eyes
Of those who wait and watch outside
The lighted no man's land of dark
In which their houseless anguish lives and dies.

Beyond the city, in the stricken grove
Of hope, and on the killing bed
Of earth and stone, like landless fugitives
They drag their last possession, common love.
Their hunger burns among the sepulchres of snow and grass
That pillow and engulf desire's pale and glowing head.
Roofless, their longing both destroys and bitterly preserves
The freedom of the poor, a frontier they may never pass.

It was courageous of Joe to insist on publishing that poem in *The Listener*. It was printed despite objections from various sources in the

BBC in those days of homo witch-hunting and secret agents – another
subject I used for a poem, also published by Joe, along with similar
themes, all reprinted in *A Spring Journey and Other Poems* – poems I
still regard as important testimonies to my experiences. 'Omens of
Disaster' was written in London, in a dank basement room at 51
Inverness Terrace, just after Bonamy Dobrée had kicked me out of
Leeds, and which was admired by W.S. Merwin, who happened to be
living on the other side of the street at the same time. We were brought
together in a curious way when one of my letters was delivered to his
address by mistake, and he kindly brought it across the road to me. The
other poems in the book are 'The Secret Agent' and 'The Questioning'.
They were not at all paranoiac; they were based on the reality of my
own and other homosexuals' lives at that period of political uncertainty
following the blessed death of Stalin in 1953, and before the very
moderate relief afforded by the Wolfenden Report in 1957. It was to
continue well into the sixties, and soon after I arrived in Sendai, Japan,
in 1959 I had a sinister encounter, in the presence of a very unhappy
dean, Professor Atsuo Kobayashi, with two so-called professors from
the University of Maryland in Japan who were actually CIA informers.
And I was to have some trouble in obtaining a visa for my first visit to
the United States. That is still all in the future, at this point in my
narrative, but I bring it in briefly here because it illustrates the political,
sexual and artistic tensions of those Cold War blues.

* * *

Contrary to general belief, the Swedes have a distinctive sense of
humour, as do the other natives of Scandinavia, though with occasional
blind spots – on their side, and on mine too. One of the first things that
caught my eye on the news-stands in Stockholm was a glossy magazine
entitled *Fart*. I knew at once that this title did not mean what any
English speaker would assume it to mean, but that it was the Swedish
word for 'travel'. But when I tried to explain all this to a Swedish
student I met by the lake, his face was completely blank; or perhaps he
was having me on, in his own humorous way?
    The beauty of the Swedish language, like that of any other, depends
on the speaker. It can sound uncouth and unmusical, but when it is
spoken correctly and with feeling it can sound as noble and melodious as
any tongue, be it growling French, lisping Spanish, robust German,
splashy Japanese, nimble Italian or class-conscious English. With my
knowledge of German, both modern and Middle High, and the smat-
terings of Old Norse that Dr Duncan Mennie at Newcastle had some-

how instilled into me, the Scandinavian languages – apart from Finnish –
are fairly easy for me to read with the help of a good dictionary.

So after a few days' study of *Teach Yourself Swedish* I could make
myself understood by using elementary grammar and an idiot vocabulary. Pronunciation was no problem – or so I thought at first. Many were
the *faux pas* I made, to the uncontrollable hilarity of my Swedish
friends, through a slip of the tongue in pronunciation. But so many of
my friends and colleagues and students spoke decent English, we always
slipped back into my native tongue after a few moments, and I never
persevered with my efforts to master a language I knew I should never
really need – a deplorable attitude, but one so universal the Scandina-
vians have become the world's best speakers of English as a foreign
language. In conversation, I found that a few formal expressions – and
Swedish formality can be very gracious and elegant – to convey greetings and thanks and little compliments in their native tongue were
appreciated by my Swedish hosts. The sophistication of such expressions
delighted me: they had an old-world grace, like the curtsies dropped by
girls and the stiff bows made by boys.

Out in the more brutal and unpredictable daily life of the streets and
parks and public transport, I never had any problems. Because of my
Nordic appearance, people sometimes stopped me to ask directions, or
to ask the time, and usually I could get the drift of what they wanted,
especially if they were just checking the time, when I could reply in
halting Swedish. But to most of the questions, rattled off in carelessly
colloquial style, I was unable to give a reply and had to resort to
English, which was nearly always acceptable. I made a few good friends
in that way, though as I am by nature a rather silent person I often had
to make a great effort to engage anyone in conversation, and at the end
of ten minutes' chat my head would be whirling and I would have to sit
down to recover from my exhaustion. This reluctance to talk idly about
nothing worried me, for I was afraid people might think me stand-offish,
and it did not seem to be a recommendation in a teacher. That was
where the exchange of polite formal phrases came in so useful for me, as
it does now in Japanese. They help one to skate over awkward silences
and embarrassing moments.

I tried to translate some modern Swedish poets, then found that their
own translations of their work into English were better than mine, and
certainly more correct. And when they translated my poems into Swedish and read them to me, they sounded much better than in English.

After a few days' orientation in Stockholm, I was considered suf-
ficiently culture-adjusted to take on the rest of the country. Nearly all
my teaching days were to begin with the first class, which in Sweden is at

eight o'clock. This did not allow me time to breakfast at my hotel, so the night before I had to take a vacuum flask to the kitchens and ask for it to be filled with hot coffee. The kind lady in charge of my engagements at the Ministry of Education, a rather forbidding institution, was most apologetic about this, but in fact I have been an early riser ever since childhood, and such a matutinal schedule posed no problems for me, though I should have liked to have had a proper Swedish breakfast before starting work, because breakfast in Sweden is just about the best breakfast in the world. However, on my days off I could indulge myself at leisure in that delicious and varied meal, though I was always up and dressed long before the restaurant opened, and had to contain my impatience until eight o'clock.

My first assignment was at a very famous public school, Sigtunaskolan, in Sigtuna, a charming small town half-way between Stockholm and Uppsala. The students I had to teach here were very mature for their age – sixteen to eighteen – and they came from wealthy and influential families who travelled widely, so their children were quite fluent in English and in one or two other European languages. The school was a kind of show-place, but there is no doubt that the teaching there was first class, and the students were of the highest intelligence, so they were a joy to teach. It was difficult at first to know what I could teach them, so I used to start a lesson with one of those informal chats about next to nothing – the weather, fashions, sport, hobbies – that I so detest in ordinary conversation. But I found that as soon as I got started, I always warmed to my task, for those students were so responsive, and so appreciative. I would spend a few minutes trying out my elementary Swedish on them, and asked them to teach me some modern slang, and in this way I picked up some rather improper words, to their great delight. In exchange, I taught them some spicy English expressions. I found a use for my naughty limericks, by cutting out all the 'dirty' words in things like 'There was an old morphy named Sparrow' and asking the students to substitute appropriate words, which they were able to do with often devastating effect. I also used some of my more serious poems in this way, removing the verbs, the nouns and the adjectives and asking the students to complete the poem in their own words, as it were. Some of the results were more interesting than the originals, in their surreal juxtaposition of images. Then they were always glad to listen to what I had originally written, and compare it with their own efforts. It was a most unconventional way to teach English – and, incidentally, to teach an appreciation of English poetry and vocabulary – but it worked, and I have often wondered why it is not used in British schools, for it can be used to teach metre, rhythm and rhyme also. I spent a happy week in Sigtuna.

After this promising introduction to Swedish school life, I expected things to get worse, but in fact they did not, for I found a fairly uniform high level of English all over Sweden. The students had always been encouraged to speak English as much as possible, and their standard of listening-comprehension was excellent: they really *listened* to what I was saying, unlike my wretchedly taught Japanese students, who have had to learn English by rote, without practical application, and so do not know how to listen, an art that is quite the opposite of the passive 'hearing' of language they encounter in those stultifying language labs that deaden all sense of English as a living tongue. But in the Scandinavian countries English is never taught as a dead language, as it is in Japan; nor are Scandinavian students inculcated with the chauvinistic idea that their own language is better than any other, and that therefore foreign languages are inferior or laughable, as I was to discover when I started teaching in Japan. Those good Swedish students and teachers completely spoiled me for my posts in Spain, Japan and the United States, and never again did I so enjoy the teaching of my native tongue to foreigners.

After Sigtuna, I started my perambulations northwards, first to Uppsala at the Högre allmänna läroverket, which was a sort of mixed high school of very good quality, with delightful students. I preserved some jottings of my lesson themes, and I am astonished at the range of subjects I covered, from classical music, Shakespeare and Hardy to discussions about the then just-emergent television; films and theatre; the inevitable 'U' and 'Non-U' which then was so fashionable; party games for the younger children like 'My aunt went to town . . .', word races, proverbs using dumb crambo, charades, 'Animal, Vegetable and Mineral' and so on – an infinite variety of diversions to keep their interest high and their listening always tuned in to my speech.

I gave a general lecture to the whole school at each place I visited, and often used a piano on the stage, playing bits of jazz or Poulenc's 'Perpetuum Mobile' or folk-songs or songs from Shakespeare. I demonstrated, quite incompetently, a grotesque fandango learnt in Andalusia, or strummed my guitar in fake flamenco. I always tried to put on a performance, and even when I arrived at an early-morning class feeling dispirited and unwell, as soon as I entered the room my depression would lift at the sight of all those beautiful, eager children with their pure, fresh, Nordic faces, their fine, athletic bodies, their warm-hearted friendliness. One of my 'Swedish Exercises' tries to capture that unforgettable joy of Swedish lessons. It is entitled 'Gymnasium', which does not mean what it appears to in English, but is the top class in a high school:

The snowboots and the skis, the fur-lined hoods
That populate the coat-racks by the classroom door
Prepare me for an audience whose moods
Are those of warm relief and cold anxiety.
They have escaped the sharpness of the world outside.
Soon they must penetrate once more
The cruel street of ice, begin the homeward ride,
The battle with the snow, the wind's perplexity.

But for the moment all is warmth and light.
Pale-golden faces smile and laugh for me.
Their lips are pale, their perfect eyes are bright.
These boys are men with voices like the sea's.
Under the fragile desks their limbs are large,
Their laughter springs from huge
Good nature that no winter night can freeze.
They are the giants of the forests that are men
Where legendary heroes lift their blond and massive heads again.
In their enormous hands a book
Tenderly flutters like captive birds,
And in their northern calmness is a generous look
Of level passion, stronger than any words.

I see from one of my notes that I persuaded some students to compose commercial jingles for radio or television, as an exercise in composition. Here is one example from my twelve-year-olds in Ock-elbo, about a popular drink, which we devised to the tune of 'Alouette, gentille allouette'.

> Try Cloetta, wonderful Cloetta,
> Try Cloetta, it's so good for you.
> Eat Cloetta, heavenly Cloetta,
> That's Cloetta, that's the thing to do!

With the younger children, we would make out long shopping lists with the ingredients in each item; or we would write about a walk describing all the animals, plants and trees with their correct English names. They would do a paragraph about the Volvo engine or a flight by SAS or campsite cooking. In doing so, I steadily increased my own Swedish vocabulary. I taught them a lot, but I learnt such a lot from my Swedish students too.

My colleagues were invariably helpful and hospitable, for I was invited out to dinner almost every night – something unheard of in the other foreign lands I taught in. In my year at Amherst, for example, I was invited to a private home for dinner only once, towards the end of my stay. As was the case with my writing, I think people did not know what to do with me or what on earth to make of me in those hidebound fifties. But it was not so in Sweden, where the traditional rules of hospitality and generosity towards strangers are ancestral in their tact and courtesy. I soon learnt that one should take a little gift or some flowers for the hostess, as a sign of appreciation, and such humble offerings were always received with a charming graciousness.

And what wonderful meals they prepared for my delectation! After a few shots of akvavit, good wines were ceremoniously opened to accompany some exquisitely prepared fresh vegetables, seafoods and rare meats like venison, mountain boar and wild hares whose snowy fur could well be made into ear-muffs or gloves, to protect me from what my hosts assumed I would find intolerable cold, but whose purity and fierceness I relished and revelled in as most people revel in baking sunshine – and sunlight depresses me. I did not have the heart to tell my hosts that I disapproved of wearing fur and disliked eating meat. But I have kept a beautiful fur hat I was given in Kiruna.

I met one extraordinary foreigner in Uppsala, a Frenchman I at first thought was completely mad. Like me, he had found the intellectual and social climate of his native land insupportable, so in 1955 he had left France to become *lecteur de français* at the University of Uppsala, where he was to stay for three years – he managed to hold out much longer than I did. This marvellous French intellectual and obvious homosexual was quite a dandy, in what I thought was a rather vulgar way. He wore gaudily checked suits like a music-hall comedian's, and blatantly contrasting bow-ties. He had a bright-red Jaguar, in which he drove me around the countryside so fast and so uninhibitedly that I refused to go out with him after my first ride. He knew many French writers like Camus, Roger Caillois, Ariès, Barthes and Bachelard, and had dined with Maurice Chevalier on the entertainer's tour of Sweden. Not until much later did I learn that this astonishing person was Michel Foucault, whose epoch-making books on the history of madness, sex and society had influenced my own thinking on these subjects very deeply. Many years later, in a lecture at the Collège de France, he evoked his ideal city in terms that reminded me of Stockholm:

A good country is one that has more or less the form of a circle, and it is at the centre of this circle that the capital should exist . . . the capital should have both an aesthetic and a symbolic relationship with its territory. The capital should be the ornament of the territory. But it should also have a political relationship with it . . . and play a moral role . . . giving the example of good manners to the rest of the land.

I was to keep in touch with Foucault irregularly in Paris, where he allowed me to attend some of his lectures. In Japan, in 1963 or so, I had a letter from him saying he was taking up a post at the Maison Franco-Japonaise in Kyoto, and asking me to find him some attractive young men: he did not want to meet intellectuals, or writers like Mishima and Kawabata, who bored him. Sadly, he never came to Japan, but went to Warsaw, where he had an unfortunate amorous adventure with a spy in the Polish secret service that obliged him to leave Warsaw precipitately for Hamburg before returning to France. I spent an hour or so with him in Hamburg, and found him quite cool and unshaken by his diplomatic incident, the main thing being, as he said, that the sex had been great, and that made up for everything, an attitude of which I thoroughly approved and always tried to emulate in Japan, Malaya and all my other temporary postings. I also met Foucault in Rome in 1967, when he was director of the Institut Français: we were both Pasolini fans and followers. I admired his lack of pedantry and brilliant independence. There was in him and his writings the sort of multiplicity of personae with which I was familiar in myself. He wrote in European and American gay magazines with the same offhand honesty and wry humour he used in his more academic writings, and with all his surprising offbeat insights that were true inspirations of liberal discourse. He made his life a work of art, but it was his own kind of *art brut*. In *Gay Sunshine* he wrote that 'the practice of sado-masochism is the creation of pleasure, and sado-masochism is truly a subculture'. And on another occasion: 'There can be no true civilization as long as marriage between men is not allowed.' Such adventurous sentiments were of course out of place in the still rather strait-laced Swedish society of the fifties. But that last remark has come true: first Denmark, then Sweden legalized homosexual marriage. When will it be legalized in the rest of Europe? I cannot see it being approved by our present sub-totalitarian Thatcher regime, that great balls-breaker of British cultural freedom and independence of expression. Foucault's death from Aids on 25 June 1984 marked the loss of one of the very few free-thinking spirits of our time, and one more badly needed now than ever. Fortunately his great and inspiring work lives on, and fine studies and biographies like Didier Eribon's massive *Michel Foucault* will always keep his genius alive in the minds and hearts of those who loved him. Hervé Guibert's *L'ami qui ne m'a pas sauvé la vie* gives a chilling account of his horrible death from Aids.

* * *

Michel had entranced his students at Uppsala with inspired amateur
productions of plays by Labiche, Giraudoux, Anouilh – his very personal illuminations of what he called *la nuit suédoise*, an expression with
a double meaning that was not lost on the Swedes, who know that long
night of the soul only too well. I felt I should never be able to equal such
exhilaration, with my limited means. All I could offer my students, and
my Swedish lovers, was my youth. So from Uppsala with its magical
rune stones I set off alone for Gävle, Ockelbo, Bollnäs, Ljusdal,
Ragunda, Umeå, Kiruna – each place so different, yet always so Swedish.
One of the joys of my job was the constant travel by train and bus
through landscapes of majestic solitude and of such unspoilt natural
beauty that my heart was often moved to tears, and to poetry:

Jämtland

The silver birch is papery, and veils
Its elbowed branches gloved in black
In a suspended shower of golden scales,
Its own light leaves, that pattern a forest track
Like narrow starshine's riddled flakes
Or coins struck from the moonlight's hidden lakes.

A river is violet beneath the deep red clouds of dark.
The ash and aspen brandish sheaves
Of fireworks, each leaf a spark,
Along a forest's evergreen black eaves.
Rafts of logs lie on the sunset like an archipelago.
Mountains, pitched with pine, hang in the reeds below.

A green swan slings himself across the vacant air.
His rippling neck hauls on his feathered vanes.
Beyond the rowan drugged with berries, there
In a yellow sky along the lake he drags the water's reins,
Making the sheeted mirror flash and shake.
The washed reeds bow to the long procession of his wake.

He floats now among impenetrable mountains furred with larch,
Sails through a lake-reflected rainbow's double hoop
That frames the northern lightnings in its melting arch,
And over his own stern image seems to prowl and stoop;

While rosy distances of ice that draw him on
Still shiver through the birch-tree's page when he has gone.

I had always imagined Sweden as a dark, forbidding land of black and white. The exaltation of brilliant colour in spring, summer and particularly autumn was a revelation to me. Not that Sweden does not have its grimmer aspects, as I described in 'The Dead Falls at Ragunda' on 18 November 1956:

> This was where a river fell away
> And left a useless fall of stones.
> Where once the mountain flashed
> With rushing waters hangs today
> A still cataract of rocks, dead bones
> Of an elemental life whose waters crashed
> And stumbled with ungovernable force,
> While over the black pine forest clouds of spray
> Marked the continuous thunders of its own applause.
>
> Now where the waters fountained trees have sprung.
> Among the boulders stained with spreading sores
> And rings of lichen, silver birches leap
> Like phantoms of the spray that hung
> And shivered with the smoke of catastrophic wars.
> – But the dead falls only seem to sleep.
> Under their arrested avalanches lie
> Ancestral heroes, gods of the epic north, whose tongue
> Lingers among the present stillness, for it cannot die.

Visits to some of the more spectacular natural sights like those at Ragunda were made possible only by the kindness of my colleagues and local people who would take me for long drives in their cars out into the vastness of the winter snows or deep into the autumn forests or along craggy coasts and the pure waters of slowly icing lakes. Sometimes they invited me to Sunday morning service in their austere, pale-lighted churches, where we would stand to pray and sit down to sing the lovely old hymns of their compassionate Protestant religion. I remember so clearly one such church in snowy Umeå, in the distant north of Norrland-Fargernas – the impressive red-brick church with its green roofs and clock-lit steeple and turreted walls, a fantastic vision in the winter twilight of Västerbotten:

In the park emptied by winter
I tread the undistinguished paths of snow and dark.
The pale bandstand adrift on scrolls
Of wind-turned music, and the metal baskets
Packed with the overflowing wastes of snow
Are frozen ghosts of unimaginable summers.

A piled church warms the sky with orange brick.
The river shuffles neon alphabets of acid green.
– I do not care where paths begin and borders end,
But in the naked birch-grove that I saunter through
The snow's calm anarchy keeps off the grass
My steps that go where no one else has been.

In nearly all my poems about Sweden the image of the silver birch
tree keeps recurring. This spiritual tree was growing everywhere with
ghostly grace, as I saw it growing and gracing the wilds of Siberia a few
years later, in a Russian summer adrift in surprising waves of wild
flowers.

Dalarna is also runic country, a magical province. At one of the
schools there was an excellent ice-hockey team, and one of my pupils
invited me to watch a match, which I made into the poem 'Ice Hockey in
Dalarna':

The player's quilted shorts are red.
Padded shoulders and sweatered chest
  Appear to shrink that golden head.
He bears a different number from the rest.

  On booted skates he's tall.
Crimson stockings muscle knees and thighs
  And make his feet seem small.
Dark eyebrows draw a vizor on his eyes.

Over the open rink the forward leans and flies.
  He holds his stick in gauntlet clutch
And weaves the puck across the scoring ice.
  Like crabs the keepers in the goal-nets crouch.

Hard on the prowling ice they thrust their blades,
  Scour the rink for danger and our hot delight.
Snow falls from the floodlights as the white sky fades,
  But still these crimson rockets shoot wet stars into the teeth of
                                                    night.

Those open-air ice-rinks are everywhere in Sweden, and the sport is a national passion. It was in Dalarna that I had a brief romantic encounter in a forest of silver birches with a tall, blond young man who never said a word. But as we parted, he smiled and said: 'Thank you, professor.' I was puzzled by this. Was he just using that universal title for a teacher much as the pimps in Montmartre greet me with 'Bonsoir, docteur?' I got the answer to the puzzle at eight o'clock in school next day, when I saw my last night's lover lolling in the back row of desks. He gave me a discreet wink. But apart from that little sign, there was no betrayal. We had shared an important secret and wanted to keep it, as I have until this moment, in the recesses of the memory palace we all construct to memorialize our triumphs and disasters.

From Umeå I took a side-trip during a week's November holiday to the Arctic, to Kiruna and Narvik. I was anxious to make my first contact with the Lapps, now more properly known as the Sami people, expert hunters and reindeer herders, and also fine craftsmen. In their native dress of blue and crimson, they were most elusive. I was fascinated by the Arctic, and by my hotel at the station in Kiruna, with its thick curtains to keep out summer's midnight sun. The room keys were attached to bits of reindeer antler. In the snow-filled streets women were using plastic orange sleds to drag their shopping home, and as baby-carriages. There was nothing to do after dark, for it was snowing heavily, and there was some doubt whether the train could leave for Narvik next morning. From my window I gazed out on a blank wilderness of snow and ice, with in the distance the lights of an iron mine whose machinery groaned and rumbled all night long. Yet I felt secure and happy there. On later visits I noticed that the streets were kept clear of snow and ice by underground thermal heat, and in the late seventies I saw that many new modern shops and apartment blocks had been built. There is now television in the bar of the hotel, mostly American situation comedies, with subtitles in Swedish, allowing us to enjoy the original sound-track. (In Japan, there is something ludicrous in the sight and sound of foreign actors whose voices have been dubbed into quite unsuitably matched Japanese ones.) I tried to write something about Kiruna, but failed: perhaps it was the bone-chilling cold that froze my brain. Yet I loved the extreme intensity of that cold, for I hate summer heat so much. In Japan I have to keep my underclothes and shirts in the freezer well into October. There were sensational, dramatic sunsets over the Arctic.

> Cold clamps the forehead
> With a band of iron. . . .

In the hilly streets of snow
Men's clothes have a sooty bloom . . .

I travelled on an express to Narvik, across mountains and along profound blue fjords, to snowbound Narvik, in the company of a jolly band of musicians, a Swedish symphony orchestra with all its instruments, with their soloist, the cellist Guido Vecchi, who has an extraordinary resemblance to Barbirolli. This 'Kiruna Express' has come all the way from Stockholm. It crosses the Arctic Circle at Murjek around 8.30 a.m. There are many exuberant young Swedes on this train going to Björkliden for a cross-country ski race. We stop at this lively little town, with its ski-lifts, cabins, skating-rinks. Children are using old-fashioned brooms to sweep the snow in wide circles on the ice of the skating-rinks, which seem to be natural pools. The static electricity at the Kiruna Station Hotel was very strong: every time I turned on the taps of the wash-basins I got an electric shock, and now I am almost afraid to touch any metal object on the train. There were also soldiers and businessmen aboard the train, whose first stop was at Stordalen, 386 metres above sea-level, 1466 kilometres from Stockholm. Then on to Abisko and Björkliden, where skiers were already swooping joyously down the mountain slopes as a weak sun came out over a snow-drifted lake.

At the border between Sweden and Norway, Riksgränsen, I was surprised to find there is no passport or immigration check, no Customs. The skies here are deep blue above the snows of the mountains. Soon we are travelling high up along a profound fjord, following its winding contours. The water and ice at the bottom of this great sea-canyon are jade green, but this colour slowly changes to turquoise blue as we approach the sea and the fjord widens.

There is no train running south from Narvik, so one has to get a bus as far as Fauske. From there I can get a train to Trondheim: the kind girls at the station information office in Kiruna had reserved a first-class sleeper for me. The bus trip from Narvik to Fauske is magnificent, through the most wonderful mountain and fjord scenery. From time to time the bus has to cross a wide fjord by driving on to a car ferry, and these short trips across the water are a delight. On a second visit to Kiruna I was able to take a sleeper from Narvik direct to Stockholm, arriving at 9 a.m., in time for my classes at the British Centre.

I dislike any contact with the British, who always succeed in making me feel frightened, and the British staff at the Centre were no exception. They behave as if they were ruling India or some other tropic colony of the last century, and always adopt such a superior attitude, simply because they speak English, and expect the Swedes to reverence them for that. In fact, the Swedes, both teachers and students, despise these British officials with their false air of authority. Perhaps things that strike one here in Sweden are the same in England. In England, if they are the same, they are never so striking, at least to a native Englishman. It is only in a foreign country that the invisible becomes plain, the insignificant suddenly has meaning, and the foreign becomes strangely familiar. Accretions of one's native customs, dress and speech fall away, and one seems to see things anew, in a fresh and analytic light.

The year was ending in colossal snows. From Stockholm I set off again for more delightful places – the Samrealskolan och kommunala gymnasiet in Avesta, the Högre allmänna läroverket in Hedemora, and a similar high school in Ludvika. It was in Ludvika, on Thursday, 13 December, that I was wakened in the middle of the night by the entry of a beautiful girl wearing long white virginal robes, and with a crown of candles burning on her long blonde hair. She was escorted by two serving maidens similarly attired, and they brought me coffee and cakes in honour of the Santa Lucia festival. I was half asleep, and their entry was like a dream or some vision of paradise. I can't quite remember, but I think that when I sat up in my hotel bed to receive the coffee and cakes, the beautiful girl placed a chaste kiss on my forehead. I did indeed feel blessed. I remembered that visit years later in Venice, when I saw the gorgeously clad corpse of the real St Lucia in her shrine near the station, and I thought of the Swedish girl's long, fine hands and cool lips as I gazed at the tubes of mouldering tobacco that were the corpse's fingers. That ancient figure from Syracuse moved me just as deeply as the modern, living one in beautiful Ludvika.

* * *

I can find no record of all the places I visited in the New Year of 1957. Was it then I saw for the first time Paul Delvaux's skeleton 'Crucifixion'? But I remember I went to Göteborg, Sweden's second-largest city, where I attended performances at the opera house, the Stora Teatern, and was enchanted by the city's excellent symphony orchestra. The performances were the equal of any I heard at the Royal Opera Theatre in Stockholm, for Swedes are celebrated for their magnificent voices. I went to Jonköping and Karlskrona, and took the opportunity to visit the lovely islands of Borgholm and Gotland. The latter, I was told, is geologically similar to Japan. The island was very prosperous during Hanseatic times, and the city of Visby is charming in its medieval domestic architecture with a fine museum housing treasures that are still being discovered from ancient trading periods. Here they celebrate the summer solstice by dancing round a maypole decorated with wild flowers and my favourite silver birch. There are Northmen runes here, too, from the fifth century. A smaller island, Stora Karlso, has been a bird sanctuary for sea-birds since 1887, and I was able to visit it by using a small ferry-boat which is free of charge, used mainly for transporting sheep and agricultural implements. It is a perfect place for bird-watchers and orchid lovers, for it is covered with wild orchids in spring and summer, as well as junipers and delicious wild strawberries. But I was haunted by Paul Delvaux's imagery of three skeletons nailed to their Easter crosses in his *Kruisiging* (now in the magnificent modern art museum in Brussels).

Back in Stockholm I was able to visit Drottningholm, where the most exquisite eighteenth-century theatre stands in a lakeside setting of great beauty. I seem to remember I went to Drottningholm by ferry from Stockholm, the Swedish flag bravely flying its yellow cross on a vivid blue ground. The theatre is unique in Europe, because it is still operated as it was in the eighteenth century, the original stage machinery being used for transformation scenes. The members of the orchestra and the theatre staff are all dressed in eighteenth-century style. It was a highly cultured man, King Gustav III, who was responsible for the perfection of this theatre, where operas and pantomime ballets were produced, and where we can still enjoy such productions in the old style. Every year there is an opera festival here, presenting usually rather rare works like Gluck's *Paris and Helen*, seldom heard since its first performance in Vienna in 1770. There is another fine old theatre that I visited in Ulriksdal, named Confidencen, north of Stockholm, part of the favourite summer retreat of Queen Lovisa Ulrica, sister of Frederick the Great and mother of Gustav III.

Such were the joys of Sweden. In that springtime, my first volume of autobiography, *The Only Child*, which I had written in my attic in Corsham, was published in London, and on the Sunday morning after publication I rushed to the station to buy the English Sunday papers, nearly all of which contained enthusiastic reviews by Raymond Mortimer, G.S. Fraser and others. Edwin Muir reviewed it fairly well for *The Listener*. Its unexpected triumph – alas, it went out of print within a week, because Mark Bonham-Carter at Collins had printed only a small edition – suddenly made me wish to be back in England. I felt restless after the long winter, in which many Swedes become devastated by melancholia and fits of depression that lead some of them to suicide. I was not suicidal, but the marvellous outburst of leaf and blossom that is the miraculous Swedish spring made me feel impatient with both my life and my much-admired Swedes. I am shocked now to find the sort of notes I was writing about them at the end of that long, lonely winter. I was desperately lonely, and when I got news of the success of my book from the British Sunday papers, I had no one to share it with. I remember that when I had finished reading the reviews, that sunny Sunday noon, I ran straight to a certain public convenience to share my transports with the startled *faux-pisseurs* who, when they had recovered from their surprise, kindly relieved me of my tensions in the pleasantest way. Brought down to earth, I adjusted my dress before leaving and treated myself to a magnificent lunch, with aperitif, champagne and cognac, before staggering back to the Eden Terrace Hotel in the Sturegatan, where I was staying at the time, to sleep off my ecstasy and restore my faculties for a further evening celebration of sexual and literary success.

But it was not all sex in the springtime. I attended concerts, including a great Chopin recital by Jan Smeterlin (Steinwayflygel). That year saw the death of Sibelius. With the last snows melting, I would wait for night in my hotel room, where a pink lamp is lit, shining on the double frames of the windows. A last snow is falling with the twilight, and through the twisty glass I watch for the moment when the snow turns blue and violet, and then fades gently down the slope into the dark of lake and trees, and the lamps go on, golden in the park where like a hunter I shall seek my love.

The birches were all at once in fresh leaf, the first spring flowers were out in the parks and in the window-boxes. The shop windows were decorated with spring flowers made from dyed feathers, and in the markets there were masses of blooms. A symbol of spring was the blue-jeaned *skinnknutte* (skinhead) on a moped with a bunch of canary-yellow feathers. I was on my last posting, to Malmö. I was staying at the Park Hotel, which had an interesting park outside. Good Friday, known here as 'Long Friday': at the Stadsteatern a meeting of the Salvation Army, which lent the only touch of colour to a moribund general election last year. On Easter Monday I went to an extraordinary performance of *Peer Gynt* at the Stadsteater – *Premiär Fredag 8 Mars 1957*, with a bewitching performance by Max von Sydov as Peer. Naima Wifstrand played his mother, with a radiant Gunnel Lindblom as Solveig, and Bibi Andersson and Ingrid Thulin in minor parts, including the latter as Anitra. It was an enormous cast, about ten times the size of the production of my own version of the play at the University Theatre, Newcastle upon Tyne, 1973, with a great Peer by an inspired Freddie Jones. An entire orchestra was seated in the wings, stage left. No national anthem was played at the beginning, but the packed audience grew gradually quieter as the time drew near for the drama to start on the vast semicircular stage. It went on for about five hours, with intervals, and I left in a state of dazed discomfort. It was the theatrical event of the season. Many of those actors and actresses appeared in Bergman's movies.

I had grown so tired of living in hotels. For the most part, Swedish hotels are almost identical. The service is bad and hard to get in this prosperous land: that is why the flood of refugees and Gastarbeiter was so welcome in the seventies, when almost a million immigrants entered the country from Finland, European countries, the Middle East, North Africa and the Far East. At first they were welcomed, then created a problem for the Swedes, as they did for Germany and Switzerland, and many Swedes turned against them. In some hotels I had a different chambermaid every day, usually of a different nationality from the day before. Occasionally there was no running hot water, the plumbing was defective – wash-basins would not empty. There was never any breakfast, not even hot coffee, before 8 a.m. It needed quite a ceremony to get a bath, which cost 2.50 to 3 kronor. Yet there was also a lot of quite useless and unwanted service, as when the chambermaid would come bursting into one's room in the evening to turn down the bedclothes, lay out pyjamas and pull down blinds. There were always only two hand-towels, like our tea-towels, heavily starched. All rooms in Stadhotellets were uniform: even the pictures on the walls were standardized, by national artists. There were meetings of Rotary and Lions International once a week, with loud music and singing – generally just under one's room – of folk-songs and comic opera choruses ('Trink, trink, Brüderlein trink,/ Lass' die Sorge zu Haus' . . .'), with lots of stamping, table-thumping in very strict time. There were women too at these get-togethers, and the musicians did not seem to belong to a union, for they played without stop. At Göteborg 'Beim Grünen Alfred' with Tyrolese orchestra of oldish men in costume, and customers, often blind drunk, joining in. In Eksjö I noticed the kind of awe, mixed with humour, with which Swedes look upon drunks. Children were fascinated by them, as if with sacred clowns, while the grown-ups gazed on them with tolerant, vacant half-smiles, regarding them as ancient gods possessed. But there is an awful violence in their drunkenness. There is a lot of surreptitious drinking of beer and spirits in lavatories, with friends sharing a bottle of akvavit in a cubicle, taking turns to sit down and drink. Behind bolted lavatory doors there was more often the clink of bottles than the pulling of chains. In hotel bedrooms groups of commercial travellers will gather to drink weak Pilsner and talk and laugh at the tops of their voices. At

Ljusdal and Hammarstrand I was kept awake all night by drunken dancers. On arrival I always ask for a quiet room, and am invariably given the noisiest available, next to a lift or a WC and right over the *Festväning* or banquet hall. I think that is sheer Swedish cussedness. Boys of sixteen drink whisky, gin and akvavit on the ferries to Copenhagen.

While I was in Malmö I was so desperate for a change of scene I often took the ferry to Copenhagen for a night. On the boat from Öresund to Copenhagen I was nearly knocked down by the sudden stampede of Swedes to the bar and the luxurious smorgasbord as soon as the boat cast off from the quay, and soon there were many unpleasant drunks. Swedish drunks are really and truly drunk: absolutely legless, incapable, thoughtless, stupid. They don't know when to stop. In one hotel there was a drunken couple next door to my room. They started arguing and fighting, and when the man went to the toilet the woman locked him out. He was banging on the door for hours, and crying, but the woman, with a voice of steel, refused to let him in. I was often kept awake by the terrible snoring of drunken businessmen – high, excited, metronome snores – which I learnt how to stop by listening with an ear to the wall for a moment of silence, then banging on the wall with a shoe. Or walking into the room as if by mistake, and going out banging *both* doors. (There are always double doors, and always both are well and truly banged whenever a drunk comes stumbling to bed.) No wonder I got fed up with living in such hotels for months on end!

Lands are like love affairs – all excitement and rapture at the first encounters. All is happy infatuation with new faces, new customs, a new language. One can see only the virtues, curiosities and beauties. But gradually enthusiasm diminishes into a more detached interest, then into indifference, disillusion, even hatred. Yet however strong and contrary that ultimate reaction may become, the initial impulse of generous, surging love is never lost, and keeps returning despite oneself, with fresh accesses of joyful insight. No love is ever completely lost: a wise affection will always remain.

I have had love affairs with many lands and many peoples, and one of the most passionate was with Sweden, possibly because of my own ancestral Scandinavian origins – Frisian Viking. I was never in love with Britain, land of my birth, where ever since early childhood I lived in a state of acute terror. But though I always felt a total stranger there, like a visitor from outer space, I shall always keep a certain mild affection for my native land, which taught me the pleasures ot exile. I return from time to time, for a few days only, simply in order to enjoy the relief of leaving it again.

Whenever I was invited to a colleague's house for dinner, I felt a sense of strain in the air of spring. Tense handshakes with relentless, steely grip and determined smiles; nervous bobbing of little daughters, jerky bows of little boys. The women here are definitely the stronger sex. They certainly know how to handle men and to get their own way without appearing to do so. The huge blond men are really like children, with a boyish, serious delight in all the latest gadgets, in new cars, new anything. So often I would see a wife stroke back tenderly a hanging blond cowlick from her husband's wine-flushed forehead, murmuring fondly 'Min Mann . . .' and planting a lush kiss on his cheek. The chemists' shops (not the *apotheker*) are full of 'How to Sex' books like *The Secrets of Love* and *Woman's Role in the Art of Sex*.

Men seem to look upon a pretty, clever wife as a special kind of expensive toy that has to be kept working properly with lots of attention, and this of course suits perfectly a certain type of matron. I grew to hate the look girls have in the street, in a dance-hall or anywhere where there are available men around: a look of absolute certainty and smug confidence in their ability to attract, subdue and tame the poor mutt of a rebellious male, so readily 'caught by the cock'. They sensibly choose their husbands after weighing up all possible advantages and measuring them against the disadvantages. A Swedish young miss is usually calculating and almost scientific in her poised selection of the male she wishes to impale.

Hotels and houses and apartments always feel overheated. There is a kind of sterile perfection about these modern homes. I was often at a loss as to which corner of a room to sit in, for the corners are obliterated by plants, sometimes trained to trail all over the walls and windows. Central heating turned on full, even in springtime. Gleaming wood-block parquet floors that produce a rich creaking sound as one walks. The 'Ornamenta' fireplace is non-functional, with a few decorative silver birch logs laid in the useless grate. I always bring flowers for the hostess, just two or three of the very choicest blooms, nothing less will do. She always goes into ecstasies over them, while I wonder where I can find a seat among all the greenery. Dinner starts with tots of akvavit and we all start skåling one another with fixed smiles. Pickled herring, raw herring, rollmops, liver pastes, cuts of ham and cheese. They hand each other the loaded butter-knife for the many varieties of rolls and bread and crackers and crispbreads. Cucumber, fresh and pickled, with nearly everything, and they call a dish of sliced gherkins a 'salad'. Delicious shellfish and other seafood, always fresh or smoked. Lobster Newburg, sturgeon, caviare. Rich cream cakes and piles of fruit. Many cups of coffee with cognac or fruit liqueur. When I offer a lighted match for someone's cigarette, a gentleman will take it from me, but a lady never does.

The country people and those who live in small towns are much nicer than the smart city folk. I admire the distinctive red colour of country houses and farmhouses, obtained by using a dye from the copper mined at Falun in Dalecarlia, a heavenly province. The deep red is set off by white-framed windows and doors, and often the house corners are also painted white. These houses make a charming picture against a deep-blue sky and dark-green pines. Some farmhouses have grass and moss and house leeks on the roof, and people joke about being able to graze their cows on their roofs. There are several fine outdoor museums in the country, like the one at Skara, a bishop's seat with a very French feeling in its great church with the venerable tombs and the rich stained glass.

But taking leave of a gathering after dinner is a long job: you must announce you are about to leave at least one hour before you really intend to, and the hostess will still press you to stay a little longer. Swedes taking leave of one another in the street do so interminably, often blocking the pavement. Most of the Swedish teachers I met worked hard in a mechanical way, actually doing the minimum – one can't blame them. They have no duties outside school. Some give the impression that they have been trapped by life, and the baffled look of unbelief in their eyes at such a heavy fate is very touching. I think this is because of the Swedish passion for individual rights, personal freedom. I noticed that many Swedes hate committing themselves to a fixed time or date for a meeting, and often a car trip rashly promised at the staff meeting later seemed to be rather unwillingly performed. Well, they must have had better things to do than tote a foreigner around. They always seem to be talking about pay, about money, and in the streets I am always hearing *tchugo-fem öre*, *Tio fem öre* and references to the 1,000-öre note. Some of my colleagues were frankly interested in how much I got as a salary and for daily expenses.

When I started my last stint at Malmö I was so sick of going without breakfast that I indicated to the school authorities that I should prefer not to give the first class of the day, at 8 a.m. This request was accepted, but I soon realized from the icy chill in the staff-room that its granting had caused a great deal of gossip and ill feeling. The atmosphere became unbearable: I was practically sent to Coventry. So I spent as much time as possible in the happier environment of Copenhagen, in the City bar, at the baths or just having tea and Danish pastries at Wivex outside Tivoli. But Copenhagen street sausages *Pölser*, are not nearly as good as the Swedish variety, *Warm Korv*, sold at every corner. Or I watch the American soldiers on leave, buying porno mags, chasing not unwilling girls, picking up boys. One lonely American sits at a pavement café, adjusts the exposure on his camera and has himself photographed by an indulgent young waiter. The Yank puts on a fatuous smirk, with appropriate, quizzically rumpled brow that is considered so boyishly appealing in their film stars.

The toy soldiers at Amalienborg Castle courtyard wear long black coats with crossed white bandoliers on chest, black bearskins (bald on top), massive steel chin-straps, blue trousers with white stripe. In the hot sun of an unusual sudden heatwave their broad cheeks are burned red like the paint on real toy soldiers. Two pace to and fro along the front of the castle between the main doors on the perron and the terribly narrow-looking, pretty, dark-orange sentry boxes. They stand at ease like released marionettes. The echoing footsteps and the heel-clicks are done in perfect unison. One bored sentry looks slyly at his wrist-watch as he turns. These soldiers are impressive from a distance, and I long to possess one. But when I get closer in the hope of making an assignation, I see that they are just very ordinary chaps, country boys with rather poor carriage and badly needing some lessons in deportment. What on earth would happen if someone actually attacked the castle?

In this intense spring heat the massive statue of Friderico Quinto gives off ominous clicks as it expands under the direct rays of the sun.

At a concert, an enthusiastic pianist with grubby-looking hands, imported from Norway, went rummaging through the Grieg piano concerto.

Now the snow has all gone, children play games in the street, a kind of hopscotch, with a design of circles inside squares done with a fresh stick of chalk on the smooth pavement: they hop from square to square on one foot with the aid of a broomstick. The pattern is marked 'Sv. Nor. Dan. Kina. (China)' – Sweden, Norway, Denmark, China. Some small children pester me to buy a little blue flower. Is it a charity? I never give pennies to beggars unless they have fine eyes. These Danish children are enchanting, so I give them more than they ask.

Dialogue overheard on the square, beside the underground toilets: 'Do you like Anita Ekberg?' 'No.' 'Why not?' 'Her feet are too big.'

Back in Sweden, a few days at Västervik: how Swedes *stare* at one another – coldly, without dropping eyes, both men and women. Working-class men in particular look at each other with obsessive interest – 'getting him weighed up' – and the one being weighed up thus is well aware of it, does not flinch. Men look at each other with unconcealed interest, with admiration or humour or respect or puzzled curiosity, just as women do: perhaps a relic of clan feeling, or wondering what part of Sweden, what part of Scandinavia a person comes from, just as North of England miners and seamen alone in pubs will steadily watch one another before speaking. In this thinly populated country the clan feeling must be even stronger.

The police appear to be unpopular, failed army officer types. Yet they were always kind to me. I even used one as a porter at a railway station. They wear swords, long coats, and give grave, considered salutes when one asks for information. I watched the tactful way they dealt with fighting drunks in the station at Malmö. Getting a bottle of booze in Sweden is quite a procedure, for it is sold only through State monopoly shops. Local committees can put chronic alcoholics on a black list that prevents them from obtaining liquor at these stores. Farmers used to run their own stills. Intoxication is an offence against the State, and there are many offenders, but there is a powerful temperance movement, though rationing of alcohol, in force since the First World War, was abolished in 1955. Perhaps if there were not so many restrictions on the sale of alcohol it would not be so mightily abused. It was only in 1956 that Stockholm got its first night-club where drinks could be obtained. But in 1967 the rigid grip of State monopoly was loosened and drinking in Sweden was liberated from repressive laws. On the whole the effect of this liberalization has been good, but temperance attitudes still persist.

The icy atmosphere in the staff-room at Malmö became so intolerable I just decided one day to leave for home without telling anyone. I got on the first ferry to Copenhagen and had a good breakfast, then a celebratory drink. My last view of Sweden was the steaming factory chimneys of Malmö, and the sight of a cargo of new cars sailing towards the port, which excited all the car-mad Swedes, who even ran from the dining saloon and the bar to gather at the side of the ferry and gloat over all the new Volkswagens. I met a young Swedish queer on board with a round, rosy face like a well-preserved granny under a would-be stylish brown beret. He did not attract me, but gave me some hints about 'gay' life in Copenhagen, to which he escaped regularly from the 'morgue' (as he termed it) of Malmö.

Before leaving Malmö I had sent a telegram to Ilona, reminding her of our promise to meet again at the same place in Hamburg. Would she be there? If so, she might change my whole existence.

After eating in the large dining-room of the ferry, people uninhibitedly pick their teeth with their fingernails, thinking no one is watching them, or, that if they are being watched, it is only by unobservant Swedes. They all have flushed faces: one man sitting opposite me had an immense flushed expanse between bristling blond eyebrows and stiff blond eyelashes in sore-looking lids. The Swedes are stocking up with duty-free chocolate, cigarettes, cigars, liquor, their open faces so eagerly covetous. If one Swede sees another buy something he hasn't got, he at once buys it himself – keeping up with the Carlsens. Well, we are all basically selfish, but the Swedes seem more so. I had become disillusioned with Sweden and I needed to distance myself from Swedes. The selfishness, inconsiderateness and thoughtlessness of Swedes strikes me more forcibly than in any other land, and is especially noticeable in their greedy, grasping behaviour on the ferries to Copenhagen. I had often heard sad complaints from Swedes about shockingly bad Swedish road manners. These faults appeared to be caused by a simple inability to understand that other people have rights too – for example, the right to a quiet night in an hotel. There is often a kind of denseness in the Swedish temper, and often an unintentional flair for doing or saying the wrong thing, without apology.

I write these words in full realization that Swedes love making fun of one another, but if foreigners do so, they leap to each other's defence. There are many good and kind people, and excellent teachers, in Sweden. But there are also unpleasant ones like those embittered spinster teachers in Malmö, thin, beaky nosed, unrelaxed, in hand-printed stuffs of a dismal cut. Waitresses are often brusque: they *never* have change for a ten-kronor note. The lovely Sami crafts and Christmas decorations are exceptionally original and pretty. But some Swedish arty lampshades are so *heavily* original. At Hemslöjd I shudder at the memory of all the awful trolls, gnomes, old men and women – hideous creatures made from gaping fir-cones. Swedish design is good, but often too slick. They have learnt all the lessons of primitivism, cubism, surrealism, yet it is all as empty, heartless, as Swedish girls tracking their willing males.

Practically the last Swede I spoke to was a young girl on the ferry, who seemed to be under the influence of drugs. She was very tall, wearing a shocking-pink new coat with bottle-green skirt, green wool ribbed stockings up to her bare pale knees, a white knitted scarf and a *diamanté* hair-slide. She had thick black eyebrows in her dead-pan mask of a face, on which the plastered make-up failed to conceal chronic impetigo. She had pale, cracked-looking lips and lifeless blonde hair, which must have been bleached. Her feet in purple court shoes looked enormous, as did her work-reddened hands in yellow net gloves, which she did not remove when eating and drinking and smoking her non-stop cigarettes. It was the feet that gave her away. She was a male, all dressed up for business with the Danes or the American forces on leave from Germany. But there was no Ilona in Hamburg. . . .

* * *

When I got back to Corsham I found that the success of *The Only Child* had somewhat raised the status of my parents, for whom status in such a place meant less than nothing. I immediately began making arrangements to move to Bath. As soon as we settled in Avondale Buildings – how that name evokes the dread Jane Austen! – I intended to take off for Spain and Jordi.

Agostin de Irizar, my former Portuguese colleague in Leeds, had kindly arranged for me to take the post of Professor of English Language and Literature at the ancient university of Salamanca, within fairly easy reach of Valladolid and Jordi. After a couple of months in Bath, exploring all the associations with one of my literary heroes, William Beckford, I was ready to move on again, to the sad bewilderment of my unfortunate parents. I could hardly understand it myself. How was it possible for me to love them so much yet find their company unbearable? We no longer had much in common, and I was beginning to feel I was less than human, a creature from outer space on a temporary mission to Planet Earth.

I was suffering, as I always shall, from what Nabokov in *Mary* calls the exile's occupational disease: 'nostalgia in reverse, the longing for yet another strange land'. Spain was not exactly a strange land to me now, but it was still to prove strange enough, as I was soon to find out.

For his summer number of *The Listener* for 23 May 1957, Joe, taking pity on my distraught state when I returned from Sweden, commissioned me to write a poem:

In Copenhagen

The level snow, that makes this city one
Of undiscovered surfaces, has gone,
And now the lime-green towers,
Domes and pinnacles and twisted spires
Exclaim upon a black blue sky whose tragic flags are furled,
Giving a pause of summer in this winter of the world.

The northern palace yards are large
With sun. Each figured rooftop casts a wedge
Of dark on which the formal statues stand
In radiant abstraction: one extended hand
Receives a dove that feathers the living word.
The other hangs in shadow, lifeless on a naked sword.

For a moment now, behold
The sun, the merchants' only lasting gold,

That batters the havens and the lakes,
Drenches each tree with green, and shakes
The distant Sound with shoals of dancing bees
That from the heavens' royal hive drop on the ambered seas.

The flowered city trembles with their weightless tread
That lays a crown of golden dust upon each mortal head
And tumbles the dazzled gardens of the deep
Where heroes and their monsters wake from sleep.
– O, soon, in every street throughout the sickened earth
May life's undying love once more bring hope to birth,
The sun's broad flags of red and white blow free
To welcome peace, the summer's longed-for majesty!

In this poem I tried to sum up my feelings about the Cold War, the refugees, the fear-sickened world waiting for the end. Joe did not accept another poem I had written nearly a year before at the Hotel Brabant in Amsterdam, on my way to Sweden, after visiting the Guernica Exhibition at the Municipal Museum:

You with the level brows,
Their dark circlet makes your gaze
As calm as a warrior's beneath a vizor.
And if I look into
Their wide remotenesses, you
Look back at me as would a conquerer.

Your eyes bestride me
Like a colossus, and reprove,
In this hated time, the free
Confusions of a wish to love.
They that are set like a mouth
Firmly, without question or response
In the visage of your warring youth
Open, speak not, for they are closed to utterance.

'Guernica' provided me with this prophetic poem about my life to come in Spain. From my Letts Diary for 1957 I find that I left Malmö – it was a girls' school, the *HAL för flickor i Malmö* – after only one week of that discouraging atmosphere, on 30 May ('Ramadan ends'). My entry for that day says: 'Left Malmö for *good*.' Yes, it was for my own good indeed: if I had stayed there much longer, I should have sunk into a real Swedish gloom and despondency. Apparently I had been home for

Christmas and New Year after all, because on 12 January I note: 'Boat train St. Pancras 3.30. Sailing Tilbury 5.30.' On the '1st Sunday after Epiphany' I note that I was 'at sea'. I arrived in Göteborg at 6 a.m. and was back in Stockholm by 3 p.m. to start teaching next day at the Högre realläroverket a Normalm and at the vocational academy, the Handelswerkskolan. Then on to Västervik, a name which suggested 'vastation', Vimmerby, Eksjö, Stockholm again, Eksjö – Jönköping, Ulricehamm – Mariestad, where I note *The Only Child* publication date was 18 March, 'Bank Holiday in Eire and Northern Ireland'. So my joyous sexual celebration of the good reviews must have been on an intercalated weekend in Stockholm, Sunday 24 March, '3rd in Lent'. But how very un-Lenten my behaviour had been!

Further perambulations took me to Lidköping, where I was taken to see Beowulf's grave at Skalunda, then on to Örebro and Uppsala again (*Försvarets laroverket*) until Maundy Thursday when I began a week's Easter holiday until my birthday on Tuesday the 23rd (St George).

It must have been at one of these stops that I had an unforgettable experience. I was sitting in some dull coffee-shop, trying to screw up my courage for the next class, when they played a record of Ella Fitzgerald singing Gershwin's 'Someone to Watch Over Me'. There was something in her spellbinding interpretation of the lyric's mediocre but deeply moving words that made my heart turn over and brought tears to my eyes. Indeed, I felt as if I were about to collapse with emotion, with overpowering surges of gratitude towards Ella for the release she brought me from all my petty affairs and inane sexual preoccupations. For a few minutes she seemed to make everything seem right with the world. It was a profoundly spiritual experience, almost religious in its intensity. But it was also a kind of literary or rather poetic revelation. In the way Ella handled those banal lines, singing sometimes on, sometimes off the beat, delaying this phrase, stressing ever so lightly that particular word, I suddenly realized how I should read my poetry in public (and perhaps in part how to write it). She seemed to lie back in a hammock of music and words, impressing it with her own considerable shape, swinging it now gently, now wildly, but always in control of her feelings, so that the emotional reactions of the listener supplied all she did not openly express but that lay deep behind everything she did.

I went to my next class that day in a state of mild ecstasy, and at once tried out my newly discovered technique on my startled pupils – eighteen-year-olds – by reading them my poem 'Perpetuum Mobile: The Broken Record' (from *A Spring Journey*). When reading poetry aloud I have always tended to be too precise, or on the contrary to be overwhelmed by emotion, to the point of breaking into tears or letting my voice quiver when it should not have done so. At times I can still hardly speak certain lines for the surge of feeling my work and the work of others arouse in me when I perform in public: but at least Ella has shown me how to overcome this defect, and it needs art to manage it. One should possess the poem entirely, but the poem should possess one too: both must be equally balanced.

Always I had loved Ella Fitzgerald's singing and her rich personality, but this was the first time I had been so penetrated by the sheer beauty and brilliance of her professionalism in performance. I later wrote an ode to her, based with the utmost reverence on the Lord's Prayer, and I was astonished that it should upset so many people. (It is in the group called 'Three Singers' – the other two are Nina Simone and Anita O'Day – in *The Body Servant*.)

My almost religious respect for her shines through that ode.

* * *

While I was back in Uppsala Ella Fitzgerald came on a tour of Sweden with the Oscar Peterson Trio, and I cut appointments and classes in order to hear her. (Michel Foucault, who adored her, was at one of her concerts, with a new boy-friend.) At the first concert she came with a woman friend into the café attached to the hotel where I was staying, making a discreet entrance on a wave of strong perfume, and sat nervously toying with a drink, trying to overcome tension and nerves. But when she got up on the temporary platform to sing her set, the stout Swedish boards cracked and she nearly fell right through before she was rescued, laughing uproariously, to give one of her very best performances. I have never forgotten the sight of that massive, billowy figure in the bright-red dress, waving the customary limp hanky, slowly sinking through the platform.

I learnt a lot about how to read poetry from several other jazz singers, most notably Anita O'Day, with whom I was to fall for ever in love in Sendai after seeing the film *Jazz on a Summer's Day*, and whom I actually met and got to know quite well in New York after her come-back at the Half Note. (She mentions it in her autobiography, *High Times, Low Times*.) I also learnt the dynamics of poetic rhythm from Mel Torme, Blossom Dearie, Nina Simone, Frank Sinatra and Dinah Washington. Extraordinary Jessye Norman, in 'With a Song in My Heart' accompanied by the Boston Pops, transforms ordinary words with spellbinding artistry and always makes my tears of joy and sorrow flow with 'My Love Is Here to Stay', 'All the Things You Are' and 'Love

Walked Right In'. As Ella did that unforgettable morning in an obscure Swedish provincial café, singing her heart out – and mine – in 'Someone to Watch over Me'. If I am grateful to Sweden for nothing else, it is for that revelation.

BACKFLASH – INTERLUDE
'Someone to Watch Over Me'

Two years a visitor at East Capital;
I detest as in the past the crafty, the unscrupulous

I, a man with a hermit's heart, scent the evil odour of wrong-doers;
I eat coarse greens for food and am often not satisfied. . . .
Tu Fu in exile

My traveller's heart is neither settled nor decided;
Many things fill it with vague unrest;
– Am on the point of doing what?
Li T'ai-po

Still, solitary, in quiet room where I write,
Since early dawn I have thought only of you.
Tu Fu to Li T'ai-po

I longed to find that someone. And there were one or two people. . . .
A postcard postscript from Joe Ackerley, dated 9 December 1954, from
17 Star and Garter Mansions and sent to me at Riette Sturge-Moore's
flat at 139 Adelaide Road, NW3. (Joe had taught me always to date my
letters, as he did, telling me of his frustration on trying to organize his
own friends' letters when he discovered that they were often not dated:
'Always keep the envelopes, Jim darling, for the where and when of
undated – and often addressless – billets doux.') So here is his card:

> My dear Jim,
>   You do sometimes write poems that positively bounce me out of
> my chair and look round for a laurel wreath of sorts – this poor card –
> to set upon your brow. Your two new poems have upon me that
> effect. The sink in particular is a masterpiece. Both are irresistibly
> good. When you strike the mark, no one strikes it to such effect, and
> you strike it more often than any other poet living. Phone me – Put.
> 1656 – and come down on Sat. eve. if you can. My women are out,
> but I may not be alone.
>
> Love, Joe

What literary editor today would ever write such a generous letter?
Joe's 'women' were of course his dear old actress Aunt Bunnie, who
had been in Frank Benson's company, and his divinely beautiful but
slightly catatonic sister, blonde Nancy, my particular passion. (Today,
Amanda Lear reminds me of her goofy beauty.) She was one of those
slightly mad girls and women who often seemed inexplicably to be
attracted to my own helpless confusions and character splits. When I
phoned Joe to say I would be there on Sat. eve. he told me he would not
indeed be alone, for Morgan Forster and his policeman friend were
coming, with the latter's adolescent son.

The poems referred to by Joe – true depictions of two aspects of my
daily life at Adelaide Road – were 'The Kitchen Sink' and 'The Drain'.
They were to appear, together with 'The Convenience', in *The Descent
into the Cave*, along with a group of poems on related themes: 'The
Drain', with deep sexual undertones – and transparent overtones too –
that Joe had to fight the Mrs Grundys at Auntie BBC to get into print. It
was about an actual event, the digging up of the garden at the back of
the Adelaide Road flat to repair a drain that was always getting blocked,
so they had to come again and again, and I had many opportunities to
observe the workmen from the kitchen window as I piled my rubbish in
that chaotic sink. The poem opens:

> Those three young workmen have had it up again –
> The drain that is the secret of my garden . . .

It goes on to describe 'their well-oiled tools' and how 'with long rods
they raked it clean/ And shot a hose of water into it . . .' and ends with a
glimpse of myself:

> While at the window stood and looked
> A glassy ghost, not breathing on the pane,
> That longed to speak, to tell them
> What perhaps they knew:
> It was my love they buried, that could have no name.

That collection contains many 'Joems' as we called them – 'The Old
Trousers' and 'Statues in the Rain', a tribute to Ken Armitage and other
sculptors at Corsham. But Joe would not have anything to do with 'The
Ashtray', a poem I wrote when I was trying to stop my very moderate
smoking habit – Joe was a very heavy smoker:

> Here are my droppings for the day:

These weightless rolls of ash, these grey
Clinkers that are the wastes of fire;
These stunted butts, the drags of sick desire. . . .

It was not that Joe did not like the poem: he did. But he was similar to many editors who, even when they like poems or short stories, do not want to publish them, and can usually give no explanation for their rejection. Joe told me: 'It's a little near the bone, dear', which seems to indicate he had guilty feelings about his heavy indulgence. He went on: 'One should always have at least one visible vice that is acceptable to the Miss Redmans in this age of conformity', and then gave his shoulder-shuddering giggle: dear old Joe could never resist the enjoyment of laughing at his own wit, which was always worth laughing at, so why should he not have relished it to the full himself? He could tell his jokes with a stern poker face simply in order to break the mask's solemnity with all the greater enthusiasm, and one could not help joining in the fun. I am not a hearty laugher, but I remember many occasions when I threw back my head in an unusually full-throated bark of joy when Joe described his unorthodox editorial approach and punctured self-satisfied windbags in authority.

For the same indefinable reasons Joe disappointed me by refusing to print another poem I still value highly, 'Ghosts, Fire, Water', about the Hiroshima panels by Iri Maruki and Toshiko Akamatsu, which had been exhibited for the first time in London. 'It's too much for *The Listener* to take, dear boy, but it's absolutely wonderful. Try Janet Adam Smith.' But the editor of *The New Statesman and Nation* turned it down also, and in fact every editor, including John Betjeman at *Time and Tide*, who had printed several of my poems, felt unable to accept it. C.V. Wedgwood said it was 'too disturbing for words', and that reaction seems to me a partial explanation of the amateurishness of modern British poetry – a fear of upsetting people. Joe was not exempt from that kind of fear himself, so it was all the more remarkable that he insisted, against strong BBC objections, on publishing those of my poems that enraged readers wrote in about condemning them as 'filth' and 'the products of a sick mind' and 'garbage'.

It was perhaps a tribute of kinds when people became enraged by my poems. Joe and I would chuckle over these irate busybodies, especially when one of them, a well-known authoress, called 'The Dustbins' 'a grave insult to the hard-working British housewife'. Joe commented: 'What about the hard-working British dustmen, darling?' Some years later R.A. Butler in *The Listener* was calling upon British poets to write about dustbins: he had obviously been unaware that the subject had

been treated, once and for all, by a fellow-contributor. Or perhaps he
had indeed read my poem and shoved it into the background of his
consciousness, as so many people had done, until it resurfaced irresistibly from the memory palace.

Joe had at first only half liked 'The Dustbins', which is one of the
poems he refers to in a letter dated 17 July 1953:

> Dear Jim,
>
> But did I not send you a note quite lately with your two poems
> which I ½-liked but did not really love any more than I love this? ['A
> Visit to Brontëland'] I am trying to give up smoking, so live in a
> constant fidget of remembering only one thing and forgetting all else.
>
> There is a man in television, whose name I never can remember
> [Royston Morley], who asked me particularly to tell you that that
> medium is anxiously awaiting your assistance. Truly! 'I do wish he
> wd. send me something,' said this nameless man.
>
> I hope you have gotten over your sordid adventure.
>
> > Love
> > J.

What my 'sordid adventure' had been I cannot now remember, but
suppose it was the usual near run-in with the plain-clothes police at
Marble Arch, or at the Hampstead Ponds, a favourite haunt of mine at
the time, where one was allowed to sunbathe naked in the all-male
enclosure, a happy hunting ground for 'rough trade' – and for copper's
narks. I never entered the rather scummy water of the ponds but would
lie in the shade as much as possible getting an indirect, subtle tan and
watching the young body-building types and amateur boxers and the
wide boys flexing their lats and waiting for a score.

On 4 January 1956, Joe wrote to me near the end of my New Year
vacation in Corsham with my parents:

> Dear Jim,
>
> If you are sticking to the dates you gave in your letter for your visit
> here [to London] I'm afraid it looks as though I shan't be seeing you.
> I'm terribly sorry, for I am agog to hear about your adventures.
> Indeed I intended to ask myself down to Corsham just for the day,
> tomorrow or Sunday, but now I have to go to Chester instead to see
> that ½-sister of mine who is so ill. It's a long train journey and I don't
> expect I shall be back in London until early Monday afternoon. By
> then will you be in the air? If not and there shd. be any chance of a
> glimpse of you, leave a message for me at my office.

I hope you are well dear – but I feel sure you are that; more to the point I hope you found your Mother and Father improved in health and spent with them a happy Xmas. How delighted they must have been with such a Xmas present as a visit from you. Nothing nicer than that ever came out of Santa Claus' sack.

Much love, dear Jim and to you all.

Joe

Yes, I had returned home for the season's festivities, bearing with me presents from Sweden and some arty-crafty but very pretty Christmas tree decorations. I remember I also brought a kind of metal roundabout of angels that spun gaily round above the thermal heat of some lighted candles. My poor parents were sick of Corsham; that was their complaint, and it could be cured only by removal to Bath in May. I was in two minds about returning to Sweden to complete my contract, so torn was I between my parents' needs and my own declining interest in that kind of teaching, which I had begun to find a great strain. I certainly intended to take care of my mother and father in their old age, and always did the best I could for their comfort in a material sense, though I could not give them what they most wanted, peace of mind. I could not find it for myself, and so I longed desperately for 'someone to watch over me'. There was no god who could do anything for me. But Joe was a fair substitute, and from many of his letters I could see that he was a god to Nancy, Aunt Bunny and many other people. Here is one of his letters written apparently during the Christmas holidays in 1950. (By the way, none of these letters appear in Neville Braybrooke's selection. I withheld them in the hope that I might one day be able to use them myself.) So here goes:

Putney

Thank you, dear Jim, for your card and its very beautiful poem, a very sure success, every word perfect and dropping perfectly into place. Is it on the market? And do, please, thank your parents for their card too: Nancy and I were most pleased and touched to hear from them. We have missed you in London: but the reason is all too easily understood. I have been lecturing Nancy on expenditure, and telling her that such items as frozen peas, mushrooms, lettuces etc. which appear at almost every meal are now taboo. Not to mention clothes.

We pass a quiet day, until the late afternoon when we walk Queenie over to the Buckinghams in Shep. Bush to spend the evening with Morgan, the Bucks., and two Americans, husband and wife, whom I like very much. If you had been about I shd. have commanded your presence. We have a turkey here too, of which you wd. have partaken – a last-minute turkey, marked up to 65/-, but reduced to 35/- because the butcher has a crush on Nancy. So my females have their uses, tho' I confess to being rather bored with them and the middleclass overcrowded squalor in which they oblige me to live. Bunny has been parked out for the holiday with a friend of hers in Sheen; if you had only asked me, I wd. have parked myself out too.

Well, I have seen some friends anyway: William [Plomer], Rose Macaulay, Henry Reed, Morgan, Black Myles and some odds and bobs. This morning I visited Morgan's Aunt Rosalie, and sat with the old dear for an hour, Penny the cat having been shuffled into the kitchen out of Queenie's way. Queenie seems well, and ought to be 'in season' but is not. Gentleman dogs begin to be interested, but the moment continues to be delayed. I thought of mating her again, but wonder if I can face it: I have 3 or 4 suitors to choose from, but *that* is not the difficulty. In a more civilized world there wd. be lying-in houses for bitches and after-care organisations for the children; but as we know all too well this is not a civilised world.

Well, God bless, dear Jim. A happy and prosperous 1951 to you all, death to Gen. MacArthur, Syngman Rhee, Chiang Kai Shek, Winston Churchill, Pres. Truman. . . . I leave you to extend the list – and a good-natured free-for-all for everyone else.

Joe

Joe was god to Queenie, his temperamental but beautiful Alsatian bitch, about whom he wrote so brilliantly in *My Dog Tulip*. He was such a god to her, she would not allow any other worshippers to come near him, and had frightened off most of his friends. She never frightened me, and I could well understand her possessiveness. Black Myles was a strange black man whom I met a number of times at the Star and Garter flat, and Joe himself admitted that he was not very attractive, though he was very good-natured and enjoyed a silly giggle about common friends and enemies. William Plomer was a less frequent visitor, though he and Joe had been lovers at one time, and lived together before Joe moved to Putney. I liked William very much, and his *Paper Houses* was the first book to arouse my interest in a Japan I then had no idea I should ever know.

I wrote to Joe about the death (on November 9) of the only friend I made on the English Department staff at Leeds University, a dear old poet, Wilfred Rowland Childe. He was someone who watched over me as best he could during those two dreary years. He often invited me to his lovely house in Harrogate, and introduced me to a mysterious Irish workman he sometimes met in Leeds. At an advanced age, Wilfred, who had known Firbank at Oxford, as well as several other exquisites, was still fond of his Terence from Donegal, who used to cuddle him on my sofa in Brunswick Place while I excused myself to go and buy cakes for tea. After a suitable interval, I would return to find them both beaming and holding hands, ready for a nice cup of tea. Terence would leave after a while, usually with Wilfred, who used to take him in his taxi to Leeds Station. I think Wilfred used to hand him a pound or two, as Terence was often unemployed. Wilfred also knew Herbert Read, to whom Joe refers in the following letter, written to me when I was in Wotton-under-Edge in Gloucestershire, where I had taken a room at Merlin Haven, and later found a small cottage for my parents:

Thanks for your starry letter, dear Jim. I'm glad your domestic affairs settle so satisfactorily and that your filial devotion now has its full blooming and reward. When you come to London come and have dinner with us and bring your host and hostess too [my mother and father] if they will come. I'm sorry to hear about Childe's death and am glad I took his poem. Herbert will be grieved; I remember that he claimed him as an old friend. I am very well and am hoping to go abroad, to Paris or Rome, for Xmas. Love J

The poem by Childe that Joe refers to was one I selected from Wilfred's latest work, written not long before he died. I could see that my friend was failing, so I loved Joe for printing it and giving enormous pleasure to Wilfred, whose work was completely ignored.

Unlike Corsham, Wotton-under-Edge was a civilized and enlightened village, set in the beautiful environment of the Cotswolds, and the wooded 'Edge' that gives the place its name. I used to drink at the marvellous old pub, The Ram, and the locals one night got me so legless on the local 'rough' cider that I had to crawl back to Merlin Haven on my hands and knees. The fruit and vegetable shop in the main street was run by a highly cultivated bachelor, Horace Mann, who took me in his car to concerts in Gloucester, and to a theatrical performance of great merit – Shakespeare, I think – by the members of the boys' club he ran there. He died a few years ago, leaving me with a very happy memory of a sensitive artist and a gentleman of learning and culture who had managed to do what I could never do: combine ordinary life and the pursuit of art.

I had taken refuge at Merlin Haven (an auspicious name, I thought) in order to set my jumbled life once more in order after the sorrows and miseries of Leeds. (I wrote to David Paul telling him I had gone there 'to forget'.) It was a delightful house, belonging to a lady named Macartney, sister of the historian. Dr Joan Evans, another historian, lived just up the lane. I had asked Joe if he knew anything about her, and at the same time sent him a copy of my new book, *A Correct Compassion*:

Dear Jim
I am most pleased with your present. Thank you *very* much. Although I only got it this morning and so have not had time to do more than peep into it, it looks much robuster and more exciting than your last volume [*The Creation*]. I *am* pleased it is out, and will get it done if I can for my Autumn Number – perhaps with Francis King's new book – tho' god knows by whom.

Yes, do of course give my name as reference if it is likely to do you any good. What fun if you got the job! I am wondering at the moment whether to go to Paris or Rome for a fortnight in early October.

I know O about Joan Evans, except that she has a large number of friends all of whom politely decline to review her books.

5/9/52   Love, J

My 1952 diary tells me the publication date of *A Correct Compassion* was 2 October. I no longer remember the post I was applying for – I was applying all over the place in those days. Often loss of nerve prevented me from keeping interview appointments. It could not have been my next job, at Bath Academy of Art, for which Cecil Day Lewis recommended me, because the Principal, Clifford Ellis, did not ask me for any references after such an OK recommendation. But I suspect the job may have been a lectureship I applied for at an Oxford women's college, St Anne's I think. I was invited to an interview, but when I got there and was sitting waiting my turn in an outer office I got cold feet and ran as fast as I could out of the building and to Oxford Station, thus giving rise to the local legend of 'the vanishing poet' and 'the Kirkup Phenomenon'. I was to run away from interviews and from jobs on so many occasions when I felt the vibrations were wrong, or when people were unkind to me, that by the time I reached Japan my proclivity had become well enough known to be dubbed 'doing a Kirkup'. I remember running out of a BBC interview when I discovered that one of the interviewers was John Weightman, a fellow-student at Newcastle, and 'always my torture' as Firbank used to say of Aldous Huxley. I was supposed to go to another room and write an essay in French, but this so reminded me of the horrors of Girdlestone and the Finals that I made off when no one was looking, and never returned to the BBC for an interview.

I remember that when I was asked by one of the BBC interviewers what kind of literary programmes I would organize, I mentioned my passion for Ronald Firbank, something that was greeted with unbelief and quiet scorn. I also tried to defend my interest in the work of Elizabeth Taylor and Barbara Pym, to no effect. But when I offered the psychological novels of Simenon, there was open hilarity, and I realized that, as so often happened, I had been invited to the interview to provide entertainment for bored officials: again I felt like the hunted bull in the bullring. I found Simenon fascinating. In some books I felt he was writing about my own childhood and youth. I had just read his latest thriller, *La cage de verre*, about one of those strangely numb, anonymous men who are often the anti-heroes of Simenon's work. I found sentences that described me exactly: 'He was never bored. . . . According to his mother, when he was a baby, he could sit quietly for hours contemplating some point in space. He never cried, and never smiled.' At school, his classmates mock Emile, who did not like sports and was not interested in people. In the school choir he pretended to sing, just moving his lips, as I had done. He lived all his life with a sense of exclusion from normal human life. Yes, such characters from Simenon were me all over. . . .

That sense of exclusion was something I knew I had consciously brought upon myself. It was a deliberate distancing of myself from other people. I could not bear too much humanity. Sometimes I would pretend to be deaf and dumb in order to avoid the attentions of unwelcome strangers and to protect myself from pointless conversation. One of the reasons why I never learnt to speak Japanese well was that Japanese conversation bored me to distraction, and I resented being bored in that way because I was never bored by my own company, and so wanted to continue those endless conversations with my other selves that were so much more interesting than Japanese social clichés and formula phrases. So I can read many languages, but will always speak them badly.

I think Joe felt the same way, though he put up with other people much better than I could. But his devotion to a neurotic Alsatian bitch seemed to me an indication of his growing disenchantment with his fellow-men. In later years, when I started studying Portuguese and Brazilian literature, I became especially interested in the work of Clarice Lispector, about whom Hélène Cixous has written a perceptive study: *L'Heure de Clarice Lispector* (1989). In certain ways this amazing Brazilian novelist, who said 'When I'm not writing, I'm dead', resembled Joe. She had a son who went mad, and was often overwhelmed by a feeling of utter helplessness in the face of his insanity, like Joe in his relationship with his sister Nancy. Clarice lived with a neurotic dog called Ulysses, a dog as horribly nerve-racked as Queenie, and, like her, always demanding total attention, jealous of all intruders coming between them. In the masquerades of sexuality, there is no ritual that allows men to embrace alterity, but many rites of exclusion for those who are 'different'. In her autobiography Laura Betti, the great Italian actress, uses the expression *teta veleta* which she took from her idol Pasolini, and which means something like 'sexual or amorous confusion' to describe her own feelings of exclusion from conventional society. My refusal to settle anywhere was one of my defences against 'inclusion'. Liszt in his letters writes that the artist has to pitch a tent only for an hour, then move on. I, too, was always 'camping out'. But Czelaw Milosz wrote: 'You who wronged a simple man, do not feel safe. The poet remembers.' It is his fate to remember every humiliation.

Joe's remarks about the distinguished Dr Joan Evans the archaeologist remind me of so many other funny letters he wrote to me about literary and academic figures. I have not followed Joe's advice and kept all his envelopes to check date and place of posting, and unfortunately not all his letters carry the date. But there is one very entertaining one dated 5 May 1950 that he wrote to me as I was moving into a cottage at Slapton near Nottingham. Things had become so hectic and so dangerous for me in London, despite the protective wiles of Madame Sheba, that I was again on the run from whatever phantoms or realities I felt were pursuing me with gestures of impending doom. The cottage was charming but very primitive, with an outdoor toilet: one had to bury one's faeces in the garden, which certainly made for a rich soil, because I could never be bothered to garden, a hateful activity for me; so it became very soon a jungle of enormous weeds, and the young folk of the village, with whom I got friendly, used to come and serenade me at night, singing that music-hall song 'It's only a garden of weeds. . . .' Sir Sacheverell Sitwell lived in nearby Towcester, and he had somehow got wind of my arrival in Slapton, for one day soon after I got settled in he came striding up the garden path, a tall and slightly sinister figure in country gentleman's tweeds, a rather haughty grin on his aristocratic face. I had quite enjoyed some of his curious books on odd subjects so I was pleased to meet him, but he waffled on so much about 'my sister, Dr Edith' that I was thankful when he left before I had the chance to disgrace myself by offering him tea in my cracked cups. But he kindly invited me to visit him at Towcester, an invitation I never took up. I was later to find one of his books quite useful when I visited Angkor Wat and other temple complexes in Cambodia. But anyone associated with Dame Edith was anathema to me, for she had once written an incensed letter to poor Joe complaining that I had plagiarized one of her poems, a letter we did not even bother to answer, the charge was so ridiculous. I remember being convulsed with almost uncontrollable giggles when I went with Joe to attend one of her poetry readings at the Lyric Theatre, Hammersmith. She made a very stagy entrance from the left, dressed in a towering brocade turban and an incredible assortment of pseudo-medieval garments with a long train – so long that it was still trailing in the wings when she reached the centre of the stage, and an assistant had to come and swathe it about her feet as photographers do to the bridal train at society weddings. Her long, taloned fingers, skeleton thin, were laden with a weight of what looked like second-hand papal rings, and she used a jewelled lorgnette to read her poems in a very deep, moaning voice – and very slowly too. The person who had come to introduce her was none other than the 'churchy verse play' actor Robert Speight, who had played in *Murder in the Cathedral* and was later to take the role of the Chronicler in my own play, *Upon this Rock* (both plays costumed by Stella Mary Pearce), for years after the talk of Peterborough, whose cathedral had played the main part with such authenticity and architectural distinction, not to mention genuine religious feeling. I liked Robert both as an actor and as a writer of rather dull books on French literature and other dismal subjects, done with exemplary seriousness. I liked him even better after this disastrous poetry reading, because when he got on the stage he found that he had left the poems he was to recite at home. Some unkind person in the audience applauded – it was *not* Joe. Whereupon Robert announced that he would render the only poem he had by heart – 'my party piece,' he joked: Hilaire Belloc's 'Tarantella'. In the circumstances he made a very exciting job of it, though it is not a very difficult thing to do with that poem. A few years later, at Peterborough, he missed his train from London for the evening performance and someone had to take over his part, which fortunately consisted only of readings from the pulpit. Robert arrived half-way through by a later train, in a state of determined calm, and I admired the way he controlled his perturbations as he solemnly mounted the pulpit for the next scene. He was a real professional.

But here are the letters Joe wrote to me at Slapton, where he visited me with Queenie once or twice:

Putney

Dear Jim

So sorry to be so late in writing you. How good of you not to complain. But I've thought of you much, and specially on that Tues. and Wed. when the snow fell, your days for taking possession of your new dwelling. And it so primitive, without being set in a wintry scene. It did seem hard.

I have been rather occupied since we met, but no, not with work, which falls on me no heavier in spite of my sister's absence; with friendship and also relationship. Spare time has been much used in looking for a room for Queenie and me, in vain, and now it matters no longer, for Aunt Bunny has acquired a new and pleasant room with another old lady across the road at Kenilworth Court. She moves in on Monday. In order to get it both she and Nancy behaved in the way that women do when they particularly want something: that is to say that when they saw the advert and visited the old lady and found that she had already had someone else after the room, a young man, and had promised to keep it open for him for 48 hours, they tried to bribe her to break her word, which she refused to do, and then visited and practically obliged the poor young man, who lives close by, to renounce his claim in Bunny's favour. Although he meant to take the room, which I believe is v. comfortable, they left him no chivalrous choice but to give it up to them and take instead a drab and uncomfortable alternative in one of the least alluring roads in Putney. Shall I send him down to you so that you can give him that love and comfort which, I know, you believe the human race stands in such great need of and is morally rehabilitated by? Anyway, my women are cockahoop.

Then Morgan [E.M. Forster] has broken down again. I spent the weekend in Aldeburgh, last weekend, and brought him up on Monday. He is to go back to his nursing home tomorrow, to have a cystostomy (if you have a dictionary) and perhaps electrical treatment on Wednesday. A second opinion has been called in: Kenneth Walker. Then Georges [Duthuit, Editor of the Paris magazine *Transition*] has again arrived – on Monday, and I have been running about with him. He has an affectionate memory of yourself. Who, indeed, has not. I was supposed to be going to Herbert Read's this weekend, but postponed it. I felt I really couldn't, without the dire thought of preparation such an undertaking required, put Queenie in a train for 4 hours with no means of leaving it – except by pulling the communication cord – for the York trains appear to stop nowhere on the way. Also, I did not feel sure of being pleased when I got there: Herbert wd. write all the time, I thought – 'Scribble, scribble, scribble, Mr Gibbon' – and I shd. be left with Ludo and the children, whom Q. wd. perhaps bite. Though considering the calamities which seem to befall the family in the ordinary course of their lives – Sophie has just been kicked in the face by a horse, for example – I did not suppose that a few nips from Queenie wd. be regarded as anything out of the way. However, I am getting old and firesideish, I daresay. Next weekend, however, I am committed to Nottingham.

So much for me. Your second letter sounds v. gay and jolly. I must come and join you in your junkettings, if you aren't expelled from the village before I can manage it. What about May 20 for a couple of nights? – or will you then be en famille or experimentally engaged with those young horses that seemed in London rather dark?

What a *bore* to have Sacheverell for a neighbour! That is really the unkindest cut of all. And only shows how right I am to determine, as I always have, that before settling myself anywhere in the country in my old age, to find out what neighbours I shall have first. To find oneself locked up in a village with such monsters as Harcourt Smith, Roy Campbell, Dorothy Sayers, Sir Alfred Munnings, Nancy Price and a hundred other such reptiles I cd. mention. . . . One can't be too careful.

Yes, I will send you some books next week (for review). I have just put in your hoary Daudet. Are your cheques to go to Chapel Lane, Slapton? I am reading Groddeck.

Love from
Joe

5/5/50

The 'Daudet' was a rather long review I did on a book about Daudet and the *Félibrige*, in which I mentioned Professor Girdlestone's innocuous book on Mistral, which had appeared some years before but was not mentioned in the bibliography. I was hoping that this mention of his name might at last put Girdle Scone in touch with me again; but, just as in the case of my despairing appeals to him for a reference, there was no response. Reviews, especially if they were lengthy, were often held in proof for a long time, until there was suitable room for them, which accounts for the adjective 'hoary'. Joe kept me fairly well supplied with books for review, which prompted him to remark, when he came to Japan and read one of my reviews in *The Japan Quarterly*: 'What a good reviewer you were for me, dear Jim. Always prompt, always well-written, and only occasionally – and usually excusably – catty. I could always rely on you for an interesting piece, even about the dullest academic rot.' Those were his very words to me in Sendai at a very difficult time in my life, and, coming as they did in a period of great doubt and despondency, pierced the gloom with such a brilliant ray of encouraging light, I have never forgotten them.

Another letter from this period bears no date but it was written while I was still at Slapton. I cannot remember what the 'nice sonnet' was that appeared in *The Times Literary Supplement*, but suspect it must have been 'Music at Night', dedicated to my doctor friend in South Shields, who diagnosed my chronic emphysema during the war, Granty – Dr Grant Sinclair. The sonnet appeared in 1951 in *The Submerged Village and Other Poems*, which was dedicated 'to J.R. Ackerley', with his amused consent, and a warning that it would make me very unpopular with the British literary mafia, especially the poetry cliques from Oxford and the provincial graves of academe. Here is the letter:

Dear Jim,

I owe you a letter and am sorry this is so late. O why, O why did you not give me your nice sonnet in today's T.L.S.? Glad tho I am to see it there – and you appearing in another journal besides my own and the N.S. [*The New Statesman & Nation*] – I am jealous of it, for it is a gem, indeed the most completely satisfying poem of yours I've ever read. How pleased Sassoon will be if he reads it – and how right he will be. There is no doubt that it is as pleasant a change in these days to read an 'anthology piece', as to go and look at a Goya or Velasquez portrait after a course of Picasso.

'The Narwhal' is just the kind of poem of yours I react against, undisciplined and self-indulgent; and as impenetrable as a cliff. Do, do give your talented mind to the making of more poems like the T.L.S. sonnet – and send them all to me.

A thick cold London fog envelopes us. We await the arrival of Mr Henry Reed to dinner – I with some reservationary (? is there such a word?) intellectual pleasure, my females with no pleasure of any sort, for if he has the art of pleasing women he troubles not to exercise it. But we are all well, and tho' Queenie is said to have an infected ovary, you wd. not take it v. seriously if you entered this flat – which I wish you would.

How are you, dear Jim. And when do you take up your Leeds appointment. I believe you are soon to visit Stonegrave House, the lair of that other and stouter reed, named Herbert.

Love from
Joe

This was my first glimpse of Joe's jealousy, which could be very virulent. But it was some time before I discovered how insanely jealous he was of my love for his beautiful sister, Nancy, whom he even accused of 'enticing' me away from him. I think one of the reasons he adored his very possesive bitch Queenie was that she was someone of whom he would never be jealous; and he must have admired her own all-consuming jealousy of all those who were close to Joe, expressed in continuous, neurotic, hysterical barkings that absolutely delighted Joe, though he would pretend to scold the 'silly old goose'. He behaved like an over-indulgent parent with a spoilt only child, much to the dismay of Nancy and of all his friends, who now considered a visit to Joe something of a penance and a real physical danger, so much so that a certain person insisted on going immediately to a doctor to have a rabies shot after Queenie gave him a little nip on the calf. It was quite harmless, and she was just trying to protect Joe by showing her loving jealousy. I myself received little nips from her in various parts of my anatomy, but I never held it against her, for I understood only too well what she was feeling. I think I was the only one of Joe's friends who ventured to pat, then stroke, then fondle her: following Joe's example, I even went so far as to play with her vulva, which she thoroughly enjoyed, lying back on the threadbare carpet in Joe's study and gazing up at me with those amazingly lovely eyes full of astonished bliss.

Joe's next letter is also from Putney, written as a thank-you letter after he and Queenie had spent a few days with me at my cottage in Slapton:

Dear Jim

Well, here we are again, as they say in the song. A very pleasant journey in a train that went nice and fast and did not rattle or bang and only stopped at Wolverton and Leighton Buzzard. The taxi (for your future use, as, for instance, when Dr Sitwell comes) cost 10/-, and I gave him a 1/6 tip. Q. had a piece of meat in the train and some of your specially bottled water, and did not thereafter natter and nag. We reached Euston in a jiffy, and I walked her to Great Portland St. station, where I continued her train experiences on to H'smith. Then I walked her over the Bridge to the towing path and down it to Putney. I had phoned Nancy from Gt Portland St., and she met me on the tow path and walked back with me. Then I changed and went up to the office, arriving at 1.15 in time for a canteen lunch. Stayed there till 5.45 trying to think of reviewers for abstruse books, while N. took Queenie on the Common.

Now I drink a gin in my flat, and you are sipping one perhaps in your pretty little pub, after an exhausting day cleaning up after us. You are a sweet host, dear Jim, and (which I did not know) an excellent cook, and in spite of weather and anxieties over Queenie and her behaviour and 'noives', it was lovely staying with you. I'm sorry we couldn't enter your wood. Still, the storm was a memorable event (no wonder, after reading the account of it in *The Times* and what it was doing, not so far off, near Leighton Buzzard) and I shall often think of us immured in your little room while Wagner thundered in the sky, and the cows, human and bovine, joined in from chapel and field.

Do get your beastly book done so that you can turn your mind to better things. It seems a waste of your nice cottage to be so using it. No plaque for you unless the Muse visits you there.

Let me know what sort of impression we left behind.

Love from Nancy and from me
Joe

P.S. And then I must bother you. I left Queenie's lead behind, and tho' not urgent for we have another, it is her favourite, and we shd. like to have it again.

I did not deserve Joe's compliments on my cooking, which is terrible, as I am not really very interested in food, and he was so particular about what he and Queenie ate. As a vegetarian, I shuddered at having to help him cook the great lumps of raw horse-meat he had brought for Queenie. His reference to a 'plaque' reminds me that I had what I thought was a good idea for providing indigent poets with free accommodation: the owner of the property would be entitled to increase its value by having a plaque affixed saying that so-and-so once lived and worked there. I sent a letter outlining my scheme to the Prime Minister and to the Lord Mayor of London, but they must have thought me a crank because I received no answer. I still think it is a workable scheme. But with the present attitude of the Arts Council towards literature, and the almost certain snub it would receive from Mrs Thatcher, I know it would never get off the ground. The 'beastly' book I was working on must have been one of my hack-work translations, possibly Paul Christian's *The History and Practice of Magic*, which an old friend, Ross Nichols, had commissioned me to do at 2 guineas a thousand words. It was interesting, but interminable.

From a short letter of the same period, written with a hangover:

Dearest Jim,

. . . I hope cottage life is pleasanter than it seemed when last you wrote – apart from the cold, which I hope this will find gone – and that you had drudged a whole lot more of your drudgery. I was on the booze last night – cocktail party at the Architectural Press– and feel pretty dumb today. Queenie is better, poor lamb; it is wretched frustrating her, but I daresay she wd. thank me, if she understood, for giving her an un-pregnant August.

I didn't give your poem to the Editor because it is rather long and a printers' strike has reduced the size of the paper. However, I will put it before him all the same.

Love

Joe

I was in the country of Dryden and my beloved John Clare, a poet very like me, but I was not happy in my primitive cottage, which was damp and kept giving me the most awful colds – to one of which Joe refers. I am really a big city person, like most intermediates. I feel out of place everywhere, but less so in a metropolis: in a small village I stand out like a sore thumb. So I am not surprised to find Joe, in his next letter to Slapton, referring to my decision to leave the cottage, and advising me to 'return to us':

Dear Jim

I am so sorry to hear you may be giving up your cottage. The fact that I did not regard it myself as positively ideal, is neither here nor there (less there, I hope, than here); but you were fond of it, and seemed to have established yourself in the heart of Slapton in a wonderfully short space of time, and I'm sorry that that filthy old harridan next door shd. have succeeded in disestablishing you. I do not like to think of the 'good' triumphing; I am thoroughly and unashamedly revengeful; do, if you have to leave, set fire to her before you go.

I sit on my terrace in the fading light and the river, quite motionless in the heat, lies below me like an Algernon Newton. Henry Reed spent yesterday with us. Today I lunched with Morgan. He will never heal up, I fear, but is writing me a review for my Summer Supplement. Dear Morgan. Poor Queenie is nine days gone in heat, and feels it, and has reached the stage of holding her tail to one side so that there shall be no obstacle. The weather is lovely, tho' too warm for Joe. I have read your poem over and think it is one of your successes. Thank you. I am grateful for it and for the review. So sorry to have missed you when you came to London. My phone number is Welbeck 5577, Ext 57, and I shall have to work hard all next week, so may be expected to be caught there. I really am sorry the cottage is collapsing – tho' not surprised, it wasn't good enough for you. The country contains too much hostility. Nature red in tooth and claw. London is drabber and sordid, but more civilized: perhaps you had better return to us.

Love J.

The poem Joe refers to in those last two letters must have been 'The Submerged Village'. The ear trouble he refers to in his next letter was the first sign of a decline into partial deafness:

Putney

Dear Jim

I meant to write – and oughter have wrote – and sorry I didn't. Partly my wretched laziness, and partly indisposition. My right ear has conked out, and I have been to see a specialist about it on Thursday. However as one falls down another gets up (Chinese proverb, Sung era), and you will be pleased to hear that Morgan is now pronounced quite cured. Nancy is well. Bunny is well. Queenie is also well, but is indulging in a 'ghost pregnancy', which makes her rather restless at night. She has been the cause of our losing a holiday, for I was to have taken Nancy to Dover last Mon. week for a week, and the rooms were booked by a friend of ours who lives there, and everything was in the bag, until the f . . .ing landlady, a Mrs Lamb, discovered that Queenie was an alsatian and refused to accept her. Nancy is now searching the map for another holiday, and is talking of caravans, as you once did.

Much interested to hear of all your activities. A good thing you have left Slapton, and I do hope you really will finish that translation, for of course you must, and it will only be an obstruction and worry to you until you do. And if you have any new versicles send one or two: your last was much praised.

News? I had 8 or 9 days with Siegfried, and Queenie caught and ate a bunny a day. It was quite pleasant really; more for her than for me. What to do with the last of my holiday I know not: perhaps the M.O. on Thursday will give me a clue.

Love from us all
Joe

I am not sure where I was when Joe wrote this letter: perhaps I had gone back to my parents in South Shields for the summer, until it was time for me to take up my Gregory Fellowship in Poetry at Leeds. Joe and I met some time that summer, again in Slapton, I think, because that was when he started talking about retirement, to give him more time for his own writing. He was drafting his wonderful novel, *We Think the World of You*, and revising *Hindoo Holiday*, and the autobiography that was to become the unforgettable *My Father and Myself* was already occupying his thoughts. While we walked round Slapton he hinted that he was looking for a literary executor, and seemed to suggest that I would be the ideal person. I knew very well that I would not be, and was glad when that onerous and thankless task was placed in the capable hands of Francis King.

The references to Siegfried Sassoon remind me that Joe, beset by certain people who even at that early stage in my writing career were bent on discrediting me with him, had appealed to several prominent writers including Plomer, Forster, Day Lewis, W.R. Rodgers, P.H. Newby and Siegfried Sassoon to give him their estimate of my worth as a poet, and they had all replied favourably. Sassoon was especially enthusiastic, and for that reason I dedicated to him my long poem 'The Last Man', which he found horrifying: he said it gave him nightmares about the future. He gave me a signed copy of his *Collected Poems* when Joe took me and Queenie to stay with Siegfried in Wiltshire at Heytesbury House. I greatly enjoyed my stay there. (Siegfried said I reminded him of his lost love, the exquisite Stephen Tennant.) Siegfried had put us, with what he thought was helpful tact, in a pair of adjacent bedrooms with a communicating door. Like many people, he assumed that Joe and I were lovers, but this was never so: we were 'just good friends'. But Joe did not bother to disillusion the matchmakers, and I could not have cared less about their ill-informed gossip. Though I was from the working class, I was not Joe's type, sexually speaking, and he certainly did not attract me physically. Our happy stay with Siegfried, who had terrible domestic troubles of his own, but was consoled by the love of his son, George, is recorded in Joe's diaries, *My Sister and Myself* (1982), so ably edited by Francis King.

Alas, in later letters written in the mid-sixties to my friend Rena, Joe showed signs of increasing old age, testiness and sheer spite, as will be seen when I come to quote the letters she received. I think it was Joe's jealousy getting the upper hand again. After the death of Queenie and his retirement from *The Listener*, he found himself increasingly lonely, as so-called friends who had been interested in him simply for whatever advantage they could draw from his power as an editor began to drop

him and call him a has-been. I was one of the few who stayed by him
faithfully to the end, and when gorgeous Rena came into my life and
swept me right off my feet, Joe could hardly bear it. I introduced him to
Rena and her equally splendid husband Roger (as soon as he met me,
Roger declared I needed 'fathering'). Predictably, Joe took to Roger at
once, and of course he was nice to Rena, a woman impossible not to
love. Even Nancy took to her, though she usually disliked any woman
who entered Joe's life, when her maniacal possessiveness would turn to
withering sarcasm and her jealousy would be inflamed as destructively
as Queenie's.

From time to time Joe would ask my opinion about a poem he had
received, and I always tried to give a favourable answer. I also introduced the work of several poets I liked to his pages – poems by Iris
Orton, David Paul (who became a book reviewer for a time), Gloria
Evans-Davies (a Chatto poet), Christopher Leach, who started off as a
poet and then became an excellent novelist, and many more. I quote
now from a letter that Joe sent me about my reactions to a poem that
had been submitted to him by an Italian woman he had met in Italy, and
to which I gave a negative response:

Dear Jim
    I have left your excellent letter on the poem until now. It showed
great penetration, and I agreed with every word. The writer was
indeed a woman – a foreigner – an Italian – whom I met in Italy 3
years ago, with her son and daughter. They were very nice and kind,
and were known as 'the mad Milanis' because they were all so
harum-scarum. Then for no known reason the son, named Micci,
aged about 25, just about to be married, just about to enter a job he
had tried to get for some time, went home and blew his brains out.
No one can explain, but I think some dark psychological reason
connected with his mother and a Jocasta complex. He did not *quite*
kill himself actually, and the hospital to which he was taken said there
was some very dim hope, depending upon a dangerous operation: but
his mother said 'No, he wished to die, let him.' There is really no
doubt that he wd. have died in any case. Since then she has taken to
poetry – a quite new thing for her – and swamped us all with the
lavish results. I have letters from her by almost every post. She is
possessed. Her poems do rather upset me, so I suppose the emotion
comes thro'. But of course they aren't poetry, as you say. I may
however publish something of hers, just as a try. A sad story. You

understood perfectly – and I have sent your letter to her. She is intelligent enough to take it.

Love

J.

* * *

Many were the ones I trusted to watch over me, but no one as much as Joe. My own parents wanted to do so, – but my father was too weak, my mother too possessive. In France before the war I had thought that Cocteau or André Gide might do the trick, but they too were ones who wanted to be watched over. . . . Andrew Young watched over me for a while, as priest and poet, but was too much of a saint. There were women like Barbara Pym, Elizabeth Taylor and Rosalinde Fuller who might have watched over me, but their attentions were engaged elsewhere. For a time, in Leeds, Wilfred Rowland Childe, Jacob Kramer and, in Wensleydale, Fred Lawson were father-figures but inadequate to my foolish wish. I first started studying Zen Buddhism in Leeds, hoping to find the all-compassionate one – a search that lasted thirty years and came to nothing in one of the centres of Zen study and Buddha worship, Kyoto.

It was while I was finishing my time at Leeds, in 1952, that I met Guy Vaesen, a theatre director of great brilliance and goodness, who was then at York Repertory. We met through an organization called the Religious Drama Society, which had asked me to be in charge of writing at their annual summer school. When the director of the Society, a vivacious young Christian woman of supposedly progressive views, asked me to London to discuss the school, and to meet the other members of the staff, that included an old friend from Wydale and Grantley Hall summer schools (run by the West Riding Educational Authority), Stella Mary Pearce. The stage director I met was Willard Stoker of the Liverpool Playhouse. He was a follower of Tyrone Guthrie. But Willard became either sick or unable to come to the summer school, and Guy took his place. Guy Vaesen was a man I took to at once, both as a professional producer and as a personal friend. He told me first of all that Willard had given a favourable report on me: 'James is a very cuddlesome poet.' This made me laugh, for I had never thought of being cuddlesome, though of course I had always wanted to be. The Religious Drama Society summer school was a terrible trial, because it was attended by a lot of very earnest Christian intellectuals.

Guy gave an hilarious account of how he had directed a disastrous production of Kafka's *The Trial*. I gave a poetry reading and daily classes in writing.

One of my classes was supposed to produce a play that would be staged by Guy at the end of the course. All I remember was that this play, which contained lots of opportunities for what was then known as 'choral speaking', was the dull product of dull students, and both Guy and I despaired of ever making something of it. When we saw the cast lined up at the front of the stage ready to let rip with their choral speaking, we got a fit of church giggles, for that all-female chorus was notable for its very thick ankles. 'What thick ankles they've all got,' I whispered to Guy as we gazed, choking back our mirth, at a few score dreary church ladies doing their best to be spiritual but staying immovably earthbound on those gross nether appendages. On the final night of the course, there was a Grand Evening. Neither of us had brought any formal clothes, and we were just going in to dinner when we saw that the school's breezy young Christian directress was clad in a fashionable long evening dress and swathed in pearls. It was obviously the great social event of her Christian year. I was furious, because nothing we had been told had prepared Guy and me for the sort of religious Lord Mayor's Banquet that we now had to sit through in scruffy jeans and sweaters, while all around us the church workers, sent to the school at great expense on grants from their parishes, had a kind of superior church social in which they all paraded about in the floor-length evening gowns seen at the annual dinners of hubby's company or bank. I was so incensed, I rushed with Guy to the bedroom we were sharing, and stripped naked, then put on a very brief pair of shorts, a French sailor's jersey and a roadman's white-spotted red sweat-rag. But Guy, helpless with laughter, persuaded me to change back into something a little more suitable. He had that sense of balance in which I was often completely lacking, and I think that was what made him such a good theatre director, as well as such a wonderful father to his angelic-faced, fair-haired little boy, the image of myself when young. We were never again invited to the RDS summer school. But it was the RDS that commissioned my play for Peterborough Cathedral, *Upon This Rock*, superbly directed by TV's Christian Simpson, and beautifully dressed by Stella. But at the end of the first performance the enraged directress of the summer school cut me dead: it was not her idea of a Christian drama at all! Besides, she had never been consulted, and she considered herself to be *the* authority on religious verse plays.

I saw several of Guy's excellent productions at York, and later at Rotherham Rep, and he took me to Huddersfield and Bradford and

other repertory theatres in an attempt to complete my dramatic education, for I had always wanted to work with professional actors and
stage directors – an opportunity that was not to be granted me until the
seventies, at the University Theatre, Newcastle upon Tyne. I adored
Guy, in the proper emotional but platonic way I felt was appropriate in
someone to watch over me, but of course he was a family man already,
and very much taken up in his career: he went on to work as a BBC
producer. But one weekend he took me to Liverpool to see a production
by Willard at Liverpool Playhouse. It was a good example of Tyrone
Guthrie's 'theatre of delight'. I loved the production, and the theatre
itself, and the robust life of the Liverpool streets and pubs. Willard and
his house manager invited me to stay at the large flat they rented in
Gambier Terrace.

   We did not know it then, but we were right at the heart of a slowly
evolving Beatlemania. Gambier Terrace was then a sort of mini-Bohemia
of art, music, sex and drugs, and John Lennon lived there for a while. It
was near the Liverpool College of Art, where he was to be a student. So
while we were feverishly absorbed by theatre productions like Eleanor
Farjeon's *The Two Bouquets*, an entrancing period musical starring
Willard's wonderful comic actor, Hugh Paddick, Paul MacCartney and
John Lennon and their classmates were learning the guitar and getting
ready to outdo Elvis when they started playing in their Liverpool cellar.
I remember so well the romance of that first night of *The Two Bouquets*.
(Those were the times of *Salad Days* and *The Boy Friend*.) I had
father-figures all round me, and one delightful lover. And when I took
my seat in the stalls, there in front of me was an old flame from wartime
days with whom I had had a long epistolary affair, and a somewhat
shorter love affair, for he was in the Air Force and not always available
either as lover or as father-figure. Now he was sitting in front of me with
someone I did not know but whom I took to be his current lover. It was
like living in a dream at Gambier Terrace. Every week I took an
incredibly complicated train journey to Corsham and back, for I had
just started teaching there, but I did not mind; I felt I was at the heart of
artistic creation, and I was in love. I had someone to watch over me, and
also to love me physically.

   This double delight was a mistake: it had to be one thing or the other.
In the end I think my intensity became too much for them to bear, and
one snowy night I was turned out of Gambier Terrace with my belong-
ings in a battered suitcase. They had had the goodness to call me a taxi,
but they did not go to the station with me. In the freezing cold of the
night train to London I cried my heart out, and vowed never to love
anyone again. A song that became popular around that time was called

'The Queers' Anthem', and went like this:

> There was a boy, a very strange enchanted boy –
> They say he wandered very far,
> Very far, over land and sea.
> A little shy, and sad of eye,
> And very wise was he.
>
> And then one day,
> The magic day he passed my way
> And as we spoke of many things,
> Fools and kings,
> This he said to me:
> The greatest thing you'll ever learn
> Is just to love,
> And be loved in return. . . .

This haunting song with its wistful melody has been sung by many fine jazz artists, and there is one of my favourite interpretations on 'In Flight', an album by George Benson. Like Anita O'Day, he can shred a lyric like e.e. cummings, then put it all together again to make it come out all fresh and new every time you hear it. The song was one in which I felt a private interest: I was both the strange boy and the person he spoke to about 'fools and kings'. It expressed all my sense of loss, and still does. It is a song that breaks my heart, and I'd love to hear Jessye Norman singing it, with all that special feeling she puts into grand opera or Gershwin.

From Liverpool (Lime Street) to London (Euston) on a train that left after midnight and arrived at Euston around 4.30 a.m. was the most miserable journey of my life, and I shall never forget arriving in a city as deeply under snow as the one I had left. I had nowhere to go. I sat in the waiting-room for a couple of hours, trying to get warm, then decided to try Madame Sheba, who was still living in her flat over the shoe shop next to Goodge Street Station – 77a Tottenham Court Road. I got there about 7 a.m. and she opened the door to me wearing a capacious peignoir of turquoise silk scattered with pink rambler roses. As always, she had her turban on: this one was gold lamé printed with peacock's feathers. She always kept her turban on in the house, and even slept in it. On the one occasion when I saw her drunk, it fell off and almost made me avert my eyes from her brown, woolly cap of hair, cut close and thinning at the temples. I felt it was a sacred mystery I should not have looked upon, and jammed the turban back on her head as I hauled her great bulk up the stairs to her little back bedroom, and hoisted her somehow on to her very high bed.

Though it was so early in the morning, Madame had already made a studied toilet and was smelling sweet and dewy. Her initial frown of suspicion, which she wore as a protective mask every time she opened that front door – for she never knew who might be ringing her bell, whether black marketeers, drug pushers, down-and-out countrymen, drunks, cops from the Tottenham Road Police Station or the sinister CID – suddenly was lifted. She gave me a radiant smile, her gold incisor glinting mischievously, held out her massive arms and embraced me. 'Here's my chicken come home to Mamma again!' she chortled, as she drew me inside – after a quick glance to left and right outside the door to see if I'd been followed – and led me up her steep, narrow stairs, her voluptuous bottom heaving and swaying before my very eyes. She was still having trouble with her lodgers, who were always in trouble with the cops. 'In the middle of the night! I of all people!' she kept exclaiming with outraged yet delighted dignity.

At once she set me down at her kitchen table and gave me a mug of tea and a bowl of her 'special made' semolina. We looked at one another. She had aged during the last two or three years, with fine wrinkles at the corners of her alluring dark eyes, and at either side of her rich mouth there were little creases like brackets. She played the vamp with me, lowering her slightly discoloured, sexy lids with their long, silky eyelashes. We told our troubles to one another. Could she be that 'someone to watch over me?' I wondered as I helped her clear the table. But alas all her rooms were taken, and Lottie from Abyssinia had been moved up to my old room. All the other rooms were occupied by people belonging to the movements for black people's rights. She could not turn them out. After a rest on her front-room sofa, where the player piano still stood among the antimacassar-draped chairs and side-tables laden with ferns, I took my leave of her and went in search of a room. But I often went back to her for a chat and a cup of tea and to hear the latest scandal about the scrapes her 'chickens' kept getting into. She had become a neighbourhood 'character'.

That was when I discovered my dank basement in Inverness Place, and where I met W.S. Merwin. I soon moved on, to a small second-floor room at 24 Kemplay Road in Hampstead, not far from Keats House, where I was a frequent visitor. The house in Kemplay Road was an interesting one, run by a gentleman of indeterminate age with a re-assuringly gentle manner and brightly peroxided hair. He treated me very kindly during the two or three months I was to spend there, looking in vain for a fellow-soul. Then Riette Sturge-Moore, who lived in Flask

Walk and was my colleague at Corsham, offered me two top rooms in her Adelaide Road flat, where I spent a happy year or so before moving to the Weavers' Cottages, Flemish Buildings, in Corsham, with the disastrous results I have described. While I lived there I found one very remarkable friend, no less than the Bishop of Manchester. He was the only member of the Church who ever gave me any support and comfort, and I bless his memory for his thoughtful kindness and sympathetic understanding. He held pacifist beliefs and was opposed to nuclear weapons, and that is how I first got in contact with him. J.B. Priestley and Jacquetta Hawkes, who should have known better, had announced somewhere in the press that there were no more good causes worth fighting for in the fifties. Priestley had been one of my heroes when I was a schoolboy, and I read through all his books in the South Shields Library in Ocean Road. I particularly liked *Benighted*, *The Good Companions*, *Wonder Hero* and *Faraway*. I never much liked his plays or his later prose works. So I was astonished by his statement, and I at once wrote him a little note pointing out that there was still one great cause left – the abolition of war, the manufacture of armaments and the banning of nuclear weapons. He replied saying briefly that he appreciated my point of view but that he did not think my concerns were so very urgent. I did not reply to this very disappointing reaction. But not long afterwards Priestley and his wife Jacquetta Hawkes started supporting the peace and anti-nuclear campaigns.

I wrote to many people prominent in literature, politics and the Church, asking them to give the peace movement their support. The only persons who replied were Naomi Mitchison, who was to be a great support to me in later years, and William, Bishop of Manchester. He was the closest I ever came to finding that real, essential 'someone to watch over me'. Here is one of the letters he wrote to me: it is the only one that has survived my endless travels and peregrinations. It will form a suitable bridge to my next chapter, because it is addressed to me at the Colegio Mayor Fray Luis de Leon, Calle de Serranos, Salamanca, Spain:

Bishop's House
26 Singleton Road
Manchester 7

15th October 1957

My dear James,

Forgive my use of your Christian name but your letter moves me to do so. Forgive, too, my long delay in replying but the fact is I have so many letters to write in the course of my work that when I have finished I have to push myself to write to my friends.

I was delighted to hear of your appointment at Salamanca for I was worried after our meeting by the fact that there did not seem to be the right job in the offing – and this seems just right for it will provide you with new paints for your palette. My chaplain, Richard Hare, has spent his holidays at Madrid acting as chaplain to the Embassy and I asked him to write to a friend of his, T.R.M. Sewell, who is at the Embassy. I thought that if you were in Madrid, as you would be sure to be, it would be pleasant to have a contact. So you may be hearing from Sewell.

Since I got back from my Lakeland holiday in Sept. I have been rather hard at it. I have to find half a million for new churches. This has meant seeing a lot of people in the business world. I like it but it uses up a vast amount of time.

I have just finished reading a proof copy of Stephen King-Hall's book *Defence in the Nuclear Age*. It is a reasoned plea for switching over to organizing defence through non-violent resistance. The book is uneven and written hastily but it should cause a stir. Gollancz are producing it in March. How I wish Britain would take a stand on this issue.

I wonder whether you have yet seen a bull-fight. Richard Hare contends that that is the real religion of Spain. What you say about religion reminds me of a saying of Baron von Hügel that 'the Christian faith is vivid yet dim'. And he goes on to illustrate what he means by referring to a dog's knowledge of its master – vivid yet obscure – so obscure that after a time in human company a dog likes to get back into the unobscure world of his fellow dogs. The Christian faith is too often presented by us clerics as too small to meet the world's needs, too confident in touching upon the ultimate mystery, and too easy in measuring up to the austerity of the Gospel claims. 'There is more faith in honest doubt etc.'

But the reverse is also true. 'There is more doubt in honest faith etc.' So God guide you. I know He will but don't become a Roy Campbell! No, I think there's no danger of that.

If you should be able to lay hands on them have a look at Herbert Farmer's *The Healing Cross* and Donald Baillie's *God was in Christ*. Both well written; the latter has a Platonic clarity. Another book well worth reading is Wm. Temple's *Readings from St John's Gospel*.

I must stop. Your letter gave me much pleasure. This bears with it my very good wishes. Please let me know how things go with you. If you are back in this country in the summer be sure to let me know for

I shall be in London from July 3 to August 10 at the Lambeth Conference.
Joy and peace to you this Christmas.

Yours ever
William M.

I am rereading Shakespeare's sonnets. How extraordinarily modern they are in phrasing. He gets so close to the object at times that his words become things.

I met William two or three times, I think once at the Houses of Parliament and once for lunch at his club in London, and each time left him with the conviction that here was one of the best brains of our times, and one of the best Christians. He was unfailingly helpful to me in all my confusions and errors. Just the way he wrote 'God guide you' reminds me of his firm handshake and fine voice. Though his God meant nothing to me, William's words never left me. There was no danger, of course, of my following Roy Campbell's kind of Roman Catholicism or his adulation of Franco. But I still regarded Campbell as a gifted poet and translator of St John of the Cross. Besides, he had been at the school in Durban that had been attended by my poetic other self, Fernando Pessoa.

I did not get in touch with our Embassy in Madrid, nor did I ever hear from Sewell. But that did not lessen the generosity of William's efforts to help me. I had indeed been to a bullfight, and had found it horrible, though perhaps not without connections with religion through Mithraic rites. In the tormented bull I had seen not only myself, as I mentioned earlier, but also the figure of Christ hounded and tortured and crucified by his enemies. I wonder if that was what Richard Hare meant? Whatever the religion of Spain, I was to find out there was little justice in it, and little concern for the poor and the powerless. That was not my idea of what the Christian religion should be, and my experiences in Spain were to destroy whatever faith I had left completely and irrevocably.

IN A POLICE STATE

Fear has many eyes, and can see things underground.

Cervantes

In me the need to talk is a primary impulse, and I can't help saying right off what comes to my tongue.

Don Quixote

There are but two families in the world, as my old grandmother used to say, the Haves and the Have-nots.

Don Quixote

The Sud Express to Lisbon leaves Paris Austerlitz at nine o'clock every morning. But it does not arrive in Salamanca until about one-thirty the next day. This was not how I wished to catch my first sight of the fabled city of Lazarillo de Tormes and of Gil Blas, who in Le Sage's novel made the journey to Salamanca only from Oviedo in the north.

So I decided to travel to Salamanca – by way of Valladolid and Jordi of course – through Andorra and Barcelona. I knew something about Catalonia but nothing about Andorra, except that it was a tiny independent principality, one of the world's smallest countries, set high in the eastern Pyrenees.

I took an early morning train from Paris to Toulouse, where I changed to a small local train for Ax-les-Thermes. There I got on a bus that took me to Le Hospitalet près l'Andorre, and through the frontier post at Pas de la Casa, over the Envalira pass and down into a land whose mountainous beauty at once put me under a spell I shall never forget. In those days Andorra was still a rather primitive country, the resort of *contrebandiers*. Accommodation was pretty rough-and-ready but the people were friendly and warm-hearted, and I took endless delight in exploring on foot the wild landscapes of lakes and forest, mountain waterfalls and paths as rich with alpine flowers as a medieval tapestry.

On that first brief visit I made up my mind that one day I would return there. I started learning Catalan and reading fine modern Catalan poets, whom I intended to translate – Foix, Espriu, Bartra and many others of the emergent Catalan school whose work, and whose very language, were banned by Franco. To be forbidden to speak and write one's own native tongue is one of the greatest punishments a cruel dictator can inflict upon a proudly independent people: it was one of the Franco regime's most despicable crimes against humanity. Today, fortunately, that dictatorship, like so many others, has crumbled into dust, and Catalan literature and culture are flourishing.

At the end of summer there were still patches of old snow on the sheltered slopes of the Cirque des Pessons, and I wrote my first poem about Andorra:

> The dark flanks of mountains
> patched with the tawny white
> of old snows, the harsh peaks
> packed with golden ice
> against a blue and amber sunset
> that stains the plaited waterfalls
> with leaping rainbow trout of light.

From Andorra la Vella, the capital with its lovely small cathedral and fortress-like Parliament House, la Casa de la Vall, I took a bus to Barcelona through stark, barren landscapes by way of Lerida and Manresa. There is a fantastic intensity and wildness, almost savagery, in the landscapes of Spain, and Catalonia, delivered from the Arabs by Charlemagne, is no exception. I travelled among grotesque rock formations, past gorges and canyons, weird spectres of fanes and fortresses on distant isolated heights, small villages strung along spines of haggard cliffs. In the Goya wall paintings today fittingly displayed in the Prado, and in many of his other works, one sees again and again these formidable elephantine rocks lowering over a cringing humanity trying to find shelter in a bandit landscape.

The piercing brilliance of the late afternoon sunlight seems to intensify the surrealism of the constantly changing scenery. The first glimpse of Montserrat is always deeply moving as it begins to rise like a vast ragged curtain on the evening horizon, mysterious and slightly sinister in its grandeur as it looms ever nearer in Goya-like menace, shifting from side to side of the bus until it vanishes behind us.

Night had fallen by the time we reached the centre of Barcelona. I stayed two nights at the Hotel Manila on the Rambla Liceu, in a side-street named after the painter Fortuny, father of the great dressmaker. This hotel was at that time a sort of private dwelling crammed with the owner's collection of Catalan works of art and pastel portraits of the great singers who appeared at the nearby Opera. In this respect it resembled another favourite hotel of mine, the Quirinale in Rome, where I like to stay in the room where Ronald Firbank died. The Hotel Manila has now been transformed into a Ramada Renaissance Hotel, with correspondingly high prices, so I prefer to stay at the Hotel Gaudi, still unspoilt, which has the advantage of being right opposite the enchanting Theatre Museum. I'm pretty sure Firbank must have stayed there, and also probably at the Hotel Manila, so convenient for the sumptuous Opera, now restored to its full glory. I attended a Wagner performance that evening, high in the gallery, and spent the next day clambering around Gaudi's towers of the Sagrada Familia. At the Parque Güell, at the terminus of the 24 tram ('Origin y final de los servicios'), after mounting the hilly Calle de Larrad, I again experienced the peculiar pleasures of this fantastic Gaudi park, the subject of one of my best poems in *The Descent into the Cave*.

Next morning, from the Paseo de Gracias station, I took the first express to Zaragoza, passing through the small seaside town of Sitges, which was in later years to become a British hooligan holiday playground. Zaragoza is the city where Buñuel was born. Buñuel, the creator of a film that deeply impressed my youth, *Los olvidados*, gives a love-hate description of his Zaragoza childhood in his autobiography, *Mi ultimo sospiro* (My Last Gasp). I stopped there only to change trains. I took the mid-afternoon express to Valladolid that goes on to Salamanca.

It was after nine o'clock when I reached Valladolid, and I took a taxi to the Hotel Moderno. Jordi was waiting for me outside after I had a bath and changed my clothes for dinner. We did not speak, just smiled, shook hands and set off walking along those dim back streets where Jordi felt fairly safe. Again we took dinner in a cheap workmen's restaurant. We were sad because he could not come to my room and I could not go to his home, where it would have been difficult to explain our relationship. So we had to go to the park where we had met under the protective shade of a friendly tree. We were both trembling with desire, afraid to make the first move. In the end we just stood holding each other close, as the tears coursed down our faces. The noises of the evening streets seemed very far away. The shouting voices did not belong to our little world of passionate love.

We stayed there a long time, until well after midnight. We had to keep drawing apart as occasional couples, and sometimes prowling single men, passed nearby. We were conscious of the insecurity of our situation. I felt that hidden eyes must be observing us from behind bushes and tree-trunks. And we had to keep an eye open for police patrols.

From time to time we strolled hand in hand, with lighted cigarettes to give warning of our presence, for we did not talk. If we did see some figure approaching, or standing in the distance, we would release our tense handclasp, fingers intertwined, and walk apart, puffing idly at our cigarettes or lighting new ones from Pablo's box of *fosforos*, as if we were just friends out for a casual stroll.

Who those single men were who sometimes crossed our path I do not know. They did not give any sign of interest in us. Perhaps, I thought, they were peeping Toms, voyeurs on the hunt for indiscreet *novios* and *novias* embracing in the shadows, as we did, at the mercy of every intruder. Perhaps they were exhibitionists – flashers. I was quite interested in flashers and their psychology, and often wished they would 'flash' me; but they always looked at me with the utmost contempt as I stood waiting hopefully for a revelation. It was girls and women they were after. 'Piss off, will you?' one of them hissed at me once on Wimbledon Common. 'Have some common decency! Mind your own business, whatever it is!' He insinuated that my 'business' must be something utterly depraved, far worse than anything he might be going to do.

Or were those men simply other lonely hunters of other men? I felt a cold thrill in my bones when I realized the implications of the word 'hunters' – perhaps those men were Franco's secret police?

At one point on the next night Jordi drew me into the shadows and to my astonishment produced a vicious-looking switch-blade knife, warning me never to look at another man in his presence. 'I use this for sticking pigs,' he said, giving me a mysterious smile, gesturing with the ugly blade across his uncovered throat, then laughing, flicking it shut and thrusting it into a long pocket in the side of his dusty black corduroys. Then he kissed me, playfully.

Afterwards we went to a bar and had some cognac. Jordi seemed frightened, and we did not stay for long. As we left, we were followed out by two men. In the street they stopped us and asked for our papers. In such a situation in a foreign country I am never able to speak the language, so when they asked for my passport I just said 'Hotel', because Spanish hotels always kept visitors' passports, at any rate for the first night. (They still do, in fact.) The men motioned me to go away, and after they had looked at Jordi's papers I saw them escort him to a car. The last I saw of Jordi was when he turned his head towards me before getting into the car, smiled, and gave a shrug. I was unable to find out what had happened to him. I dared not go to his house, fearing

that it might cause further trouble for him. I left Valladolid for Salamanca the next day. I was frightened, too.

I did not see Jordi again, except for one brief encounter in Salamanca. I was never to return to Valladolid, a place of fear and heart-
break, until long after the death of Franco and the end of his regime.

* * *

Towards sunset I was travelling towards Salamanca from Medina del
Campo. In that pure evening light of late summer the plains were brown
and golden, with here a crumbling village with women nearly always in
black, and here a straggling group of toylike, stunted umbrella pines.
No birds. A shepherd with his stick, solitary, was already wrapped up to
the eyes in his striped poncho, the only true centre of his eccentric flock.
There is an unutterable sadness around Medina del Campo, where I had
to change trains for Salamanca.

It was the perfect moment to arrive in the city where I was to spend
the next year. I first saw Salamanca at a certain moment of dusk when
the setting sun still casts a deep red glow over the city's rosy stone. At
the station there were several little buses. I entered one full of nuns,
their winged white coifs illuminating the dim interior, making it like a
candle-lit church. They sat silently. When the bus started, they all
crossed themselves, as I had seen nuns do in Ireland when setting out on
a journey, however short. I think they noticed that I did not follow their
example. They were so different from the lively Irish nuns, who, when
they were passing some workmen unloading crates of beer into a
pavement hatch in Nassau Street, Dublin, burst out laughing when the
jovial brewery workers called out to them: 'Now, girls, steady up!'
There was something faintly sinister about these speechless nuns; but
perhaps they belonged to a silent order. Yet if so, whey weren't they
cloistered?

The driver and conductor made up for them by shouting and singing,
and the little bus itself was extremely noisy as it rattled along the bumpy
streets. We had started off in grand style, rattling right round the station
plaza with a great tooting of horns. Now we were rumbling and petard-
ing up a steep brown-earth road with long, high convent walls on each
side, towards a little square with a few dimly lit small shops and
pollarded trees like headless ostriches perched on one knobbly leg.
There were a few houses whose wrought-iron balconies were crammed
with plants: great pots of geraniums, full and dark, the flowers looking
down at me like tiny faces, intently.

At various stops nun after nun silently descended. The RENFE train

station must be a long way from the centre, I thought, just as we began
to enter the acid neon groves of the darkening city, through a narrow
glade of brightly lit shops, the Corrielo, then through a vast archway – a
policeman's shrill whistle – and the bus was rolling and swinging right
into the grand Plaza Mayor, which it circled slowly, triumphantly
hooting. The sight of the noble stone arcades with hanging lanterns, café
tables, people sitting smoking and drinking, waiters wearing long white
aprons balancing trays of bottles and glasses and highly coloured liqueurs,
the busy shops, a glimpse of a sombre church – it was all enchantment.
The bus trundled out into the Avenida Generalissimo Franco, a name
that made my heart sink – again the sharp, imperious police whistle –
faces looking in on us from outside, where the slow-moving crowds were
talking and laughing. The bus shuddered to a stop.

I hauled my luggage to the nearest small hotel and took a cheap
room. Before term started I wanted to live anonymously in this city
where no one knew me, just for a few days. Then I would announce my
arrival to the university authorities. And I would have to meet the head
of the English Department, Professor Ruiperez, who had sent me kind
letters of invitation and welcome, in faultless English.

After a fashionably elevenish dinner at my *hostal-pension*, in a small
green dining-room lit by blinding neon, I strolled out into the streets
where the sellers of lottery tickets were still in full cry – 'Para hoy! Para
hoy!' – and the blind beggars and cripples crouched and complained,
some of them small children left squatting on a bit of cardboard and
bawling their heads off. I tried not to let this interfere with *les très riches
heures de* James Kirkup, but the wretchedness and misery were overwhelming. Some of the beggars knelt in the middle of the pavement,
arms raised in an attitude of crucifixion, their rheumy eyes lifted
heavenwards like the imploring ecstasies of El Greco saints. But people
just walked round them. There was a legless young man on a cushioned
board to which roller-skates had been fitted, and he propelled himself
along with hands encased in old cigar-boxes. He had developed a fine
pair of shoulders, and his biceps bulged under his short-sleeved singlet:
his arms seemed to have grown unnaturally long and appeared simian.
He held a metal cup in his teeth, which were perfect in his bearded face
and glittered as brilliantly as his big, dark eyes under the street lamps.
Occasionally a small coin clattered in his tin. There were blind men
begging, selling lottery tickets.

I left these agonizing streets of beggars behind and entered the Plaza
Mayor, a magnificent example of eighteenth-century Spanish baroque,
dominated by the superb façade of the Churrigueresque Town Hall or
Ayuntamiento. There are spacious arcades and galleries on all sides of

the square, and on these I could see nobly sculpted medallions of famous Spaniards. On its eastern side stands the grand Pabellón Real (Royal Pavilion), facing the Ayuntamiento. The whole Plaza was ablaze with floodlighting, and big globes of pearly lamps hung in every arcade. The fine statues on the topmost balconies of the Ayuntamiento and framing the moonlike clock-face gestured against the midnight skies, and at once I was under the spell of the past. All this dazzling illumination was in honour of my arrival? No. It was for the great annual festa of 3 September, with its cattle fairs, bullfights and *zarzuelas*. There was dancing and singing at various points – the chatter and whir of castanets, the hoarse yelps and anguished arias of flamenco, the pistol-like crepitations of *zapateado*, the sharp slow hand-claps of café patrons calling waiters.

Gerald Brennan, writing just two or three years after the war, says in *The Face of Spain* that the slow hand-clap to attract the attention of waiters had died out, but I heard it in several places in the north. As his book is mainly about the south, perhaps it had died out in Andalusia, though even there I remember being startled by its male authority as I walked past a café in Seville. The hand-claps sometimes seemed to be keeping time with my leisurely steps as I wandered under the arcades in the hot night, but that was just a coincidence. I slightly lengthened my stride, feeling self-conscious as I always do if I find myself marching in step with martial music, when I deliberately break step and try to walk between the beats, as it were, in as unmilitary a way as possible.

After a while I sat down at a pavement café table and rather shamefacedly clapped my hands, but produced such a ladylike patter that no one heard me. So I just sat watching the passing scene until I caught the eye of a waiter and ordered some wine. As I sat there and sipped my Valdepeñas I observed the ladies in their flounced festival attire, plying elegant fans, escorted by dignified caballeros wearing black sombreros. There were small girls selling roasted melon seeds, shoeblacks clacking their cloths over hand-tooled Spanish leather boots. Extremely pretty young women, still in their teens, advanced from table to table, offering baskets of roses and carnations to couples. As I did not have a woman companion, they tended to ignore me, but I called to one and bought a little bouquet to put in my hotel bedroom's tooth-glass. There were fewer beggars under the arcades, perhaps scared away by the patrolling police, and by the awe-inspiring Civil Guards in their black-lacquered headgear and solemnly swinging capes. The constant presence of police I found rather intimidating. I was also depressed by the sight of rich, elderly couples strolling along laden with jewellery, the man's arm laid lightly round his spouse's shoulder. But always at the back of my mind there was the memory of Jordi, his knife, his smile, his helpless shrug. Why could he not be walking with me here? I saw there were some middle-aged men, single or in small groups, who all wore very dark glasses and pencil-thin moustaches, light raincoats hanging effetely from their shoulders in that Spanish fashion of male superiority that is elsewhere considered the mark of a homosexual. Younger people, because of the unseasonal heat, were wearing sweaters tied round the hips, another typically Spanish style that has been imitated by the Irish. I was once or twice approached by stony-faced nuns begging for charities, but I gave nothing because I felt sure that some of those nuns were fakes, possibly men in drag, for their big, dark, hollow eyes, dyspeptic noses bright red in chalk-white faces, compressed, colourless lips and faint moustaches were hardly the signs of religious penance, and they were all wearing rather large boots. I glimpsed a pair of shimmering transvestites in a back-street bar.

Despite all the illuminations, the thrilling flamenco and the shrill life of the streets, there was a sense of menace, a feeling of insecurity. I was made uneasy by those parading men in smart suits and dark glasses, who appeared to be a kind of confraternity of Falangists, ardent nationalists and supporters of Franco, whose picture was everywhere. Life here, I could see, was going to be on an even more perilous tightrope than it was in Britain. As I expected, there was no evidence of an alternative culture, and there were no obvious homosexuals, though I received a few long looks from passers-by which I was careful not to return. My mood was briefly lightened by the arrival of a *tuna* group of university students in traditional academic robes decorated with flying coloured ribbons who played guitars and mandolines and sang cheerful folksongs, accompanied by the antics of a virtuoso tambourine player. These strolling minstrels are very popular in Spain, and the *tuna* in Salamanca is one of the best. I was often to meet these apparently carefree young men parading the streets and lanes of the city well after midnight, or serenading pretty girls beneath their lighted windows, their only reward a thrown rose or carnation. Their music was both charming and professional.

I returned to my hotel around 3 a.m. My sadness over and fear for Jordi would not go away. The front door was locked, and that was when I made my first acquaintance with a venerable traditional figure, the *sereno*, an old man with a stick, a big brass badge and a large bunch of keys. These *serenos* patrol the streets at night, acting as watchmen and guardians of the peace. But they are also authorized to open street doors for people who have neglected to carry their often very ornate and heavy antique front-door keys with them. Here again the slow hand-clap is the signal one gives for a *sereno*'s help. He would usually appear in answer to the signal within a few minutes, for each *sereno* has a certain section to patrol. Their name is derived from the 'all quiet' or 'all's well' cry ('sereno') that the men used to give after calling the hours, just like our old English tradition – 'Two o'clock and all's well' – which has unfortunately died out. The *serenos* receive a small salary from the shopkeepers and private houses they keep an eye on, but it is considered proper to give them a tip each time they open a door for one. I found them to be cheerful, reassuring old men, and delightful conversationalists. They were a contrast to the ever-present police and Civil Guards. But they are all old men, and theirs is a dying profession. (They were still patrolling the streets of Madrid as late as 1973, when they were officially retired.)

As I turned to say good-night to my *sereno*, and to press a tip into his palm, the deep-blue sky held a brimming star – Orion.

*   *   *

Breakfast was a bowl of weak, milky coffee and a tasteless roll of bread. The small block of semi-refined sugar, like cement, took a long time to dissolve. Outside, at eight o'clock, the streets were already busy with sweepers, a watering-cart, shop assistants, police blowing whistles, bicycles, scooters, not many cars, the voices of the lottery ticket vendors, schoolchildren screaming as they ran to school, carts pulled by donkeys braying, trucks hooting, an ambulance siren – it all added up to utter confusion. But it was an early-morning bedlam that soon died down. The Spaniards are by nature noisy and vociferous, especially in the mornings when, like cocks crowing, they have to announce to the world that they are alive and doing. The stout, middle-aged men in black glasses do not appear until ten o'clock, with brief-cases or small leather bags. They were smoking cigars, hawking and spitting and shaking hands with friends or associates. There is some kind of conspiracy of bureaucrats: they all have their fingers in the same profitable pie. Their thin black moustaches were glossy with cologne, which wafted sickeningly behind them as they strolled to their offices.

It was a heavenly morning, not too hot yet. I wandered all over the city, getting lost then finding myself again where I had started. I saw some of the places that were to play an important part in the later dramas of my life: the great Clerecia church where I was to be sitting one momentous morning, and beside it the lovely Casa de las Conchas, its walls decorated with rows of carved scallop shells – seven rows adorn the upper storeys. I admired the main door of the Catedral Nueva –

comparatively new, that is, for it was started in 1513. The splendidly ornate style and the wealth of carvings in the soft-tinted stone were to be the subject of a poem. For the moment I kept away from the university. I strolled down to the Tormes and its Roman bridge: in the Plaza del Puente at its northern end stands an ancient, battered statue of the Roman lion mentioned in *Lazarillo de Tormes*. The bridge was constructed in the first century BC and is attributed to Trajan. Its many arches reminded me of the perfection of the Roman aqueduct at Segovia. I walked along the banks of the Tormes, sucking a native sweetmeat called *Piedras del Tormes* – pastel-tinted boiled sweets imitating the pebbles of that great river. Here and there were crowds of men bargaining over cattle and horses. These were magnificent, but in my eyes the men were even finer, with their dark, hollow cheeks, taut, slim bodies in tight-fitting black corduroys that vividly outlined their considerable sexual equipment. Some of the men, when they saw me looking at them, smiled shyly, and as if automatically scratched their swollen codpieces. This I knew was not a sexual invitation but a protection against the evil eye. Their warm Spanish eyes in luxuriant black eyelashes melted my heart which had been chilled by the dark-glassed fascists in the city streets. They sported knives like Jordi's. They all reminded me of him.

All the churches are closed for lunch and siesta. But I can hear nuns singing quietly, sweetly, invisible behind thick wooden grilles. There are little street altars, devotional carvings in the most unexpected places. Inside the churches I could feel intense devoutness, and recalled the ejaculations shouted after La Macarena in Seville, so truly reverent yet passionate, reminiscent of medieval mystery plays' earthy realism and at the same time resembling the way men call after girls in the street. Yet there is a firm respect for women and for the relations between men and women in daily life. Behind the reserve of the Spaniards there is warmth and passion. As in Ireland, there are many frustrated bachelors and spinsters, and there are frequent late marriages. Sometimes in the parks I see sweethearts, *novios* and *novias*, showing one another great respect, walking sedately together, not even holding hands. During the evening *paseo* the atmosphere is more relaxed, but still quite formal.

They have a frank and friendly interest in foreigners, in machinery, in clothes. They ask me how much I paid for everything I was wearing, how much I pay for my room at the *pension*, how much salary I shall be getting at the university – a salary to me ridiculously small, little more than pocket-money, but for the majority of working-class Spaniards a fortune. There is such volubility I find it hard to follow what some people are saying, and they make no compromises for non-native speakers. Like the French, they expect everyone to understand their language. Even when I can understand all they are saying, they give me little opportunity to reply, so anxious are they to keep up the headlong momentum of their own speech; then they complain that I say nothing! They are great gossips, the men as much as the women, whispering behind raised hands, then bursting into sudden excesses of rage with wildly waving hands, flashing eyes, curled lips spitting torrents of invective. Then it is changed in a moment, and they are all sunny smiles and playful pats on the arm. A few determinedly modern young women eat snacks in the street, but no girl or woman in Spain dares wear trousers or skimpy bathing-suits. In the Franco era Spain is the least modern of all European countries. This may be partly due to its isolated geographical position, which has helped to give the country its intense feeling of national uniqueness, and its deep conservatism. George Borrow, in *The Bible in Spain*, called it 'the genuine spirit of localism'. Although the country is one of astonishing variety in landscape, climate and speech, it is everywhere itself, unmistakably Spanish. In his work on Spanish cathedrals John Harvey comments on the Spaniard's national pride, often so abrasive, so aggressive and disdainful of foreign ways, modern ideas of internationalism. But without that pride the Spaniard would not be Spanish, as Harvey writes: 'It is profoundly to be hoped that he will never allow these sharp angles to be smoothed off by the modern cult of "all things to all men", and a false catholicity of taste which is no taste at all. Spain is the last country of discrimination; long may she retain this priceless gift.'

The woman who sells you a ticket at the bus office crosses herself for you as she makes it out. Beggars, when you give them money, bless you and wish you good luck, a gold tooth flashing surprisingly in a dusky smile suddenly lighting a dirty face. There is something medieval in the way the Spaniard can reconcile earthy realism and practical common sense with soaring fantasy and spiritual exaltation. To most Englishmen such a conjunction will be unbelievable; but, on returning to England, he may find himself wondering how he has finally accepted the Spanish view. It is impossible to live in Spain and not be radically changed, not to discover profound truths about life, and about oneself.

A FATAL ENCOUNTER

The Poem in the Pencil

This pencil has a poem I could write.
It lies asleep within its woody shade,
A fountain that the forest leafs to light
And thins to nothing but the wish I made
To cast a shadow down the page.

The pattern is disguised within a cage.
I cannot bring its meaning to escape
Although I tease it with a tender rage
And pledge with love its naked shape.
– It will not lie down by my side.

Because I call it out of pride,
Its veins run cold within my hand
And leave the narrow page too wide.
– When will it let me understand
My wish to share the words we hide?

Salamanca had been Franco's headquarters in 1937. Something of the secret terror of that period in the Civil War remained. The beautiful tawny stone of the great churches and university buildings seemed to me stained with the blood of Republican idealists in the British battalion of the 15th International Brigade. They were fighting for justice for the workers, a fine cause but one that had already proved useless in Russia, where the same old bureaucratic hierarchy held sway as it did in Spain. There was another iron dictatorship in Germany, whose Condor Legion bombed the working classes in Guernica on 26 April 1937. Kim Philby had been a war correspondent in Salamanca, sending dispatches to *The Times*. As the newspaper's special correspondent with Franco and his troops, Philby had a watertight cover for his clandestine operations. Guy Burgess had told my Gateshead chorus-boy friend, Jack Hewit, that Philby must have had very good reasons for going to Franco in Salamanca. Pablo Merry del Val, whose father had been Spanish Ambassador in London, conducted briefings for the correspondents and censored their dispatches. Their briefings were held in the airy first-floor gallery of the university quadrangle.

This was where the offices of the English Department and several lecture-rooms were situated when I arrived in 1957, twenty years after Philby. The beautiful old building in neoclassical style is called the Palacio de Anaya, situated on the square of that name, and it was built in 1760. There was a bust of Miguel de Unamuno at the bottom of the staircase, and it seemed to have been defaced. He was a fine writer, essayist and philosopher who wrote *The Tragic Sense of Life* and who was persecuted by Franco and put under house arrest by Primo de Rivera because of his liberal views expressed fearlessly while he was the Rector of the University. He died in 1936, and despite the Franco oppression he was venerated by many of the university staff. Professor Ruiperez of the Faculty of Letters spoke to me quite openly of his admiration for the man and the writer. He died under house arrest in Salamanca, uncompromising to the end.

It was Unamuno who wrote: 'Only in solitude do we find ourselves; and in finding ourselves, we find in ourselves all our brothers in solitude.' This was an idea that appealed strongly to me, though Unamuno had not been thinking of some of the 'brothers in solitude' – the outcasts from social and sexual 'normality' – who were the brothers that first sprang to my mind on reading that sentence in Corsham. But I was one with the solitaries of the spirit, too: with St Teresa and St John of the Cross as well as with humbler dissidents like Jordi and one or two other men of the working class I had known in Spain, the young bank clerk I had met in Cordoba the previous spring, among the orange and lilac blossom of Las Tendillas, where we walked and whispered, hardly daring to look at one another, and separating at the sight of police. My own solitude was as nothing compared with their constantly patrolled loneliness, without hope of escape.

Unamuno also wrote: 'Love is the child of illusion and the parent of disillusion' – a very Zen Buddhist concept of which I was to learn the truth in Salamanca.

Nothing had prepared me for the overwhelming architectural beauty of Salamanca, and in particular for the grandeur of the university, the oldest in Spain and one of the oldest in Europe, with its noble façade in plateresque style. Some of the ancient lecture theatres had been well preserved, like the Aula de Fray Luis de Leon, named after one of the many notable scholars who have graced its pulpit-lectern. Founded in the thirteenth century, Salamanca was the equal of Paris, Bologna and Oxford, became internationally famous and attracted students from all over the world. It fell into intellectual decay during the eighteenth and nineteenth centuries, from which it was rescued by its famous rector, Miguel de Unamuno. The great library contains one of the best collections of ancient manuscripts of the Hispanic civilizations, including the most complete copy of an extraordinary medieval poem, *El libro de buen amor* (The Book of Good Love) by Juan Ruíz, dated 1343 in its second version, which Menendez Pelayo praises thus: 'Juan Ruíz, Archpriest of Hita, wrote the comic epic of an entire epoch in his multiform book, the Human Comedy of the 14th Century. He managed to reduce the variegated and picturesque spectacle of the Middle Ages to the unity of a humoristic concept at the very moment it began to dissolve and crumble.' The university chapel and the grand stone stairways with carved reliefs on the ornamental balustrades are extremely fine. I was deeply imbued with the historic and cultural spells of this monumental structure when I took my first walk round the cloisters of the inner courtyard, whose first-floor gallery, open to the sky, is beautifully panelled and wainscoted.

I had called Professor Ruiperez from my *hostal*, and at once he came to take me out to lunch at an expensive restaurant featuring all the local dishes, including a hearty paella and fine Rioja wines. He was a very kind, youngish, amiable scholar of great distinction, and a power in the university. I think he was shocked to find his new Professor of English staying in a cheap *pension*. But the place he took me to after lunch, the Colegio Ponce de Leon, where I was supposed to have rooms, was a rather stark student hostel, and my little room was very small, with just a narrow bed, a table and a chair. But my windows commanded charming views of the city. I stayed there only a few days, and then for some reason I was removed to the Colegio Fray Luis de Leon, where I was given a somewhat larger and more comfortable room. The toilets and bathrooms and showers were at the end of the hall on the second floor, and from my window I had a splendid view of the cathedral, whose Gothic, Renaissance and baroque styles mingled perfectly in the dark-rose-and-amber stone to give it almost the appearance of some natural rock formation. There was a multitude of bells – solemn, melodious, hasty, irritable, angry, tinny, noble, girlish – an infinite variety of calls to worship and memorials of passing time.

The students had not yet arrived, but I took meals in the refectory with a few of the college authorities and professors who had already started the new term's work. They seemed to me very distant, almost suspicious. There was no kind of social life. Indeed, all the time I was at Salamanca, I was never once invited to anyone's house.

One by one the students returned, filling the corridors and the public rooms with cheerful noise. They were male students. It would have been unthinkable in the Spain of those days to have male and female students living under the same roof. The majority were Spaniards, but there were many from South America, particularly Venezuela, and these were better dressed and better off than the other students, a fact that caused some resentment. Some of them were mature students studying medicine, dentistry, law, engineering. They were in their early thirties, so I did not feel too out of place from the point of view of age, and at first no one took any notice of me, as if they thought I was just another mature student. I intended to study, and registered for courses on Spanish language and literature.

It was on the morning when registration began that I had my fatal encounter. I had registered for my classes, and Professor Ruiperez had shown me my lecture-rooms, where I had introduced myself to large classes of students, mixed men and women, with a preponderance of women, as is usual in foreign arts faculties. They seemed quite pleasant young people, who listened intently to my greetings, my introductions and my little jokes. I announced the titles of the textbooks we would be using. These included Jespersen's *Primer of the English Language*, a book I had not opened since my student days, and then only to shut it immediately, never in the intervening years opening it again. Now I should have to study the English language in earnest, keeping one chapter ahead of the students each week. I expected to hate it, but in fact I enjoyed my lectures on English language history and became an enthusiastic advocate of exercises in parsing, syntax and dictation – the very best test of listening comprehension. In literature I was going to offer both British and American authors, both prose and poetry, so that was no problem, though it did mean that I should have to read authors I disliked – Conrad, Hemingway, Woolf, Graham Greene, C.P. Snow – but I leavened this stodgy bunch with those I felt more in sympathy with, though they were not officially on the syllabus – Waugh, Firbank and Forster at their head.

Between two classes I went out into the beautiful gallery on the first floor, open to the cloisters and the courtyard below. I leant back against the stone balustrade and lit a cigarette. What happened next is something I shall never forget, and I have thought of that moment incessantly ever since it happened. Jordi was still very much on my mind. He knew my address at the university but had not written. His long silence worried me and made me frightened. Among the throngs of passing students I was thinking fondly of Jordi when someone who was obviously an American passed by, and our eyes met for a split second. He was a little shorter than myself, rather stocky with broad shoulders and that slightly duck-toed walk I find so attractive in athletic young men.

He was dressed casually in jeans and T-shirt and sweater, and his eyes in his sun-tanned face were very blue. He had not shaved for a day or two, and there was fair stubble on his cheeks and jaw. But the most remark-able thing about him was his hair, unusually long for those days, and abundant – of the palest, curly blond, exactly the moonlight platinum colour of my own hair when I was a little boy. I thought I detected a faint smile on his lips, but I did not smile back because my heart was in a turmoil. I thought he was the most beautiful creature I had ever seen – certainly the most beautiful male. *On the Waterfront* and *Rebel without a Cause* had appeared in 1954 and 1955, starring Marlon Brando and James Dean respectively, and I had fallen for them both. The person I saw that morning in the sunny gallery of the Palacio de Anaya reminded me of James Dean, not so much in physical appearance, though they were alike in presenting the essence of a certain youthful American type of the period, as in an instant personal magnetism, a cocksure and irresistible sexual charm. I was stunned. It was almost as if I had received a blow to the heart. He was the ideal of all the friends I had ever longed for, the elder brother that, as an only child, I could never hope for – though he was at least fifteen years younger than I, his assurance and absolute maleness made me feel like a younger brother by contrast. I returned to face my next class with wildly beating heart and in a state of utter confusion, of mingled joy, misery, hope and despair. Fortunately it was the first class in English literature, so I did no more than introduce myself and give the reading assignment for the next week. Then I dismissed the students and turned myself loose on the streets of Salamanca, under the burning sun of an Indian summer, trying to get my emotions under control.

Who was he? Why had he come to Salamanca? As far as I knew, he was the only American student in the Arts Faculty. At least I had seen no others. These were foolish and unnecessary questions anyhow, because I was sure such a divinity would never have anything to do with someone so much older and so much less good-looking than himself. All my life I have seen that type of person, handsome and self-assured, who knew he could have me just by crooking a finger and beckoning me to follow. They had caused me many heartaches and disillusions, and I was determined that it should never happen again. My readings in Zen, too, had shown me the folly of love, analysed it as an illusion among all the other illusions of this floating and temporary world, an emotion that by its very nature created suffering. For Zen teaches us that love breeds fear, and fear breeds hatred, and hatred breeds violence, in a never-ending, vicious circle. I was certainly not going to allow myself to suffer all that hell again. In any case there would be no occasion for that to happen. The person I had seen could have not the slightest interest in a beat-up old poet like me. Or so I thought. . . .

A day or two later I had a free morning, in which I intended to follow a class in Spanish language. When I got to the classroom, I found there were only about six students in the class, and we chatted idly until the lecturer arrived. The class started, and I was in the middle of reading aloud a prose passage from Galdós when the door opened and in walked the fair-haired god I had glimpsed in the gallery. My heart lurched and seemed to miss a beat, but I went on reading calmly, though the print was blurred. At the end of my reading, the lecturer asked the newcomer his name, and I heard his voice for the first time – a soft, warm American accent, with the rich, furry tone the English find so attractive. I stole a quick sidelong glance, and saw him turn his head at the same instant to look at me and give a faint smile. I turned my head away quickly, but I had had time to take in another feature – his rather sharp, small nose that looked as if it might have been broken in a boxing match. Then he gave his name, one of those Midwest American names, I guessed, probably originally Ukrainian, from Kansas or Montana.

The class dragged to its end. The other students stayed seated, all turned towards the newcomer, anxious to make his acquaintance, and I knew only too well that he could have any one of them he liked as his friend. He was one of those people who are instantly popular, and I felt sure he must know and relish his power over others, the power that only exceptional physical beauty can give, especially when it is allied with intelligence and strong animal magnetism. I felt very much the wall-flower as I crept out of the room without speaking to anyone, my books held tightly against my chest in a way which, I was to learn, was feminine and wrong for a man.

Something made me linger at the bottom of the grand staircase, near the bust of Unamuno, pretending to read some notices about student societies. After about five minutes I heard a voice behind me say: 'Hi, there! I'm Dana.' I turned round, knowing already who it was, with sinking heart. Yes, it was he, with a broad, sunny grin revealing perfectly white, rather small teeth in a friendly smile. I was British enough not to want to reveal my name to a stranger, so I just said, rather coldly: 'How are you?' A slight cloud on his smile, then it passed, and he asked: 'Where can you get a cup of coffee in this place?' I took him to a nearby café. I knew I was hooked. And I knew he knew it. But I was determined not to allow myself to be hauled in like a helpless fish as he reeled in his capable line. On that day we became friends, yet for a long time I kept my distance, afraid even to shake hands with him.

* * *

About twelve years later, when I was looking back on that meeting with Dana, I wrote the following poem:

Christ Rejected

In the life of the ugly,
the plain, the lonely, sometimes
a stranger of great beauty comes
with an ease almost holy.

They who were never loved,
who worshipped from afar with scorn
the beauty of the nobly-born
for a moment felt themselves moved.

How can it be? Who is he?
A stranger of great beauty,
with limbs perfect, smile all purity,
comes, and gives his love to me?

It is as they tell us of
Jesus, loving the halt and the dumb,
who, laying his hands upon lepers, did come
on earth, to give us of God's love.

How beautiful are thy feet with shoes,
the joints of thy thighs are as jewels,
the smell of thy nose like apples.
His legs are pillars of marble, his lips lilies . . .

The ugly believe, and know
that this is the love of Christ.
– But put an arm about the stranger's waist,
he melts away like snow.

The stranger of great beauty comes
and goes in lives that are plain,
bringing love, but also fear; hope, but pain.
Ours are the hearts, but his the drums.

None can resist him, who are not
as perfect as he, but those sad fools
who turn away as he comes with smiles,
and seek the comfort of the brothers he forgot.

(from *White Shadows, Black Shadows: Poems of Peace and War*)

I did indeed see him as a kind of Christ figure, perhaps as someone who had come to save me from myself, from my ineradicable loneliness of mind and soul. For despite all the passing lovers and the casual one-night stands or five-minute fantasies, I was always essentially alone, a solitary. Because of them, perhaps. Each fevered quest for a true love left me more adrift than ever. And long after Dana had left me, I still thought of him every day, and from time to time wrote poems about him, like this one which came to me after several viewings of a film that greatly disturbed and fascinated me, Pasolini's *Teorema*:

On Pasolini's Teorema

Glimpsed in a courtyard, a gallery, a cloister, a garden –
yes, we know him all too well,
that plausible young male demon,
unscrupulous messenger of hell, fair angel of our fate,
handsome, mysterious, understanding,
and inexplicably loving,
who comes one day from nowhere
and takes our hearts, our minds, our souls,
in exchange for – what?

For loneliness and desolation worse than anything we knew
before his coming; for a persistent sense of loss,
an ache of separation, a bitter, loveless isolation
in a world to which he brought
a temporary joy, a passing sweetness.
– But was it worth it? A brief time
of unforgettable pleasure in a life of pain?

For now the pain grows worse,
the isolation more intense,
and he who came and took our souls
when we least needed him
does not come now, now that we need him most.

Instead, a hollow shadow walks beside us
and haunts us day and night
with visions, madness, dreams
of impossible and unimaginable love
that, even if we knew it once again,
we should reject, knowing it untrue
and foul: and unavailing, hollow

as the words and smiles with which
he first approached us, come from nowhere,
to take us back there with him, and leave us there alone.

(from *Ecce Homo – My Pasolini: Poems and Translations*)

The star of that upsetting movie, Terence Stamp, reminded me of
Dana at his most perverse and enigmatic, half-god, half-demon, lover
and destroyer. Yet he was a kind of Christ figure, who entered the lives
of ordinary people in a rich, bored, bourgeois family, made love to them
all indifferently, both male and female, inexplicably, then left as mysteriously as he had come, deserting them in the hours of their greatest
need.

Sad to say, I had learnt to be suspicious of good-looking young men
who for no particular reason seemed to take a sudden interest in me. I
knew I was not attractive. Yet I had such a deep longing for the
romantic friendship, for the *ami amant*, for that 'someone to watch over
me', that I was often half tempted to succumb to the wiles of youths I
felt pretty sure were plain-clothes detectives from the Vice Squad or
undercover agents for MI5.

In that cold war atmosphere that was mingled with the chill dictatorship of Franco, I felt that the American 'innocents' of Henry James's
novels had become the sophisticated manipulators his Europeans had
once appeared to be. So Dana was my European exploiter; I was his
Daisy Miller.

This was how I regarded Dana from the start. What was behind his
apparent friendliness? At that first meeting he told me something about
himself. He had been a student of D.J. Enright at the Freie Universität
in West Berlin, and that information immediately put me on my guard.
Were the British literary mafia on my tracks again? Had Enright told
him about my appointment to Salamanca, and instructed his student to
infiltrate my literary and private life? There is always such intense
jealousy among members of the British literary establishment when
someone who is not 'one of us' is favoured by an appointment, a prize.
A few years later Enright came to see me when I was working in Kuala
Lumpur and he was Professor in Singapore. We met in the old Majestic
Hotel, where I was staying, and I asked him about his former student in
Berlin. Oh yes, Enright remembered him very well, and when I mentioned the name a puzzled look fleetingly crossed his face.

Dana had travelled from Berlin to Salamanca on an old motor bike
that was to play a large part in our lives both in Spain and in England.
He had put up at a cheap *pension*, the Hospedaje Lisboa ('Camas,

Comidas' – Rooms, Meals), where he had an even smaller room than the one assigned to me at the Colegio. He told me he had been studying poetry with Enright, and that he wrote poetry too. One of his poems had been published, he said, in *The New Yorker* by Howard Moss, the Poetry Editor, who – though I did not know it until Dana told me later – was a well-known homosexual. When I told him that Howard Moss – whom I never met but whose poetry I greatly admired – had already published several of my poems, Dana appeared surprised and a little put out. I could not remember ever having seen one of his poems in *The New Yorker*, but it was a magazine I saw only occasionally in those days. We started talking about poetry and about our favourite modern poets. We neither of us had much interest in contemporary British poets, but were united in our enthusiasm for Elizabeth Bishop, Marianne Moore, W.S. Merwin, Wallace Stevens, William Carlos Williams, Charles Reznikoff, Theodore Roethke and Richard Wilbur. He did not share my passion for Frank O'Hara, Robert Duncan, Denise Levertov (whom I had met in London and Paris), James Merrill and the early Pound; nor did I agree with his high estimate of Robert Lowell, Howard Nemerov and T.S. Eliot. But we both agreed that Robert Frost, Allen Ginsberg, Kenneth Rexroth and the rising tide of repetitive Beat poets were not worthy of consideration.

Dana did not ask to see my own poems, which at once made me suspect that he had some knowledge of them already. But he seemed anxious to show me his own poetry, with which he had filled several notebooks. I agreed to take a look at these efforts, and we arranged to meet next day after my morning lectures.

The first thing that struck me about Dana's poems was his incredibly tiny script, an almost minuscule handwriting that was often difficult to decipher. This queer way of writing filled me with foreboding, because it seemed to indicate a cold, self-centred nature, the reverse of the outgoing geniality he displayed to one and all. His writing looked crabbed. At the time I was interested in graphology, and had experimented with various styles of handwriting. My usual script looks like demented knitting, but among my manuscripts I am still surprised to find poem drafts and diary entries in neat italic calligraphy, painstakingly produced with a special calligraphic pen, or 'disguised' and backsloping hands, or the 'progressive' styles I had copied from my art students in Corsham. My multiple personality required multiple scripts, and from my study of graphology I tried to create individual scripts that conformed to the analyses of heavy down-strokes, 'pasty' loops and uncrossed 'ts': I was especially interested in 'pasty' strokes, which are supposed to indicate a rich sexuality, and disconnected letters, indicative of 'inspiration'. By adopting various graphological forms I hoped to fool the editors to whom I submitted my poems with a covering note, often under a false name. I was particularly keen to give my handwritten lines an upward slope – a sign of success, according to graphologists. But I also remembered that André Gide's letters to me had shown this tendency very clearly.

As for Dana's poems, at first I thought they were pretty feeble. We sat down together at a café table and went through some of them together. As we sat there in that noisy, smoke-filled place I was deeply conscious of his physical presence, so close and so disturbingly animal, almost electric in its restrained, pulsing sexuality. I tried to keep my eyes off his muscular thighs in their tight blue jeans, but as we bent over the café table it was easy to cast occasional surreptitious glances at his powerfully outlined sexual equipment under the much-rubbed fly, which seemed to be almost bursting at the seams. I was conscious, too, of his fine, tanned hand holding the pencil, and of the occasional play of warm breath from his mouth, wholesome as home-baked bread, though he was a heavy smoker – much heavier than I. It was I who introduced him to the Bisontes brand, a Spanish version of Lucky Strike, with a similar 'toasted' flavour. Today, having given up smoking about twenty years ago, I find it unbelievable that I should have smoked as many as ten cigarettes a day; but they were one of the things that helped to create a bond with Dana, something we could share. We would each bring out a packet of Bisontes with the bold bison emblem and a little box of those peculiarly Spanish waxed matches called *cerillos*. I remember the first time I offered Dana one of these cigarettes: he accepted one, and I then took one myself. But by the time I had got it out of the packet and placed it between my lips, he had lighted a *cerillo* and was holding it out to me in cupped hands, smiling above the soft yellow flame whose elvish reflection danced in his blue eyes. As we pored over his crippled handwriting I felt a steady heat coming from his body like an aura which slowly enveloped me and seemed to penetrate the very marrow of my bones. I knew I was being bewitched, laid under a spell so intensely personal, so thrilling, I did not have the power to resist it, or to judge if it were good or evil. From time to time I took in little details of his face: his small, neat ears round which the moonlight-blond locks curled; the light golden stubble round his laughing mouth; the rather dry, sensuous yet slightly cruel lips; the perfect column of the neck and throat emerging from his open shirt, unbuttoned to give me – was it deliberate? – a shadowy glimpse of a dark nipple in a hairless chest, the beautifully smooth breast of an ancient god. I felt myself falling, falling, as if for the first time, deeper and deeper into mysterious pits of passion and anxiety, longing and despair. He moved a leg to scratch – innocently? – his bulging crotch, and the knee just touched mine beneath the table, as if accidentally, and I felt as if I had been touched by lightning.

And all the time, in this turmoil of sexual ambiguities, we were talking about words, about poetry. I was trying my best to correct his style without imposing my own upon it, and he seemed genuinely grateful when I pointed out what I thought was a weakness in rhythm, a word to be changed, an image to be further developed, a form to be tightened or relaxed. . . . Yes, in poetry I felt I could stand at least as his equal, and indeed what started off that day as a sort of master-pupil relationship soon became a strange kind of poetic collaboration, in which we played equal parts. We would work on one of his poems, then turn to one of mine and work together on it. Then we started finding our common subjects and composing poems together, a double authorship. I stopped writing my own poems. He had taken them away from me and was making them his own. Our voices were mingled in poetry. But though he had taken all my poetic power, and gave me some of his in return, he still remained himself, his own man, his own poet. At times I felt I was just a kind of palimpsest, or a blackboard that could always be wiped clean to make room for his own work. Even my handwriting changed, and started to become small and stunted, like his. Yes, I was possessed, but happy to be so, if it allowed me to be with him, to feel him near me for a few hours every day. We became inseparable, and I was so proud to be seen walking with him, to enter a concert hall with him and let others see us sit down together at café and restaurant tables. His Spanish was almost non-existent, and he did not know how to study a foreign language, so I gave him lessons. I, too, was studying Spanish; but soon I had abandoned the classes for foreigners in the university and was studying on my own. The classes were so slow for me. Dana soon dropped out and came to study with me.

All this time I was trying to make a little money by doing hack-work translations of French and German children's stories. I translated Schiller's *Don Carlos* and revised my version of Heinrich von Kleist's *Prinz von Homburg* for Eric Bentley's anthology of classic German theatre, for which I was paid a pittance. Dana got an allowance from home: his father was a government official; his mother worked as a teacher – she sent him wads of onion-skin typing paper that were then unobtainable in Europe, and also drugs, bottles of Dexedrine.

Because the cafés were so noisy and crowded, we had started working on our poems in my room at the Colegio. And because I had only one chair, we used to sit on the edge of the hard, narrow bed and draw up the table so that we could write on it together. One day, after we had been working together all afternoon without much success, Dana without warning lay back on the bed, his head on the pillow. 'Lie down and relax,' he told me. In absolute terror, I lay down beside him. On that narrow bed we were so close together. I did not dare move, and yet I did: I put my hand on his thigh, and slowly moved it up towards the centre of my desire. After a moment he gently took my hand and moved it away, saying nothing. We lay there silently, then he got up and left the room, leaving me lying there in an agony of frustration and guilt, furious with myself for having given way, yet curiously glad I had finally done so.

Dana did not reappear for a few days, and during that time I felt I was going mad. I wandered the streets of Salamanca, hoping to run into him. I went to our favourite cafés, but no one had seen him. At night I would stand on the pavement opposite the Hospedaje Lisboa and look up at his window. Sometimes it was lighted, and I would wait there, watching until the light went off, usually long past midnight. Then I knew he was writing poetry alone, without me, and that hurt me to the depths of my being.

Among the unpublished poems I wrote at that time there is one that tries to express my feelings of loneliness and abandonment by my beautiful god. I wrote it one late evening, sitting at my window, looking out into the rainy darkness of autumn and at the great black bulk of the cathedral:

> The rain beats on the window
> As the bells beat down the dark.
> I wonder where you are, and if
> You walk in rain, or under stars.
>
> The bells beat into my memory
> The days and nights we knew
> In this one room, among the city's
> Mysteries of stone. To you
>
> I send this whispered message
> Through the fastnesses of wind and rain –
> To you, whose face begins to fade,
> And hear your voice again.
>
> Stay true to our belief
> In one another and our singular art.
> If the rain beats for me, it beats
> For both of us. I hear it falling in your heart.

The bell-laden streets were haunted by the fume of roasting chestnuts. Now whenever I smell roasted chestnuts in Shijo-dori in Kyoto, or in Zürich Hauptbahnhof, I remember that aching void in my life.

* * *

But after all you came back one day, and it all started again. You were unchanged. You made no reference to what had happened. You did not tell me what you had been doing, or where you had been, and you were not interested in whatever I might have been doing. You were joyous and friendly and warm, and full of your own poems. You had come back to me in order to show me your poems: there was no one else to whom you could show them. That at least was something, something I could cling to, something I could use to keep you close to me. My poetry had never been of so much practical use to me before. I was half proud, half ashamed to be using it in this way. No wonder it kept deserting me! But just to have you near me I was willing to give it all to you.

Your second-hand motor bike was always breaking down. One day, with me clinging to you – what rapture! – on the pillion, we made a trip to Zamora, a small medieval city to the north of Salamanca. It was one of those heavenly, crisp autumn days, all sunny chills and skies of broken clouds whose grotesque shadows went moving slowly over the bare brown earth of the fields and hills. You were always a late riser, quite unlike me, so we did not start on this little adventure until after lunch. So we were late in returning, and night fell when we were only half-way home. The road was deserted and we were throbbing along at a moderate pace when suddenly the engine sputtered and stopped. I had not the first notion of mechanics, but you with your capable hands worked on the machine until, after running with it, pushing it along, we were able to make the engine tick over again. We got on, and started off again through the lonely night, in pitch darkness, not a house or a lantern to be seen. Then after a few miles the engine stopped again. Again we worked on it and pushed hard, and again got it to start, jumped on before it changed its mind and sped away. This happened about a dozen times. Finally the engine gave up the ghost completely and nothing could persuade it to start again. We were left in the middle of nowhere. So we took turns in pushing the bike along. You wanted to abandon it by the side of the road, but I made you push it on, with myself taking short spells of pushing. I was no match for your proud, muscular strength: after a few yards I was exhausted, and you would take over, shoving the burden along with tireless energy. At last, in the far distance, we glimpsed the first lights of Salamanca. From there the road was downhill, so we were able to coast noiselessly down into the sleeping suburbs, then dismount and push the bike into the city centre. It was an experience that bound us more closely than ever.

I had been studying a guide-book to Zamora before we left. (Dana would never dream of doing such a thing – he would just take off into the void and somehow find his way around.) In the book I found a Spanish proverb that runs, *No se ganó Zamora en una hora* – 'Zamora isn't reached in an hour', which is the equivalent of our 'Rome wasn't built in a day'. We learnt that by our own experience.

Our friendship had been noticed, as I had hoped it would be, for I was so proud of having a friend. The atmosphere in the college was becoming strained, and mealtimes in the refectory were agony. One Sunday afternoon, when Dana and I were sitting on the edge of the bed working over versions of various poems, the door, which we always left unlocked, suddenly burst open and a group of surly-looking students entered, led by a big bully who was not Spanish but Venezuelan. We looked up from our papers in surprise. I felt afraid. The group strode over to our table in a menacing way, and the Venezuelan growled: 'Why are you always together? What are you doing? Why is he here? He does not belong to this college!'

I replied that we were studying and writing, a fact that was obvious from the books, dictionaries and papers scattered over the table and the bed. With sulky faces, the students turned to go. But the Venezuelan turned at the door and ordered us to come downstairs and drink with them. I did not want to go, but Dana said we had better do as they asked. So we spent the whole afternoon in aimless beer-drinking and student ragging, singing student songs to stamping feet and clapping hands. It was not at all my idea of pleasure, but I did it for Dana's sake. Unlike me, he at once felt at home in that charged, aggressive, almost militaristic atmosphere, joined heartily in the drinking and singing, and soon had all the students on his side, which was fortunate for me, because *el Americano*'s prestige deflected a terrible submerged violence and hatred that might well have done me harm. I was astonished, and a little dismayed, by the ease with which Dana entered into the spirit of things, giving Indian war-whoops and clowning and laughing in a way I thought was rather contemptible. But perhaps he was doing it to save me? Or was it just another side of his character I had not seen before, but that I may have suspected was always there? Those students were all right-wing, fascist bullies, ardent supporters of Franco and his regime. They were out to destroy me, I was sure. So a few days later I moved to an hotel, the Hotel España (*solo apartamentos*) on the Plaza España. I had an apartment on the third floor, overlooking the square and the end of the Avenida Jose Antonio de Rivera round which I would watch Dana coming to join me for another afternoon of poetry.

Day after day, night after night, we spent sitting together at my table in that apartment. Now we did not have to sit on the edge of the bed – a much wider bed – because there were two chairs, and I had my own shower and facilities for making coffee and snacks. Now that I had left the college dormitory I used to look fearfully from time to time out of my window, expecting to see that gang of fascist students coming to beat me up. One day when I went to give my language class at the university I found the word *maricone* (queer) chalked in large Gothic letters on the blackboard. I pretended not to notice it, and, as the students listened with bated breath, instructed them to turn to page thirty in Jespersen. I gave a good class: there is nothing like teaching well for making one forget oneself and one's petty troubles. I did not wipe the offending word off the blackboard, but as I was packing up my books and papers at the end of the class, a girl got up and without a word erased it, to a scattering of applause. I did not tell Dana about it.

But I did tell him about Jordi. I do not remember now how or why I did so, because despite my infatuation I still sometimes thought Dana was a Franco spy, or from the FBI or the CIA or even the CID or the KGB. Then I would tell myself such ideas were unreasonable: why would an American half-poet want to betray me to any government agency? It was absurd. But I knew that absurder things had happened in America and Britain – and in Spain. When I told Dana about Jordi, he said something I found revealing: 'I like working men too.' What exactly did that imply? Was he, too, after all, as I half suspected, a bisexual? He had already told me about his girl-friend, an American student of modern dance in West Berlin. But he had also hinted at a sexual relationship with one of his American university professors, and with the editor of a certain American music magazine, with whom he had spent a vacation in Haiti. He showed me photographs of them together in a boat there, on a beach, in a restaurant. But as far as I knew, he had no other friends in Salamanca, though he had only to lift his little finger and both men and women would have come running at his bidding.

He was unfailingly modest in behaviour and appearance, though his luxuriant hair used to excite the cupidity of the two hairdressers in the little barber-shop opposite the entrance to the Hospidaje Lisboa. I was letting my own hair grow too. The barbers would playfully wave to us as we went by, motioning towards their empty chairs.

I wished I had said nothing about Jordi. At times I would wake up in the night, streaming with sweat, from a nightmare in which I relived that terrifying night in Valladolid. I shall never forget Jordi's face, his rueful smile, his fatalistic shrug as he was pushed into the car. At times of the greatest mental stress I would wander into some cool church and try to pray in the dimness scented by peasant sweat, cold candle-grease and stale incense. Sometimes Dana would come and sit with me on the hard little chairs. Sometimes I would sit in the deserted church of San Martin, a small twelfth-century romanesque building just off the Plaza Mayor, on the Plaza Poeta Iglesias. At other times I went into the much larger, colder Clerecia and watched the glib little gilt pendulum of an old-fashioned wall-clock next to the altar silently swinging my pain away. I gave alms to all the blind beggars, lit candles without believing at all in their efficacy. I just wanted to add a little light to illuminate the darkness of my soul. When we came out of the Clerecia, after dipping hands in the holy water stoup and placing a drop on each other's brows, as we had seen the *novios* and *novias* do (the boy on entering a church would dip his hand in the water and transfer a drop to his fiancée's fingertip so that they could cross themselves in unison), we would go into La Casa de las Conchas next to the Clerecia, with elaborate wrought-iron window-grilles and its tranquil courtyard, and sit there quietly for a while, thinking of the next poem, or of the one we were working on. It was in this splendid fifteenth-century monument to the high architectural taste of the Catholic sovereigns that I read a message written by a fifteenth-century schoolboy on his classroom wall: *Aquí supo lo que es bueno, y lo que es malo,/ Lo que es dulce, y lo que es amaro* (Here I had knowledge of what is good, and of what is bad,/ Of what is sweet, and of what is bitter). It seemed to apply to my life in Spain.

The ornately decorated and sculptured churches were parables and sermons in honey-coloured stone, miraculously preserved. Like the French cathedrals, they were Bibles for those who could not read. One of our poems was about the great carved tympanum over the main door of the Catedral Nueva, an incredibly detailed, deeply undercarved Nativity in two tall arched panels. A typed version tells me the poem was written in December 1957. I had written to Joe Ackerley about Dana, and how we were writing poems together, and he asked to see some examples of this unusual collaboration. I sent him our Christmas poem, 'Adoration of the Shepherds and the Kings' (Puerta del Perdón, Salamanca), which he printed in the 19 December issue, his 1957 Christmas number:

> Under the cathedral's leaning cliff, the caves
> Of darkness slam their doors. Above, in high relief,
> Twin arches, flocked with angels, open up their graves

Of rosy stone upon the gospel's double leaf,
Where kings and shepherds offer gifts to their belief.

Below some angels carolling an arch, the star
Steps out in front of formal clouds,
To light a tardy shepherd down the stable's far,
Rooftopping hill into the other panel's night –
With a curly dog, two camels and three trees in sight.

* * *

Off to the manger – to the boy whose little sleep
Is carved of brighter stone that leaves the starlight dim –
The shepherds run: one brings a basket, one a sheep
That tumbles round the wicker cot; one in the brim
Of his dumpled hat is kneeling; another kneels with him.

Behind them, dumbstruck in a wattled stall,
A donkey breathes into their frosted hair;
A baffled ox has horned in through the wall.
The mother kneels and tends the infant air
That He has warmed by lying naked there.

* * *

Inside the other arch, three wise, outlandish kings,
Extravagantly groomed, are kneeling to adore
A child, the lodestone of their wanderings,
With gold and frankincense and myrrh.
They cast a crown before him on the briared floor.

Joseph to the background lends an honest charm.
A page is peeping round his master at the Son
Of Man, whose mother stands Him in her arm.
– Michael, geared for battle, guards the little one,
Whose clouds of angels blaze his star into a sun.

It was something we could barely understand, but I had a growing feeling that without my love the whole project would collapse. It was love that kept me going; it was ambition to be a poet that fuelled Dana's labour and yoked it with mine. At the same time I think there was a certain kind of love – detached but concerned – in the background of all he did, a love that steadily grew, without display, without spoken devotion; and I, too, never spoke of 'love'. I realized I just had to accept him for what he was, and when I learnt to do that, he did the same to me

– accepted me without question, in all my imperfection, in all that made me unworthy of him.

Another poem that I have dated in the typescript 'December, 1957, Plaza de Anaya, Salamanca', is one I was able to write for myself, and that I never showed to Dana. It was just about the last poem I wrote on my own for the next six months or so; it is called 'Believing Is Seeing', and it was also about a carving, the sculpture illustrating the miracle of Christ healing the blind man:

> In this little park, beneath the blind man's door
> That made our separate visions one,
> I walk again alone, and all is dark.
> I am afraid to find belief has gone.
>
> In this moment, I try to see,
> But cannot. Light is set apart
> From the reality we both restored
> To one another. I am blinded to the heart.
>
> Each moment that once brought me
> To yourself abstracts me more and more.
> I stare dumbly from behind a glass
> At snow falling down the blinded door.
>
> Pray now no more for you and me,
> But only for that one identity
> We give each other. Let us believe
> Its miracle will always make us see.
>
> In the little park beneath the blind man's door
> That blessed us with the vision faith had won,
> The day now is wrapped in snow,
> And it is brighter than the sun.

I still recognize that poem as being utterly my own. In our Nativity poem, I can still, thirty years later, recognize the contributions made by Dana to the poem, and those that are mine. Dana's words and phrases are unmistakable; they have that slightly cute, American ring: 'Twin arches, flocked with angels', 'some angels carolling an arch', 'a tardy shepherd', 'the star steps out', 'a curly dog', and so on. The inherent American way with words is everywhere evident.

That poem, 'Believing Is Seeing,' refers to one of the first poems we wrote together. It was one about another exquisitely detailed carving on a cathedral door, the Portada de Ramos – the Palm Sunday Doorway. I did not date the typed copy I made – for Dana could not or would not type, and after we had finished a poem to our common satisfaction, I had to type it out while he rested on the bed – but I am fairly certain it was written soon after I met Dana in that Spanish class for foreigners, which I have noted in my 1957 Letts Diary: 'Wednesday, October 16. Moon's last quarter. Met Dana in class.' So here is our first poem written in collaboration:

Portada de Ramos

Here in a country where so many men are blind,
We pass a daily miracle performed in stone:
Followed by the three disciples he loved best,
And bridling his ass beneath a wall and by a bridge,
Christ gentles out of stone into the arc of sight.
Two palm trees frond the background of the day.

A halo rich with rust is lofted round the heads
Of James and John and Peter. Thinned by time, the rings
Still dip and float above their brows, with grace
That perfectly restores their master's perished crown.
His robes are loosely folded in the clouding stone.
His missing hand is lifted and its blessing stays.

A crowd of two or three lay down their cloaks
And strew palm branches beneath the donkey's hooves.
In a corner by a bridge, Zacchaeus climbs a tree
To match the fame of Jesus with his face.
Two boys, perched upon a wall, surprise
A gesture and believe the miracle.

A shaft of metal weaves the light of Jesus' eyes
Into the blind man's stony gaze and makes it His,
A sight that lets the others see across the dark
Their faces lifted to the light. Their arms are stayed
Between the questioning and answering of faith
That still projects itself along the rusting shaft.

The blind may never see this proof of hope.
They cannot find it here in stone as soft as sand
Whose dusty roses shroud the scene and shell their eyes.
They count their steps along the darkened streets,
Fumbling a lottery of falling leaves, and crying to the stones
Their message for the day, which is today.

That last line was a memory of all the blind lottery-ticket sellers we had heard crying 'Para hoy! Para hoy!' Our ideas about faith were taken from my readings of Unamuno, and in this poem from one of the essays, 'Faith, Hope and Charity', from *The Tragic Sense of Life*: 'A faith that does not doubt is a dead faith.' This was one of the unequivocal statements that aroused in 1913 the ire of the traditionalist clergy of Spain. I preferred Paul Delvaux's macabre vision of the Crucifixion.

In my diary, some time after our first meeting, I wrote the date of Dana's birthday. He was a Libra, or the Balance, the seventh sign of the Zodiac whose name indicates that day and night, being of equal length, are being weighed 'in the balance'. It is an autumnal sign and one in which the 'balance' might be tipped one way or another, and in sexuality could hover between male and female, with one sexual scale dipping, then the other rising obediently and almost passively, distantly, independently, in an alternation of identities and desires that I knew so well. Dana was always balanced between the two, whereas I would fluctuate for long periods – a year or two in the male, a year or two in the female scale, with often sharp and distressing adjustments of behaviour and character. I always thought that my Taurean nature – though on the cusp with Aries, looking forward towards another double-image sign, Gemini, which made for imbalance – was far from typical; but certainly the bull was well and truly there in my strong sexuality. Dana was steadily centred right in the middle of Libra, and so could be regarded as a perfectly balanced human being, with a true equivalence of male and female, physical and intellectual, animal and spiritual, and I think it was from this delicate balance, never upset, that his magnetic force of personality derived. I secretly longed to upset his balance but never succeeded, except in the making of poetry, in which he was compelled to tilt towards me.

Another diary entry, in the same black ink, written with my calligraphic pen, was for 2 November: 'Day of the poem "Fall, a Flock of Sheep, a Roman Bridge".' This was the first poem Dana showed me, and one of the first I reworked with him. My typed version is signed with our pseudonym. In the 'Notes' under the same date I have written something I always wanted to remember: 'The walk at night. Dana. Viva! Todos Diffuntos (All Saints).' There is also the name Angel Kirvor, which was the first pseudonym we thought of for our combined poems. After we finished that poem, late in the evening of 2 November, we went walking through the streets of Salamanca for most of the night, for the poem had persuaded us that something remarkable was really happening to us, that some kind of poetic grace had been bestowed upon us. We had been careful until then not to think that way. But this poem seemed to us incontrovertible proof of our poetic twinship.

*   *   *

And we went on writing poems, in that luxuriant air of mingled spirituality and sexual anguish. Dana always sat with his legs wide apart, as if inviting the touch of eyes, if not hands. I was sure he knew I could barely contain myself or restrain my trembling fingers that longed to run their tips along the insides of those meaty thighs that were spreadeagled enticingly over the edge of his seat.

He had few clothes – a 'good suit' of dark-blue lightweight dacron that was the badge of every American in those days, a couple of shirts, a long, shapeless tweed overcoat of German origin he wore when it got colder. Then there were those brown corduroys and blue jeans: the very seams of his old, faded pants enraptured me, seeming to underscore the seductive outlines of his lower frame, running from the back of his thick leather belt down along that mysterious, rich intercrural channel, and coming out at the other end of the tunnel at the tense crossroads orienting the scrotum's heavy bag with its blissful raphe, or subtly defining and underlining the inside and outside of the long, smooth thighs and the stocky, bulgy, athletic calves. He had been a very successful amateur boxer, and sometimes would try to relieve our tension by sparring with me, teaching me basic moves of a sport I knew nothing about and instinctively detested. But as I tried to follow his instructions, keeping my fists up and my chin tucked in and learning a new kind of dance on the balls of my feet, the sight of his bare, hairless chest, so brown and muscular, would suddenly fill me with more than muscular weakness, and I felt I would collapse, not under the playful blows he landed on my discombobulated body, but under the sheer spell of his magnificence. I never landed a single blow on those perfect shoulders, that sun-tanned thorax, that laughing, mocking, taunting face; but I was only too happy when he slipped through my feeble defences and gently pummelled me all over with his bare hands, until my all-too-vulnerable defence degenerated into a giggling slapping match.

He was fully aware, I now realize, of my absorbed interest in his loose-limbed, perfectly proportioned body, its stocky compactness, and exploited my obsession, my helpless longing to touch the untouchable. As we spent hour after hour sitting at our work-table, all curtains drawn to intensify our concentration beneath the old-fashioned fringed standard lamp, he would from time to time ease his buttocks and balls, pulling and tugging on the firm seams of the taut, well-worn jeans or the well-rubbed brown needle cords, scratching and stroking himself idly, as if unselfconsciously in the most private places with those delicate fingers with the bitten nails and his big, warm palms. Was he just a common cock-tease, I would wonder as I suggested a new word, broke an overlong line, or did he sometimes really desire a more intimate contact? If so, he never gave any definite sign of it.

All through that October and November, in my claustrophobic college room or in my dark-curtained hotel apartment, I grew to desire more of him than just his presence at my side as we wrote. Sometimes I would try to withhold my gift of words as the only way I could convey to him that he was withholding something I needed as badly as he needed my poetic ability. At once he would sense my withdrawal, and was sad and silent for a while. He would go out for a walk, leaving me alone for an hour, then return full of high spirits, shouting from the doorway: 'Back on form now?' Was he taking drugs? If so, he concealed it from me. But sometimes he seemed unnaturally flushed and lively – and it was not with drink. Was it marijuana, which he told me he had smoked? Or something more sinister? The very idea of taking drugs disgusted me. As I had told Dr Grey Walter, a poet is born 'high'. He needs at all times to be in full possession of his faculties, or that extra, unpredictable poetic thrust would never declare itself – that heart-lifting boost that rockets mere words into the outer spaces of true poetry.

I loved working with Dana, and yet as time went by and we produced more and more collaborative poems I began to long to get my own poetic and personal identities back. From the very first day I saw him I began writing poems to him that later grouped themselves into the sequence entitled 'Suite Salmantina' which, with other poems about Spain, forms the central part of my collection called *The Prodigal Son: Poems 1956–1959*. They were not all written at the same time, or in that order: I had to keep struggling to write my own work as Dana's poetic demands became more and more insistent.

TURNING IT ALL TO POETRY

The satisfied, the happy, do not love; they fall asleep in habit, near neighbour to annihilation.

Miguel de Unamuno, THE TRAGIC SENSE OF LIFE

'I'll turn it all to poetry!'

Myself, when threatened with arrest by the British police

Like Unamuno, I am all contradictions. Poetry is my only defence against a world I detest and celebrate, my only weapon against a life I love and abominate. Being bisexual is a simple duality. But to have a multiple personality, in which one self may suddenly be overthrown by another and one mind may be torn in several different directions is sometimes so intolerable, I long for extinction. But would even physical evaporation bring peace to warring souls and contradictory afterlives? I doubt it.

My infatuation with Dana did, however, bring a certain simplicity to my existence. As I became more and more obsessed by him, and as he absorbed more and more of my being, all else seemed to start retreating into a permanent, one-dimensional background, against which only he and I stood out as more than stick figures. We had made our own Garden of Eden.

I wrote dutifully to my parents every week. I kept in touch with Joe – there were no other friends. But they appeared to me as if seen through the wrong end of a telescope, muted and unreal. Students, colleagues, passers-by all faded into deceptive distances. Even Jordi and his knife withdrew slowly from my consciousness. All was excluded by this all-exclusive passion. All those I had loved in the past – Richard, Marjorie, Alain, Madeleine, Leo, Muriel, Alan, Sandro, Erich, Jordi – all loved more or less in vain, hopelessly – were now without substance or meaning.

I could see this condition coming upon me relentlessly from the first moment Dana cast his eyes upon me: he was another who knew how to use the power of the evil eye, almost casually, to enchant total strangers. Against his magnetic forces, my own 'evil' eye, which had anyhow long since started to abandon me, could put up no resistance.

After my first sight of him that sunny autumn morning in the gallery of the courtyard in the Palacio de Anaya, his face haunted me all day, and I dreamt of him during the night – a long, ecstatic dream of such acute sensual pleasure I woke up aching and exhausted by too much bliss. The dawn was just breaking. I got up and, sitting at my window, looked out over the still-sleeping city, and wrote my first poem to this unknown god:

> The dawn strikes up its music in the dark.
> Behind the black cathedrals of the square
> Cocks shout, and wake the grumbling dogs.
> Great domes compose their masses on the air.
>
> A flock of doves, cast from the breeze's hand,
> Crockets a pinnacle with wings on wings.
> Bells beat at the morning stars like fans,
> And in between their silence rings.
>
> Street-lamps still illuminate
> Each level, long façade.
> But the roofs' inventive arabesques
> Turn black against a sky of jade.
>
> Translucencies are brushed with clouds
> And furred with feathers, with the bloom
> Of dark and fronded trees.
> The city breathes, and flows into my room.
>
> I lean from a window like a statue from a wall,
> And dip my face into the fountains of the east.
> A chimney slowly hangs out smoke.
> My eyes are brimmed with the horizon's feast.
>
> Now jade is blue: grey distances are slashed with red;
> The fretted spires are pierced with white.
> – I look towards these preparations for the sun,
> And see your face lift from its dream of night.

The night before, I had gone for a long, lonely walk along the banks of the Tormes, crossing and recrossing the Roman bridge, hoping against hope that I might somehow find you also walking there. But all was deserted, and I took comfort from a star:

The first star, liquid Sirius,
Drips in the river's glass its slender
Chandelier. Its lustre, long as light,
Drops brimming candles deep
Into the melting mirrors of the night.

A swimming creature undulates across the sky, and shakes
The limpid evening to a pulse of cool desire,
A weeping star that mends itself in time
With lost light that trembles round
The bend of space, and barely breaks.

The next day the unbelievable happened, and you entered the
Spanish class for foreigners. I heard your name for the first time. And at
the end of the class, near the bust of Unamuno, I heard your voice
calling to me for the first time. We went to that café with the tourist
postcards rattling on their metal lattices in the dusty wind, on the street
called Libreros. We talked for the first time about poetry, poets and our
own poems:

Your eyes first looked into these words
With that steady honesty you give
To cats and ballads, food and birds,
To fields and faces, sticks and stones,
And only then they seemed to live:
I felt your body in my flesh and bones.

Was it a case of demonic possession? I began to think it must be, for
every hour of my waking and sleeping was occupied by thoughts and
images of you, in every expected and unexpected situation and attitude.
In my day-dreams and nightmares you were always clothed in those
washed-out jeans: I can still see their frayed, ravelled seams with their
bleached, raggy threads softened by countless abrasions and grindings,
the frazzled button-holes, the worn buttons showing the cheap metal
underneath. I often saw you sprawling on the floor or on a park bench, a
joyous sunburst of creases radiating from your abandoned crotch, your
jumping fly. But mostly I imagined you asleep, left utterly to yourself in
a situation where my own absence from your life did not matter:

I dream of you asleep:
A contained sweetness,
Warm, and full, and deep.

I think of your completeness,
And the way you place
A gentle strength, a neatness

In a line that orders grace
With wildness; the unexpected break
Of phrase that lights your face,

The seafarer's eyes that shake
Their pale blue fires on the prow
Of poetry, your sparkling wake.

We were looking forward to the vacation, to Christmas, to what you called 'New Year's'. Secretly I was planning to take you home with me to show to my parents. I had already written to them about you, in guarded terms, and their lack of response to my enthusiasms in the way of friends never discouraged me. I had learnt, however, never to tell them much, to keep the best parts hidden, as indeed I often had to. But with you, there was nothing to hide – at least so far. We were 'just good friends', however much I wished we could be more than that. The closest I ever got to you was when we went for a spin on your motor bike, with me like a ravished flapper on the pillion, legitimately clinging to your lissom waist, to those two wonderful hip-bones I loved to hold, as if they were the very hinges of heaven, whose wind blew your hair back into my ecstatic face:

Each day now is Christmas,
With the present of the day before
Still with me, past being broken,
And the present day's own gift
Still to be given and received.

Love gives each morning's air,
Cleansed by the sun's wide sweeps of blue,
A breath of celebration, spicy
As the wind-thrown fragrance of your hair,
The very essence that is only you.

The 'presents' and the 'gifts' were those we exchanged daily when we were writing poetry together – presents which, unlike those of my childhood, did not break as soon as touched. Life had become spiced by my longing, by the sheer happiness of knowing I would see you that morning, that night, next day:

At five of the stars I wake
On a rare October morning,
And a poem overflows
My candid dark.

I keep my eyes closed,
Happy, pretending sleep,
With a gift in my head for you,
Another in my heart.

Suddenly both are one.
I am writing with open eyes
The words I dreamed for you,
As if the familiar were new.

The paper warms to them
And to my flowing hand
With the untidy fire
Of the bed I burned to leave.

Looking to where the dark
Shelters the house in which you lie,
I feel my heart beat like a boy's
On Christmas morning, in a house of toys.

After I moved to my apartment in the Hotel España I kept hoping I might be able to persuade you to come and share it, or at least to take the one next to mine, which was empty. But you always evaded this question, saying your allowance from home would not stretch to paying the extra rent. And you seemed to have become attached to that awful little room in the Hospedaje Lisboa. I think I obscurely felt relief that I would continue to live alone, to have at least a few hours of the day and night when I could try to regain one of my mixed-up selves. For I was still struggling in the web you had woven, like a helpless insect wanting to escape, yet hypnotized into acquiescence and adoration by the spider's malefic eyes and enveloping threads, wound slowly one by one round my resistless mind:

Love blinds, but makes me see
Life's folly clear as day.
My self has gone away from me
And nothing come to stay.
Only the love I flee
Is true, and will not go away.

I was convinced of one thing: of the purity and truth of my love for you. Then why did I want to run away from it? There were bitter memories of broken love for Alan, a good-looking Londoner I had fallen for while I was still at Madame Sheba's. With her penetrating instinct she did not like him, and was so angry with me for, as she said, 'wasting myself upon such rubbish', that in the end she turned me out of my room and I went to live in a tiny, freezing attic in a house in Morningside Crescent owned by a friend of hers, a white woman. I was very unhappy there, away from the love and warmth Madame had always given me, and the love affair that accompanied the change soon turned cold: Alan exhibited a certain kind of treachery, casually throwing me over for someone else who 'was better in bed'. It was a common experience for me to fall in love with love and then be led up the garden path, only to be rejected and mocked. That affair left a permanent scar on my heart and I was afraid of reopening it. So I clung to the concept of ideal love for you, at the same time hoping for the even more impossibly ideal physical fulfilment and completion that would seal our closeness for ever. Each time I saw you coming dancing towards me along a sunny street, moving lightly on your toes like a boxer, with your slightly duck-toed run that I, a turned-out-toes walker, found so male and so sexy, my heart jumped in my throat and I wanted to run towards you and throw myself into your arms. But we never even walked arm-in-arm, as was the accepted way for conventional Spanish male friends or accomplices like the black-glassed Falangists. I struggled to keep my love pure, remembering at the same time something Madeleine had told me and that Rena was to repeat: 'What you need, Jimi, is the love of a bad woman.' Well, I did find that, and the love of bad men, too, but it made no difference. I was an incurable romantic and yearned for a romantic friendship before it would be too late, for I believed in those days that romantic friendship was possible only in youth. So I strove to keep our relationship 'true' – on a true course:

> True love alone can write
> Because it asks no more
> Than its undemanding light
> To burn out passion's core
> Of self, with care for others' sight.
>
> A pure flame burns my snow.
> I melt and freeze,
> But I am water, too, and flow,
> To give my driven spirit ease,

In a single tear, that is the joy I know.

My hand runs like a delta through
These maps my soundings make.
Although I draw them all for you,
And keep a lighthouse for your sake,
All men may use them, for my love is true.

From time to time, walking in the crowded arcades of the Plaza
Mayor, my heart would miss a beat as I fancied I saw Jordi mingling
with all those similar dark heads and slender figures. Something about
the back of a man's neck would remind me of him. I have always felt
that character is most clearly expressed in the back of a person's head,
and especially in the nape. From a swift glance at the back of a person's
head I can at once estimate the intelligence and sexuality of that person.
For me, intelligence and sexuality go together, and it is usually with the
intelligence in a person's eyes that I first fall in love. Jordi's head was set
beautifully on his broad shoulders, and there was something in the way
he held his neck to support that head which was unmistakably intelligent
and sexy. I like big heads that are flat at the back, not pointed, and for
that reason in recent years it is Korean males who have attracted me
most, with their rich, straight black hair laid perpendicularly on that
square-backed skull – always, to me, the sign of a male good at
mathematics, the sexiest science. There were many heads like that in
Spain, and I would follow outstanding examples gazing in admiration at
that nape, that neck, that flat-backed skull, until the head turned and let
me glimpse the face, which was never disappointing. But each time my
heart stood still, expecting to find Jordi: yet it was never he. One short
poem in 'Suite Salmantina' applies to both you and Jordi:

Instead of a despair, believe
True love is never lost.
Though no hand will receive
Its foolish gift, its ghost
Will not go wandering without release
Along the rivers of the midnight air.

Although the body finds no peace,
True love is in the spirit's care,
And is not wasted in a selfish sigh.
– This one truth I find in you
Is gathered by the waters and the sky,
And is not lost, because my love is true.

Most of the square-skulled men I followed in this way in the streets turned out to have very macho faces, conventionally handsome, proud, even disdainful, as if they felt they alone were the lords and masters of the earth. That always disappointed me. I have never cared much for men who are all man: they are the ones who smugly believe they must be irresistible to me, and take elaborately cautious steps to protect their priceless male virginity from what they seem to imagine will be my marauding hands. I can understand so well what women feel when they are subjected to a male-dominated society – an almost intolerable urge to scream at those smirking, swanking Don Juans who think no woman can resist them. I prefer men who have some feminine tact and delicacy and sensitivity, and women who have some of the better masculine qualities – tenderness, protectiveness, a good brain and a humorous way of dealing with all the practical impossibilities of life. And I could sense this feminine quality in you. Sometimes I even thought of you as one of my favourite fictional heroines, Maggie Tulliver in *The Mill on the Floss*, while I was Philip Waken, though not such a limp type. It was the sort of relationship I had with my earliest girl-love, the tomboy Isa, when I was about three or four years old, described in *The Only Child*. Then our relationship to each other would change, and you would be a more boyish Philip Waken, and I a less hoydenish Maggie. Willa Cather's *My Antonia*, which along with her other novels I was absorbing with great delight at this period, provided another couple with whom to identify, Antonia and Jim Burden, and I kept switching sides with these characters also. I wanted so much to put into words, in a novel or a play, all that you and I felt for one another, not just to love love but to inscribe it as George Eliot and Willa Cather had done. So I felt inexpressible gratitude to you for giving me the support and care of that relationship, however attenuated it appeared to me at times:

> You are the only ghost
> I ever truly loved,
> Because your presence moved
> My heart with more than lust.

> With not a single touch
> And with no human kiss
> You brought my life to this
> Wild calm that holds so much.

> Not only gaiety and trust
> I learnt from your repose,
> But that true passion grows,

Like art, because it must.

O, with a single look
I felt the darkness change.
And it was nothing strange:
The opening of a book.

In the brightness of the sun
You bring a moonlit air.
– No ghost had ever gifts as rare,
Or love more substance, than this only one.

And always, when we were apart, I kept bringing you beside me in my imagination, in the poems I was writing all alone, writing for you as well as for myself:

I seem to hear you stir, as if
You were only in the other room.
Distance has paper walls.
The air between us
Is your breath and mine.

Though you are close,
You are most far away.
But because you are so dear
I bring you through the paper wall
That is neither there, nor here.

And often, as I sat writing such poems that helped me cling to the last shreds of my many identities, I would suddenly sense that you were indeed approaching. You could not be in the room next to mine, but you were in the same city, coming towards me, turning the corner of the square, entering the same street! And I would rush to the window and look down and see you turning the corner to cross the square below, or walk round it to the hotel door. I never went down to meet you, for I was always afraid those right-wing student bullies might be waiting for me – you they could not touch, but I was an easy prey. It was only when I felt safe with you, and after we had spent some hours working on our poems, that we would go down to the restaurant for late dinner, which always ended with either banana or 'flan'. Then, when it had grown dark, we would go out to join the *paseo*:

I wait for the drown
Of evening, when we go,

Together and together, through
The sinking town,
A meeting that is not a rendezvous
With loneliness and dark,
And stiff knives thicketing a naked park.

Slowly the roofs go down,
Releasing buoyant stars
To mark the watered sky with spars
Of light, a splintering crown
That binds our hidden scars
With stone, and keeps our heads above
The wrecks of solitude and love.

Yet as our relationship deepened, you seemed to abstract yourself, and sometimes I would not see you for days on end. Then when we met again, you would be full of all you had done – a ride on your motor bike to Alba de Tormes or Ledesma, a strange church you had discovered, or a new book someone had sent you from the States. Even worse, you would tell me about new poems you had started to write, and it was like a dagger in my heart when you described working on them without my help – though the real reason you had come back to see me was to labour over them with me, adding my suggestions and excisions in the margins in your minuscule script. When you stayed away from me, I would try in vain to will you back beside me: then, long after the dinner I waited for you to share but had to eat alone, I would wander out into the stony streets, hoping to bump into you, to glimpse you sitting in a bar or on a park bench:

Wandering alone at midnight
Along the streets we walked together,
I was a stranger once again,
For everything was unfamiliar,
Changed by the loneliness as much
As by your presence at my side.

Even the stars were altered.
The fixed positions that I saw with you
Now seemed obscure.
I could not find my orient,
Or the pole that keeps its compass in your hand
At meeting and parting, night and day.

> – Then I found myself beneath
> Your window lighted from within,
> And for a moment watched
> Your shadow move across the glass.
> I gave a shout: but as I looked,
> Even that last star went out.

Still, I waited patiently, and wished you well. I wanted your poetry to be better, wanted to show you the way into a wider perspective of words and feelings. After long days and nights alone I would wake in the mornings wondering if this new day would bring a new poem from you, a new smile as you ran dancing towards me on your boxer's turned-in toes. When I awoke and started getting ready for my classes, which now passed mechanically, as if in a vacuum, the students suspended in time and space, and my own voice seeming to come from somewhere a long, long way away, I would write a poem for you as a kind of incantation to bring you back that day:

> Now you are waking to our common air
> That is the same for sleepers and their mates,
> For those who watch and wonder at the rare
> Bright morning that combines our separate fates.
>
> Let this long day be full for you,
> Filled with your working sun
> That makes the heavens white and blue
> Above the brown horizons where your poems run.

Although you always came to me brimming with news of where you had been and what you had done, I do not think you told me everything. And you never asked me what I had been doing.

*   *   *

And suddenly so much was happening to you and, by extension, to me. You got letters from home, from your father asking when you were going to settle down and get a proper job, or were you going to be an 'eternal student'? Packages of that rare onion-skin typing paper which made my erasures of mistypings so easy came from your mother, who also sent you boxes of drugs, chiefly Dexedrine, those shocking-pink amphetamines which, I later discovered, are bad for the heart. The Spanish laws against drug use in those days were exceptionally severe, and I was terrified in case you should be found out by the police or the drug squad. I had heard awful tales of Spanish prisons. You persuaded me to experiment with Dexedrine. I still remember the night we started, sitting in the brasserie on the ground floor of my hotel, downing Dexedrine with San Miguel beer. They were supposed to heighten our perceptions, but really I could see little difference between my ordinary vision of life, which was fantastic enough, and what the pills apparently produced, mainly a nervous sleeplessness shot through with incoherent babblings and bursts of laughter alternating with floods of tears. They also made me extremely randy, an effect I pointed out to you, who seemed unaffected in that department and were astonished that they should stimulate my already overwrought sexuality – 'oversexed and under seventy' is how I still think of myself. Under the influence of the drugs we exchanged a few playful cuddles and kisses, just for a lark. It went no further, despite my insistence: you always gently repulsed me. But our complicity in taking those dreadful little uppers, of which I thoroughly disapproved, as I do of all narcotic stimulants, drew us closer together, so I submitted to their influence.

You rarely received letters yourself. I never received one from you, though you had many from me, of course. That you did not write letters to me I sometimes attributed to the fact that you must indeed be a secret agent, unwilling to commit himself in writing. I think the postman would never have been able to decipher your scribble, your own version of Walser's MS, *Bleistiftgebiet* or Kingdom of the Pencil, which we were to describe in a later poem, 'The Poem in the Pencil'.

But you certainly received some letters. There was one from an American girl in Berlin. I believe she was studying modern dance and had been a pupil of Mary Wigman, or of one of her disciples. She announced, to my dismay, that she was coming to Salamanca for a week or so. I could so clearly see her coming between you and me, between us and our poetry, and I felt furiously jealous and unhappy but tried not to show it. After all, I had no real claim upon your attention, and I knew I meant so little to you I could be dropped at any moment without a second thought.

The young woman arrived late one evening after having driven all the way from Berlin in her Volkswagen Beetle, at that time the 'in' means of transport for young Americans. To my surprise, I liked her very much. She was tall and dark and pale, and looked very mysterious and romantic. She had a beautiful figure which she used in subtle movements of unparalleled grace. The only thing I did not like about her was the flat ballerina-style slippers she always wore, to reduce her height I think, because she was taller than you. We all three had dinner

together, then you went off with her to your room, where she was to
stay, though how you managed to accommodate yourselves in that tiny
room with its narrow bed was something I preferred not to think about.
I suffered agonies of suspense in silence, for I never knew when or
where I would see you again, or whether she would be with you.

One morning, to my intense embarrassment, you brought her to my
poetry appreciation class – which you had never bothered to attend
yourself. You came without warning and without asking my permission
and sat with her at the back of the lecture theatre, exchanging glances
and comments. My poems that day were Hopkins's 'Heaven-Haven'
and 'The Habit of Perfection'. You ruined them for me, and I have
hated them ever since. In Japan I refuse admittance to the many
foreigners who try to barnstorm my classes. I inform them that my
classes are intended 'for Japanese only'. For native English speakers I
would give a quite different kind of lecture, and I did not want to be
judged by the standards of my lectures to the Japanese, which were
nearly always basic and very simple in expression. Yet 'The Habit of
Perfection' was once my private vision of our own poetic relationship.
And as Hopkins writes in a letter to Bridges: 'Now it is the virtue of
design, pattern, or inscape to be distinctive and it is the vice of distinctiveness to become queer.' I was already queer, and had known too long
the vice of distinctiveness in my personal life as well as in my poetry.

The young dancer put a stop to our writing, as I had expected. You
went for rides with her in her VW, and made an extended trip to Lisbon
– to Madrid also, I believe. I behaved with great dignity and showed
none of the resentment I may have felt. But it was a relief to me when
she left and, I was thankful to discover, it was even more of a relief to
you.

We took up the lost threads of our writing together with even greater
dedication. After that long interval it was hard to get started again. But
as soon as we had found our voice again, we were once more interrupted
by visits from Berlin. A group of your former fellow-students at the
university, all Germans, and all extreme radicals, arrived on the scene in
Salamanca and proceeded to disrupt our lives and shock the Spaniards
with their outrageous behaviour, in which you joined.

One of the things we were involved in remains in my memory with
shocking force. It all started out as a silly student prank, but it was to
mark me for life.

We had been conducting the German youths on tours of our favour-
ite places in the city – to the bullring, the restaurants, the bars, the River
Tormes, the Casa de Santa Teresa, the Antiguo Colegio Mayor de
Irlandeses, San Martin (where we were nearly locked in for the night)

and to the conventual church of San Esteban. The Convento de San Esteban is a magnificent plateresque sixteenth-century edifice on the Plaza Santo Domingo, approached by a small arched bridge which provides an impressive forefront to that immense carved façade, with the arcaded convent standing at right angles to it on the right. It was one of my favourite churches, because the interior was so vast, so gloriously ornamented, and nearly always empty. That altar is one of the greatest works of José Churriguera.

As usual when we entered a church together, I dipped my finger in the holy water and gave you a drop from my fingertips, so that we could cross ourselves together, like a *novio* and *novia*. Our gesture was not really a religious one, for neither of us believed in the Roman Catholic faith and detested its oppressive hold on the Spanish people, particularly the poor. We used to do it almost as a social thing, a conventional Spanish gesture which for us had a special meaning – or at least it did for me, because I looked upon it as a seal on our friendship. I think you did it just to please me, or perhaps to satisfy your own deep-seated urge to be conventional in outward things.

But when your German friends saw us doing this, they hooted with derision. Fortunately, the church was empty: there were no priests, no sacristans, no black-mantillaed old ladies worshipping in front of the gorgeously gilded altar with its six twisted baroque pillars framing the blue heaven of the inner sanctuary. It is one of the most imposing interiors in Salamanca, and the atmosphere of utter devoutness that informs every inch of stone and ornament is overpoweringly strange and haunting.

We all trooped up to the altar, behind which your Berlin friends discovered a mysterious opening. I think it must have been left by workmen who had been preparing the crypt for the disposal of some saintly relic or the body of a recently deceased priest.

The young Germans went down into the crypt, pulling you after them. You looked back at me, and I knew I had to follow you. When we got inside the dimly lit space beneath the main altar, we found an open coffin, in which a partially decomposed skeleton was lying. The robes were stained and torn, but there still seemed to be some blood on the bones. There was what may have been a bishop's mitre on the skull, which grinned amiably up at us. We gazed at the figure in the utmost fascination. Then you cried: 'Anyone who doesn't touch the bones is chicken!'

Immediately you touched those bones, and all the others did the same, laughing and jostling to get at the coffin. Again you just looked at me, and I knew I had to do as you had done, so I stretched out my right hand and touched the bones, which were slightly sticky. But in touching them I tried to bless them, in a spirit of reverence. I prayed silently for peace to those venerable remains.

We left the church without being seen. After a few more days in Salamanca, during which you and I could do no work in common, your friends left in a great uproar of drunken invective, shouting political slogans – which fortunately were in German – against the Franco regime. Though I agreed with their political views, I could not condone the way they acted and was glad to see them go at last. So, I am sure, were you. But the memory of those sacred bones remained engraved upon my memory for the rest of my life. They had been defiled, and I expected punishment.

                              *   *   *

There was a curious incident when a man from the British Council in Madrid came to see me. This was to be the third of my many run-ins with that typically British authoritarian institution, which is never happy unless making trouble. The British Council abroad is bent on getting everything connected with British education and culture under its tyrannical control, and outsiders like myself who found their own positions without passing through the old-boy network and the rigid screening system of the Council were always given a hard time.

I don't know why our man in Madrid came to see me; just idle curiosity, perhaps – so few people have ever met me, so many seem anxious to do so. Or perhaps he had heard rumours of my goings-on, and had come personally to find out 'what Kirkup's up to now' – the traditional BC phrase wherever they have the misfortune to discover my presence. He was a typical British Council smoothie, with a fatuous grin and an ingratiating manner. To my surprise, he invited me to give a poetry reading in Madrid. I agreed, provided Dana were allowed to go with me and share the reading. He was rather taken aback but said he would report to head office and let me know about it in the New Year.

Dana and I had already spent a few weekends in Madrid, travelling by bus via Avila through wonderful country. On our first trip together we had visited a café of a very old-fashioned kind, called Cafeteria Varela Reposteria in Preciados, and I had noted an inscription saying *En este lugar escribió sus mejores versos el gran poeta Emilio Carrere 1881–1947. Homenaje de los poetas españoles, Madrid MCMLII.** An

* 'In this place the great poet Emilio Carrere 1881–1947 wrote his best verses. Homage from the poets of Spain, Madrid, MCMLII.'

ancient waiter had come to take our order. I wanted to introduce Dana
to Pernod, so I asked the old man for 'dos Pernod'. I was expecting the
usual French style of service, with an ice-bucket and a carafe of chilled
water, and two glasses containing a small amount of Pernod at the
bottom. Instead, the waiter brought us two full glasses of the 'green
fairy'. It was probably the first time he had been asked for such a drink,
despite his long years of service. I should have sent the drinks back, but
instead looked upon them as a windfall in our rather straitened circumstances. After calling for some ice-cubes which we popped into the straight
Pernod, we drank them down, with predictably weird results (we had
already had Dexedrine). We staggered out into the Madrid evening 'full
of piss and vinegar', as Dana said later, and somehow made our way to
the Puerta del Sol, where there is a large circular fountain. Its waters
proved irresistibly attractive to us, and we playfully started splashing
one another. We grew more and more excited. Then I saw a stern
policeman standing nearby with suspicious and disapproving stare. He
looked so miserable I decided to cheer him up by inviting him to join
our little game, and started throwing handfuls of water over him. But he
considered this an unforgivable insult to his dignity and marched us both
to an underground lavatory on the edge of the square, followed by a
curious and gleeful crowd waiting for the *extranjeros* to get their come-
uppance. In my elevated state I was afraid only that the cop might
search us and discover the Dexedrine in Dana's pocket. We were both
carrying packets of condoms, too, as an extra precaution, should we be
granted the favours of some fair *señorita* or visit the red-light district,
the *barrio chino*. However, after haranguing us and making me mop up
his uniform, the outraged policeman indicated a couple of wash-basins.
I had tried to excuse our conduct by telling him we had just needed a
wash. He turned on the taps and thrust my face and head into the water
and completely soaked my shirt and jacket. 'If you want a wash, that's
the way to do it!' he shouted, his face contorted with fury. I have since
learnt that this kind of treatment is known as the 'water torture' in
Spanish prisons. Then we were allowed to go, to the disappointment of
the crowd. That lavatory is still there. . . .

But once outside, Dana and I became quarrelsome and started to
fight with one another, releasing heaven knows what accumulated stores
of fury and resentment. I was knocked to the ground, and a kind
passer-by picked me up and dusted down my soaking clothes as I
watched Dana walking away into the night. I was too proud to follow
him and beg forgiveness. Anyhow, we were both at fault. After trudging
disconsolately round a few bars, I went back to our cheap hostel, where
to my relief I found Dana snoring in the double bed we were to share. I

crept in beside him and lay for some time with throbbing head. Then I felt Dana squeeze my hand, and he said: 'Buenas noches, amigo Jim.' That was all. We drifted into sleep.

I was up early next morning with a clanging hangover, and as I sat beside the bed watching Dana sleep, I wrote one of the several poems of that period about insomnia and my vigil over my sleeping friend's form, 'The Lonely Insomniac':

> While you enjoy sound sleep,
> I the insomniac am deep in light.
> My head is full of blazing night
> That mocks the vigil I must keep.
>
> I wrap myself in lamps and fires,
> And the four walls are a shining jail.
> The blinded windows rattle in my pale
> Bones, the skeleton that never tires.
>
> The dark is lit as bright as day.
> I watch your dreams with open eyes.
> The planes are heavy in my hanging skies.
> My love's asleep and far away.

Late risers always exasperate early risers like myself, who hate to miss what they know is the best part of the day. As soon as it was light, I crept out of the room and went downstairs for a coffee at a nearby café. Then I strolled around the city for a couple of hours, knowing that Dana would not be awake before noon. When I got back to our hostel, our bags were in the hallway and Dana was waiting for me. Apparently we had made so much noise when we returned separately the night before that we had wakened everyone and we were being thrown out. Dana was pale and still half asleep. We trudged around for an hour or so, unable to face the thought of lunch, and found another small hotel near Chamartin (we were going back by train the next day by the last evening train). Dana felt so sick, he went straight back to bed, but had been there only a few seconds before he leapt out with a scream of agony: an autumnal, sleepy wasp had been brought in by the chambermaid among the bedclothes which had been airing at the window and had stung my friend on the bottom! The sting proved a lightning cure for his hangover, for he stood rubbing his arse while I rushed to the *farmacia* for a remedy. Then he allowed me to rub it into his injured posterior, a great thrill for me. But I was even more thrilled by the fact that our little tiff had been meaningless and that we were still good friends. We went out for a lunch that was late even by Madrid standards, then went to a *zarzuela*. That night, before we fell asleep – stone sober this time – Dana again gave my hand a squeeze. I was in heaven. But we were to have several more arguments in the months to come, and not all of them about poetry. That weekend is also memorable for something Dana said to me in the train on the way back to Salamanca: 'I knew you were gay as soon as I saw you that morning in the *galleria*.' Then, in response to my crestfallen look, he added kindly: 'Of course you did not *look* gay – you're no screaming queen – but nevertheless I just knew.' Then I realized he must have known many bisexuals before me, and many homosexuals too. I think at times he found his own handsomeness an awful burden: people just wouldn't let him alone. He told me he sometimes hated his face, hated his body because of the ease with which they helped him to dominate others. He told me he was also in revolt against his strict puritan upbringing, a fairly common case in the sons of God-fearing Americans. People were always taking him in hand, hoping to reform him, to make him conform to their own self-centred ideal of what he should be. I was the first person to take him simply as he was, and for that he showed his gratitude by giving me a light kiss on the cheek in the darkened carriage.

November. We sang together those heart-rending popular songs about the season: 'The Autumn Leaves' and Trenet's French version from which it was taken. We also sang 'Longtemps, longtemps, longtemps, après que les poètes sont disparus . . .', also by Trenet, one of the most beautifully upsetting songs for poets. And we were finding poets everywhere. In Salamanca we often smiled at each other as we passed along a street called Street of the Two Poets – or was it a little plaza? We fatuously wondered if a street or a square would ever be named after us – 'two spooky old Villons,' as Dana once described us.

Then came December. The dancer, on her way back to the United States, took Dana in her VW to Lisbon, Porto and Bilbao, where I met them, then we drove all the way to Paris. Dana went on with his friend to see her off at Le Havre, while I made my way to London, where I was joined by Dana a few days later. We were in Bath to stay for a couple of weeks with my parents, in time for Christmas and 'New Year's'. So far, I had behaved with great restraint. But in Britain things were to take a new and not unexpected turn.

WELCOME TO BATH

Oh! who can ever be tired of Bath?

Jane Austen, NORTHANGER ABBEY

We stayed a couple of nights in London, in a small hotel situated in the street extending from the top of St Martin's Lane. Again we had a double bed, and I made one or two tentative sexual advances, to no effect. But we would fall asleep in one another's arms – that romantic image which is in reality so uncomfortable and painful. Dana would fall asleep immediately he put his head on the pillow, and after a while I had to try to extract myself from his embrace. I thought of us as the little princes in the Tower, and of the city of London as the cruel torturer Hubert who at any moment might come and put out our poetic eyes.

While we were in London I took Dana to meet Joe Ackerley in his office in Marylebone High Street. Joe looked on us both with quizzical amusement, no doubt savouring the incongruity of our companionship. He also looked rather envious. I could see that he was wondering just how far we had gone in our relationship, and how long it might last. Would it, he was thinking, be like the ending of Forster's as yet unpublished *Maurice*, a somewhat tame homo novel of which he was to say, commenting on the male lovers setting up house at the end, 'I give it three weeks?' Well, we had already lasted three months, and I was keeping my fingers crossed for our relationship to continue for ever.

Joe invited us out to lunch, which was what I had been hoping for, because we were both more or less on our uppers. He conducted us to a new restaurant, the Hungry Horse, which was pronouncedly 'gay', with all the young waiters in tight-fitting cotton trousers of small blue-and-white checks. Joe obviously thought it was all very daring and suitable for us both. When the waiter came to take our orders, I could not help noticing the massive sexual equipment outlined by his soft cotton pants. We were sitting on rather low chairs, and he was very tall, so that when he placed himself at my corner his impedimenta were almost on a level with my nose. He caught my astonished stare, and paused as he was jotting down the orders, glancing down at himself in apparent wonder at what I could be looking at.

Joe was in good form, though the time for his retirement was drawing near, and he was already beginning to feel a bit lost and abandoned by people who once fawned on him. Now that they knew he would be leaving, the literary confraternity had already started to turn their backs on him, and had begun to scan the possible replacements in the current British intellectual mafia. Joe was trying to be bright and cheerful, but there was a deep undercurrent of sadness, and later, when he had gone back to his office, Dana said: 'I think he's terribly lonely.'

During lunch Joe kept us entertained with anecdotes about his friends and contributors – old Wyndham Lewis, half blind, who was one of his art critics, and who, when taken to eat at L'Escargot, just pushed his gourmet food around on his plate. He was concerned, as always, about Morgan Forster's health and his own sister Nancy's extravagance. He talked about Elizabeth Bowen, a dear friend whose unhappy marriage had upset him. 'All the people I know who have married, have ended up unhappy,' he told us. Then, laying his hands on our shoulders, he added: 'Never get married, dears. Marriage is the death of art and freedom and self-respect.' I wondered if he thought Dana and I were about to tie the knot, or whether he was thinking of us individually – the latter, I think, because he had warned me against marriage once or twice before when I had shown what he regarded as too much interest in a woman friend. In this he resembled Bonamy Dobrée at Leeds, who reacted with the utmost dismay when his pet student, Robin Skelton, announced his engagement to a fellow-student. 'Marriage will be the end of his talent,' Bonamy predicted, though I had not seen much talent in the poems Robin had so far shown me. They showed promise and were not as mediocre as all the other stuff inflicted upon me at Leeds, but I could not see any real future for Robin as a poet. He has proved to be an excellent literary scholar.

Yes, Joe must have been desperately lonely at that time, because he asked us to dinner the following evening at Chez Victor's, one of his favourite restaurants. After dinner he took us to the Royal College of Art, where he seemed proud to be an honorary member of the faculty club and students' union. He took us up to see the students, and the very first ones I saw were Sonia Lawson, already a highly gifted artist, daughter of my friends Fred and Muriel in Redmire; and one of my best students from Corsham, the vivacious, beautiful and witty Helen Dear, the shining light of my so-called 'duds'. She was far from being so, and I always remember her with affection for the way she enlivened my drama classes. Sonia and Helen flung themselves into my arms, to Joe's great astonishment. But the girls had eyes only for Dana's beauty and sexy demeanour, which that night was particularly James Deanish.

Next day we were off in the train to Bath. I had borrowed ten quid from Joe – later repaid, and the only interest he demanded was a chaste kiss in front of the BBC in Langham Place. The Thames at Maidenhead – a name that provoked Dana's hilarity – looked wintry, and there was snow obliterating the white horse at Uffingham. But Chippenham and Bath were milder, free of snow. We gazed enraptured at the city of Bath from the train as it drew in to the station – it was all laid out on the slopes of Lansdown like an aerial map of a moon landscape. 'How very different from Spain' was Dana's first comment as the bus took us from the station to Avondale Buildings.

My mother and father seemed glad to see me, and they welcomed Dana warmly. My Aunt Lyallie was also spending Christmas with us, so our little house was rather crowded. Dana and I slept together in the double bed in my bedroom, next to my parents' room, where my mother was sleeping with Aunt Lyallie. My father put up on the sofa in the big living-room next to my bedroom, which I had claimed as my study. It was the first time Dana had stayed in an English house, and I think he was delighted with the difference between it and his home in the United States. He said we were much more Spartan. It was perhaps the small electric heater in my bedroom which made him say that. The cold was intense, but I welcomed it because it gave us an excuse to lie close together for warmth. And on that first night at home we had our first real sexual encounter, a rather one-sided one, with Dana quite passive. Trying not to make a sound, I achieved a long and delicious orgasm, a heavenly mixture of sheer physical bliss, emotional release and satisfyingly agitating anxiety. I was 'over the moon', as Joe liked to say in imitation of his working-class friends' picturesquely idiomatic Cockney. But was Dana?

I could see at once that my parents and Aunt Lyallie had taken to him. He was so attentive, and so polite, and we loved the way he addressed them as 'Sir' and 'Ma'am'. They were happy, I think, that I had found such a good friend, and did everything they could to make him feel at home. My aunt and my mother were particularly fond of him, and when he had a stomach upset they fussed over him all the time, preparing special bland food for him, making him swallow Milk of Magnesia and advising him not to drink too much Christmas sherry. Under their ministrations he soon recovered. They loved to 'baby' him in a way they could never do with me. I sensed that they approved of him whole-heartedly, and that by comparison I was no longer the blue-eyed boy of the family: I did not come up to scratch. I did not mind. I had no desire to change anything as long as Dana was around. I was happy with him just as he was, without affectation. 'He has no "side",' my Aunt Lyallie said approvingly for she had always thought Americans were a stuck-up, boastful lot. My father and mother perhaps saw in him the son they would have liked to have, not the peculiar failure they had produced in me.

Just to look at Dana fully clothed was enough to give me an erection. When I was with him I was in a more or less permanent state of sexual excitement, and I could bring myself to orgasm just by looking at him, without the aid of hands. In my love-making I simply held him close and let the rest take over, rounded off with a simple kiss. That was always enough for me in my homosexual role. I could prolong the ecstasy as long as I liked, even after he had fallen asleep in my arms and continued sleeping right through my climaxes. It was that simple. The purity of my love was something that to me remained undefiled.

But did Dana see it the same way? Did he, too, feel undefiled? On the morning after that first sexual experience we walked after breakfast up the street, past gossiping garden gates and twitching lace curtains to the fields at the top. We walked in silence for a long time. Then we sat down for a rest under a hedge, and Dana asked that typically American question: 'Do you want to talk about it?' This came out without any warning, so I answered, with fake innocence: 'Talk about what?' A pause. 'Last night,' Dana replied, with a rather grim note in his voice. 'I'm not blaming you,' he went on. 'But I'd just like to know where we stand.'

I hardly knew what to say to this, so remained silent.

'If we are going to continue to be friends and write our poetry, we must come to some kind of arrangement,' Dana said. 'I don't find you unattractive, but I think you might consider my feelings as well as your own.'

Another pause.

'The only important thing', he continued, 'is for us to go on writing our poems. That's all I care about. If it brings us closer together, and helps us to write better poems, I would be willing to trade some sex with you. You help me, and I'll help you. And let us help each other get this thing into perspective or it's going to ruin our collaboration.'

It was an unusually long speech for Dana. I was speechless with a mixture of fear and embarrassment. I did not want to 'talk about it'. That seemed to me unnecessary. Then he gave me a smile and a playful punch on the arm: 'You were pretty good last night, you old sex maniac.' Thankful to hear the change in his tone, I responded with a less playful punch, and soon we were on our feet slapping at each other with a wild hilarity, a contest in which inevitably I was the loser. But we had saved the day, and our long friendship. And from then on, Dana became increasingly responsive to my love-making. Months later he was to admit: 'Don't you realize, Jim, I was just egging you on all the time? Why were you so slow? And: 'You are the *purest* person I've ever known.'

But on that morning my happiness was clouded by something he said to me as we were walking home to lunch: 'Your parents know about you, Jim – you know that, don't you?' It was something I had never admitted to myself. Of course, deep inside me, I knew all along that they knew. But we would never have dreamt of talking about it. Dana's words struck at my heart, as he had done, quite deliberately, when he had told me: 'The very first time I saw you, I knew you were gay.' At lunch I was sad and subdued, and I could hardly face my mother's and father's happy faces, or the rather more knowing glances of Aunt Lyallie, who I later discovered had put my mother wise to many things.

After lunch we went up to my study to work on our poems. But we did not create much poetry: we held each other tenderly, and he comforted me with kisses. 'Just wait, Jim. Don't let's do it here in this house with your mother and father watching and perhaps listening. . . .' I nodded in agreement, saying: 'We'll keep it for our New Year's present.' He hugged me in consent. My Christmas happiness was complete.

We all went to the carol service in Bath Abbey, where I had difficulty restraining my tears. I was too choked with emotion to sing the carols of my childhood in that glorious fane. Though I had always disliked Christmas, because I knew it made my mother unhappy for some reason, that was one Christmas when I was happy, and I have never forgotten it.

After a week at home I began to get restless, as always in the company of my parents. I felt ashamed of feeling so bored with them. But I knew that it was time to leave, and we said goodbye to them on New Year's Eve. That morning I met my father on the middle landing of the stairs, and we were alone together for the first time in the holidays. We stopped and looked at each other, then shook hands. 'Well, good-bye, then, Jim,' he said, with a little smile. 'Goodbye, Daddy.' It was the last time I saw him alive.

Dana and I spent a few days in London again before travelling to Spain. We spent a lot of time in the National Gallery and at the Tate, and wrote some poems about the pictures there, including Verrocchio's *Tobias and the Angel*, Piero di Cosima's *Mythological Subject* and Titian's *Christ Appearing to the Magdalen – Noli me Tangere*, whose theme had a special significance for me now: Dana was Christ, and I was the Magdalen. 'Or can it be the other way round?' he asked. 'It can be either,' I replied, 'now that we know who we are and where we are with one another.' It is one of our best collaborations, so here it is:

On the distant ocean, burnished
To a passionate blue, the tree is bent,
And in the kindling sky, whose benison
Of green and golden leaf transcends
The sepulchres of dark, the winds of light
Now wash the living wood.

The tree leans patiently away
From habitations on a dusky hill,
Whose pathway lights a shepherd and his dog
To a greening valley white with sheep.
– The foreground of the quickening day
Confronts the Magdalen with her risen Lord.

She kneels to him along the leaning
Tree of her desire, and reaches out
A hand whose hesitations beg to touch
The gardener's unearthly robes.
Tenderly his perfect body fends
Her gesture with the faith of love.

He leans above her like a leafy bough
That frees its gentle body from the grave
Rhythm of a bitter tree. – *Touch me
Not.* – His face makes sweet
This quiet admonition, and his hand,
In blessing, hangs above her head its dove.

I remember we sat there all afternoon looking at that wonderful picture and planning our poem in our heads. After an early dinner we went straight back to our hotel and wrote it. Then we undressed each other, lay down on the bed, and made our first, fully reciprocal, passionate love.

MY DISTRACTED WINTER

*Nur an den beiden Polen menschlicher Verbindung, dort, wo es noch keine
oder keine Worte mehr gibt, im Blick und in der Umarmung, ist eigentlich
Glück zu finden, denn nur dort ist Unbedingtheit, Freiheit, Geheimnis und
tiefe Rücksichtslosigkeit.*

(Only at the two poles of human relationship, where there are no words,
or no more words, in the looking and the embracing, is happiness really to
be found, for only there lie unconditional surrender, freedom, mystery
and profound irresponsibility.)

O n the back of a piece of paper where we had worked on a poem
called 'The Word' I found the quotation that begins this chapter. I do
not remember now who wrote it, but it is no doubt from a modern
German author, perhaps a philosopher, and it expresses exactly my
state of mind at the beginning of 1958. As if in answer to the prophecy I
had written in Amsterdam in the Hotel Brabant after visiting the
exhibition of Picasso's *Guernica*, I was now in the very presence of love
itself, in the form of the hero imagined there and then. The poem we
were working on was one of several left unfinished, but I can quote here
the first three verses, for their expression of our condition at that time,
our sense of being so close together that we were utterly apart from all
else:

> A cool, real thing,
> The object of our art,
> Has the unsounded life
> Of all that is apart.
>
> We look into its heart,
> And see a meaning there.
> We take its strangeness in –
> The familiar, too, is rare.
>
> We whisper it across
> The table of our looks;
> A kiss exchanged in time
> Is the seed of books. . . .

Our love had become completely exclusive, in its lookings, embracings, kissings, from all but 'the word' of whatever poem we were writing together. It was a strange, hothouse life in my shuttered and curtained room at the Hotel España. I rarely went out. The weather was bitterly cold, and because there was no heating in Dana's little room he used to spend all day, and nearly every night, in my warm apartment. We would sit hour after hour on either side of my table, exchanging glances, kisses, embraces, smiles – and the words of our poems. I was always conscious now of the mocking presence of those fascist student bullies in the streets, following me with laughter and taunts. Sometimes they would come and lunch or dine in my hotel, sitting at a table next to ours. These goons did not attack Dana – it was me they were after. Sometimes they broke into my classes at the university, carrying pictures of Franco and Primo de Rivera and chanting Falangist slogans or singing army songs, and shouting *maricone! maricone!* There were some students, mainly girls, who protested. In particular, Manuela, the girl who had wiped the word *maricone* from the blackboard, stood up to the rowdies and lashed them with her tongue. This girl seemed as if she wanted to become our friend. We sometimes met her in the street on her way from classes, and she always stopped to talk to us.

But we were beyond friendship. We were totally absorbed in one another and in our work. We used to take showers together in my apartment and then wander around naked until we were dry. We were still writing our own separate poems, and one I did started:

> The naked body turns a room
> To jungles where the panther prowls
> In black and green and yellow gloom
> And blood in walls of darkness growls.
>
> Within the hunter's furry loins
> The sun-flexed muscles play.
> Showered with movement's leafy coins,
> The level haunches lightly sway. . . .

Sometimes the shutters of my room, raised slightly to let in streaks of sunlight between their horizontal slats, made our winter room seem tropical.

Then we would fling ourselves upon each other at all hours of the day and night make love upon the unmade bed, for often we refused to let the maid in to make up the room:

I love your nakedness displayed
In bored abandon on the tangled bed,
The dark nipples starring the wide, smooth chest,
The rough lips parted in your sun-tanned face,
The strong and slender hips,
The navel's little cup of bitterness,
The blond-tinselled thighs,
The well-set neck's warm spoon,
The feet's long fans,
The arms curved round your radiant head,
And the dark treasure at your body's heart
That beats and leaps for pleasure. . . .

Reading Unamuno, I found this passage which gave me comfort among all the mockery: 'The greatest height of heroism to which an individual, like a people, can attain is to know how to face ridicule.' I hardly knew how I was able to face it, either then or at any other time of my life in this mocking world, but I did, though it did not seem to me that I was in any way heroic – just the opposite, in fact. I sometimes felt degraded and cowardly to be so different, and the object of so much taunting and discrimination.

When the life of that one room became too oppressive, we would go for a spin on the motor bike to Bejar, Miranda del Castanar, Sequeros – places where no one knew us. We also went to Madrid again and saw a performance by the famous travelling circus, the Circo Price, about whose clowns I wrote a poem in *The Prodigal Son*. I was in a very black and negative mood, I remember, and waited for the trapeze artists to fall and kill themselves, for the female contortionist to twist herself into such a knot of meat that she would never get disentangled. Dana was shocked by my attitude, but I was not in my right mind. The Circus Price, the oldest in Europe, was a marvellous popular institution. It was founded in the mid-1850s by an Englishman, Thomas Price. The elegant old Price building stood in the Plaza del Rey, right at the heart of Madrid's banking and commercial district. It was a family show. One of the stars was the trapeze artist, Señorita Pinito del Oro, a gypsy who learnt her art on a clothes-line strung between two Madrid apartment buildings. Josephine Baker and such well-known and beloved clowns as Grock, Ramper and Charlie Rivel appeared regularly with the circus. The tyrant Primo de Rivera loved circuses, and loved big cigars, which he smoked during the performance, though it was forbidden. On being reproved by a humble usher, Primo de Rivera had a law passed making the Circo Price the only theatre in Madrid where smoking was allowed. And that law was still in effect when the building finally had to close in 1972, on the expiry of the lease, after which it was transformed into a bank.

Naturally I was sleeping badly. My insomnia became chronic whenever Dana stayed the night, simply because I could not take my eyes away from his sleeping form beneath the bedside lamps. There are several poems I wrote about this fixation, and some unfinished ones like this:

> I who cannot get a wink of sleep
> Sit by the night's large window watching you, naked,
> Adrift in the moonlight on the bed,
> Your tanned face drowned in the dew, the foam
> Of pillows, and brown arms cornering your head
> Like wreaths of sand about your hair's blond sheaf.
>
> How can I ever drop my eyes as deep
> Into the swimming dark as you . . .?

Our love-making was of the purest, simplest kind, without extreme erotic refinements and *recherché* positions. We would hold each other in an embrace, exchanging long kisses, and rock our bodies together until they overflowed. Dana was much more experienced than I: he taught me a form of *carezza* by which we could indefinitely prolong erection and contain ejaculation. We were like a couple of shamans. It was utterly delightful. I wanted nothing more, though I think Dana must have wanted other things that I never thought of offering him; with him alone I would have been happy to do what I had always denied others. I got some insight into this when I was telling him about my readings in Zen, and trying to explain the principles of yin and yan. I drew a small diagram of the interlocking male and female principles in their embracing circle. I saw that next to it Dana wrote 'Sixtynine' (the amatory position the French call *soixante-neuf*) and changed the 'comma' shapes into '69'. It was only towards the end of my time in Spain, when we were in Ciudad Rodrigo for the Festival Taurino, that we once, quite by accident, found ourselves in the 69 position and went through with it successfully. I had no desire to try it again.

From time to time we visited the old *barrio chino*, the red-light district, which formed a kind of everyman's land at the heart of the bell-haunted, church-loaded city. I am not sure why this quarter was called 'Chinese' except that perhaps its apartness from the regular secular and religious life of Salamanca made it seem like another country, and a far-off, exotic one at that. The place was all tawdry bars, dance-halls and flop-houses that were also houses of assignation. Besides the 'straight' prostitutes, there were a few transvestites, heavily made up, trying to swallow their Adam's apples and speak in wheedling, fluty voices. They deceived no one, but I felt a bond with their strange sisterhood. Indeed, I had always, since living in the red-light district of Leeds, Brunswick Place, had a fondness and respect for prostitutes. It was the prostitutes in Douai and Lille and Paris who gave me my first induction into their ways and wiles. In the sixties my heroines were not Bardot or Monroe or Vivien Leigh, but Christine Keeler and Mandy Rice-Davies. I admired them for doing openly what many women do in secret or under the respectable cover of marriage. I felt like those women and men who openly sold their favours. Why should not people do as they pleased with their own bodies? And I thought some of the girls were extraordinarily attractive in their outrageous costumes and theatrical make-up. I envied them their sexual freedom and their self-assured dignity, and I despised the British vice squads that ran them in and were not above enjoying their charms for a consideration. Since I hated the police, it was natural that I should feel myself aligned with the prostitutes.

The girls in the *barrio chino* of Spanish cities were of all ages, sizes and nationalities. We used to go to a certain bar and sit at our favourite table, where we would be joined by a pair of bedizened harridans with dyed orange hair and chipped scarlet fingernails. In their almost dead-white, overpowdered faces, the mean little eyes looked red and sore in their crusted pits of mascara; their great painted mouths with lipstick smearing over the fuzzy edges gave them a touchingly clownish look. They wore over their sagging, wrinkled breasts flimsy, lace-up bodices with nothing underneath, and from those cleavages arose a fume of mingled sweat, baby powder and cheap scent. They were always smoking. Every five minutes they would cadge a Bisonte from me, or a Lucky Strike from Dana. They did not seem very interested in business, though they ran up big drinks bills for us and would occasionally ruffle our hair or squeeze our balls with an experienced touch, weighing us up, as it were. I'm afraid we did not measure up to the standards set by the well-hung Spanish men who drifted around with flies bulging to the point of bursting their buttons. But the women liked to talk to us, as we were foreigners, laughing uproariously at our accents and our mistakes in Spanish. Sometimes they would read our palms, finishing by giving them a little scratch that signified they were available – one scratch twenty douros, two scratches fifty douros and so on up the scale from an 'in and out' in the toilets or a 'short time' in a back room to a whole night in the brothel, with champagne and bath.

I remember well what one of these old hags told us. They were great judges of character, and her analysis of Dana was: 'You are good enough to be a film star.' Then, turning to me: 'And *you* – you think much, too much. . . .' I think we were both put out, for Dana, though certainly James Dean material, hated to be valued for his looks alone, while I resented the ease with which he attracted praise and disliked being thought of as an intellectual with nothing else to recommend me. We left in a strange, silent huff, the women running after us into the street and trying to pull us back inside. It was always a Toulouse Lautrec evening in the *barrio chino*: grotesque, horrible, funny, depressing, exciting and often pleasantly relaxing. I never forgot those women, their hard lives with their superficial glitter and laughter concealing untold tragedies and disillusions. I felt respect as well as affection for them. But we could never bring ourselves to be bedded by them, though there was a little gypsy flower-girl with her gilded basket of faded carnations, stolen from a grave, who announced a sudden passion for Dana. As she was only about fourteen, we always bought a few dark-red carnations from her, but that was as far as we would go, to her surprise and indignation. She had lost her virginity when she was ten, so she told us, and she was popular with some of the Spanish men who would perch her on their knees and allow her to fondle their private parts as a joke. But everyone took care of her, from the brassy madames to the scruffy young page-boys and the sinister young bartenders. The *barrio* was a place where I felt freer than anywhere else in Salamanca, for it was really a land outside the law, where outcasts at last could feel at home.

All the time, we were making love as we wrote our poems, in a great wave of inspiration and tenderness that seemed as if it could never end. Then one night towards the end of January we had had too much Dexedrine and San Miguel, and we started exchanging acrimonious words. We did not exactly quarrel, but we started unloading pent-up resentments and frustrations. Poetry was forgotten. Dana went back to his room at the Hospedaje Lisboa, leaving me in tears on my bed, sunk in despair. That evening, before dinner, we had sat together in the Clerecia, watching the glib little gilded pendulum of the antique wall-clock wagging away. It was while we were sitting there that my father must have died of a heart attack in Bath. The hotel manager woke me at 10 a.m. with a telegram from my mother, which had been delayed. It simply said that my father had died: it asked me to come home. I dressed and rushed through the streets to Dana's place, and after prolonged hammering on his door managed to wake him and tell him the news. It reconciled us: he took me in his arms and comforted me. Then I hurried back to pack my things. There was some kind of *festa* that day, for the narrow streets and the Corillo were dense with merry throngs of students and the *tuna* was playing in the Plaza Mayor. The manager of the Hotel España was very kind and thoughtful: he would have to let my apartment while I was away, should anyone want it, but promised to let me have it back when I returned after the funeral. Dana saw me off at the station.

I reached Bath next morning, after travelling all day and night. My poor mother was grief-stricken and all alone. She managed to tell me what had happened. There had been a heavy fall of snow, and my father, clearing the path in front of our house, had suddenly felt a terrible pain in his chest. He lay down on the bed, with my mother beside him, and he died in her arms, saying: 'You've been a good wife to me, Mary.' We had no telephone, and in any case there was no time to call a doctor. She took me into the first-floor front room, where my father had already been laid out in his coffin. The room was filled with a strange, sweet smell. He looked so dignified, so calm, so thankful to be gone from this world and from his troublesome son. I remembered the last time I had seen him, on the half-landing on the stairs, and how we looked at one another – as if he had sensed it would be our last encounter – and had shaken hands and said goodbye. My mother smoothed his perfect brow, so broad and noble, and I laid a final kiss upon it.

'It was really Corsham that did it,' my mother said. 'He never recovered from the way people treated us there, all that spite and unkindness and the way they spoke of you, Jim.' Then she told me that during the last winter, while I was in Sweden, my father had already had an attack, but they had not told me. Years later, after my mother's death, I found out what had caused that first attack and precipitated the fatal one. There were anonymous letters to my parents, postmarked Chippenham, Corsham, Bath and London, telling them to watch out and do something about their son or there would be trouble for them. But they had never mentioned these despicable attacks to me; they had kept cheerful faces and shown me all the love and care they had always given me, their prodigal son.

A few months after his death I finally was able to write an elegy for my father, 'died 21st January, 1958', which is the final poem in *The Prodigal Son*. The shameful outrage committed by the German students in the crypt of San Esteban inevitably was echoed in the conclusion of the poem.

I had to return to my classes in Salamanca. My Aunt Lyallie came to keep my mother company until she recovered a little from the shock, which seemed to have worsened the condition of her eyes, for she was slowly going blind. I often thought her blindness was not entirely physical: she wanted finally to shut her eyes to the sorrows and miseries of the son she still adored, for she could not bear to see me suffering.

Before I left, I bought a large-screen television set for her and Aunt Lyallie. Television was then just becoming very popular, though the screens were still only black and white. My father would not even allow a radio in the house, and when I suggested getting a TV set for him and my mother he adamantly refused, saying that the wireless had been the death of good conversation, and that TV would be the death of the family. The first programme we watched after it was installed was one my father would have loved, about old sailing-ships and the life of our ancestor, the poet-sailor William Falconer, who wrote a long poem, *The Shipwreck*, which was popular in its day. My mother sighed as she peered at those crowding white sails and topgallants: 'If only he were here to see that!' And our tears flowed again.

Here are the first two verses of my elegy for my father:

> In a cold season you suddenly left our home
> When I was far away, and sick in mind.
> Those harsh days in my distracted winter
> Must have touched you, too, and the heart
> That failed you as my own gave up the ghost.
>
> My dark nights blazed with sleepless candles
> In my drugged room shuttered tight against the bells,
> The stars, the snow, the people thin as burnt-out sticks,
> The black and iron-frosted gardens of a city that was once
> A rose of stone, and now was only stone. . . .

My father's favourite flowers were dark-red carnations. The night before his death I had bought a big bunch of red carnations to put in my room with the lighted candles we were now writing by, to please Dana. I must have been arranging those flowers, and setting the lighted candles round them, at the very moment my father was dying. 'O, Father, let my last touch rest your ashes, love. . . .'

My Father's Rule

Brass-bound boxwood
with the two triple brass hinges
and, on the eighteenth inch,
the big brass sun,
the folding centre.

'Rabone Warranted Boxwood
Made in England
No. 1380.'

At the tenth and fourteenth inches
brass points fit into holes
at the twenty-second and twenty-sixth inches.
On the inner seventeenth and nineteenth inches,
two tiny brass pins protrude,
linking with holes on the thirty-fifth inch and the first,
the holes worn with use
into slits that cannot hold.

The four nine-inch lengths
smooth and neat
folding together, opening
like a fan: the noble numbers and
the halves, quarters, tenths –
dark on the outside,
dark with the labour and sweat
of my father's hands,
the inside numbers clearer,
the wood paler, like his palms.

•

When I was a boy
often I played for hours
with this rule –
opening it and shutting it,
folding it, extending it.

The rule became so many things to me –
the holding centre was a crown of gold,
a coin of undiscovered realms:
the steel rivet at its heart
was the hub of every thought and act.

Sometimes, a solitary child,
I unfolded it to make
the oriental zigzag fence
of our Willow Pattern plates.
Sometimes, opened upright
and covered with a duster
borrowed from my mother Mary
it became an American native wigwam.
Or it grew into a tree
of angled branches like an ancient plum –
in my imagination
I could make anything
of its flexible inflexibility.

•

Three feet of honesty and pride
in decent workmanship –
thirty-six inches divided into four
stained, worn wooden slats
that measured more than wood.

The hands of the carpenter have blessed them,
and the skill of the craftsman hallowed them
all the days of his life.
For every time he used them
he gave them grace, his touch
each day was left upon them,
part of his very self –
in work and out of it.

•

I see still
the way he used to slide his folded rule
into the long side pocket of his dungarees,
and how, as he strode along,
it knocked against his thigh.

I see him draw it out to measure
my height, marked on the door-jamb each birthday
by his flat carpenter's pencil with its chisel point.

Now, a lost child,
and more alone than ever,

I hold my father's rule
in helpless hands, holding it for dear life,
and holding on to it, like grim death,
a last plank in
the wreck of a drowning world.

– And where is his spirit level now?

*   *   *

On another of our jaunts to Avila and Madrid we admired the Velas-
quezes and Goyas in the Prado. But we were not moved to write about
them, possibly because they were so very much themselves, any personal comment of ours might seem an intrusion. And the complex,
ever-absorbing detail of *Las Meninas* was really beyond words – pure art
underlying mysteriously the brilliant surface, where literature has no
place. But we loved *Los Borrachos*, those working men drunk on the
ambiguous beauty of Bacchus as well as on the wine.

It was on this visit that Dana did something I found surprising and at
first puzzling. I had always believed everything he did and said to be
sincere and genuinely personal, but gradually small cracks began appearing in his carefully constructed persona and well-tended integrity.
On this occasion we were sitting late at night in a small park somewhere
in Madrid. We were the only people there. I forget what we had been
talking and arguing about, but probably it was something connected
with our continuing confusions about poetry and sex. He may have been
genuinely distressed by the pain he was causing me – something he later
confessed he had deliberately provoked, with subtle sadism masquerad-
ing as friendly frankness. Now he was starting to cry, and I had never
seen him cry before. Were these real tears, or was he just squeezing
them out after too much cognac? I observed him quite coldly but with
my usual hapless concern. He looked really wretched and crestfallen. So
I said: 'It would have been better if we had never met.' And he
answered: 'Yes, I have been waiting a long time, waiting to hear you say
that. It's what they all say to me in the end. They always say that.' Who,
I wondered, were 'they'?

Then, out of his overcoat pocket he produced a safety razor-blade,
with which he sharpened the pencil he always used for his often indeci-
pherable, cramped little scribbles – a sign, a psychiatrist later told me, of
someone wanting to attract as little attention as possible, as in the case
of Robert Walser. My own feeling is that Walser's microscript was a
symptom of abnormal modesty and self-effacement or self-depreciation

in an unbearable modern world where, rather than seek fame, he preferred to be a servant. In Dana's case, as in my own, there was a withdrawal from normal or so-called normal society. Dana was often embarrassed by his good looks and their power over everyone who met him, so his tiny writing may have been a kind of Walserian camouflage.

With that dulled little blade in his right hand, he began drawing it slowly across the inside of his left wrist. His tears dropped on the blade. Beads of blood appeared along the cuts, which alarmed me, though at the same time I could see that the wounds were superficial. Nevertheless, I rushed him back to our nearby hotel, where I cleaned the wounds and fixed three or four large Band-Aids on them. I remember the helpless, almost childlike way he submitted himself to my ministrations. He, too, needed someone to watch over him. At that moment my feelings of love for him became somewhat abstract, like a mother bandaging her little boy's playground cuts and sores. I gave him some aspirin, undressed him and put him to bed.

Next day, when he awoke at noon, he was as bright and cheerful as if nothing at all had happened. And indeed nothing had happened. It was all play-acting, a bluff to get attention, but he never admitted it nor apologized for anything he had done or said.

I wonder how many times I was taken in by his Yankee sincerity, his B-movie honesty. How many times had my heart sunk when I asked if we could go somewhere or try something new in our poems and he had answered with the excusing phrase 'I guess not'? Perhaps unconsciously I willingly let myself be fooled, just in order to please him and keep our relationship going. I was so terrified of losing him, for I sensed there would never be another love like this in my life.

But he always wanted to be the one in control, the top dog, to be the one who could take off on a whim and relate his volatility to democratic individual freedom to do as one pleased – a special privilege to which only Americans were supposed to be entitled.

But I needed his love so much, and he knew it. Always at the end of any love affair I had wondered if there would ever be another, and there always had been. But now I feared I was getting too old for romantic friendships. If Dana left me, I knew I would never love anyone again – or at least, not in the same way, with the same intensity. So I clung to him through the poetry I went on helping him to write. If only he had started to write in a larger script, I might have felt I had succeeded with him, made him a poet.

There was only one thing I was ashamed of in my love for Dana, which had sprung from poetry, and from sources I knew were pure. After all, it was he who seduced me. But then I tried to seduce him with poetry. I wanted our collaboration, strange as it was, to continue for ever, just so long as it kept him beside me. I think that he, who could have had as many friends as he wished, never realized how much it meant to a lonely and friendless person to have a friend, to be seen walking with him in the rose-red streets of Salamanca, to be able to go to a concert or an art museum with him, to have him opposite me at dinner in even the meanest, cheapest restaurant.

So I used to encourage his own poetry, and his ideas for poetic themes, even when I knew they were poor or did not interest me. I was terrified that if I criticized him he would take offence and leave me, if not permanently, then for a few days, without giving me a sign of life, and so leaving me in anguish.

We discussed my pacifism, and on one occasion I denied my convictions, just to be on his side. He had been just too young for the Korean War, and one day he told me that it was one of the experiences he regretted having missed. He said he could understand my hatred of war, and why I rejected all involvement in war and the governments that perpetrated it. But he added that in the case of the Korean War the Allies were justified in fighting against the communists. I cravenly agreed, simply in order not to antagonize and perhaps lose him. But immediately my heart was suffused with shame. Now I am never ashamed of anything, for I consider shame to be a bourgeois and petty emotion, but this was the one occasion when I felt ashamed of myself, and I have never forgotten how sad it made me to have denied my principles for the sake of friendship and love – or what I imagined to be love. Was it not infatuation, rather? But this incident gave me an insight into Dana's mind. If he was an anti-communist, could he not be some kind of spy or agent of the American government? The dread Pentagon . . .? That possibility, always present in my mind, became, I must admit, an added thrill.

Dana was opinionated and liked to have the last word in an argument. As I have never been interested in argument, he must often have felt frustrated by my silences, my refusal to rise to the bait. Sometimes he immediately pounced upon whatever I said and showed me in a psychoanalytical way how wrong I was, and how right he was.

He could always find fault with something, either in my writing or in my personality – something not difficult to achieve because I have always laid myself open to easy attack. I remember one instance, after we had been making love, when he took my hands very tenderly and turned them this way and that, pressing them gently, kissing the palms and the wrists. Then, out of the blue, he pronounced 'Jim, the backs of your hands are very ugly – did you know that?' in a tone that suggested I might be surprised and hurt. I was silent, for I could not understand in what way he meant that my hands were ugly: I had never considered whether they were beautiful or not. But at once I saw that perhaps he was right, that perhaps the backs of my hands were indeed hideous and strange. But after turning them over to reveal the palms, he declared: 'But the palms are so beautiful, the lines so clear and simple, the shape so pure.' Was I supposed to be pleased by these comments? I did not know what to say in reply, so I took his hands and held them beside my own, showing first the backs, then the palms, then measuring them one against the other, palm to palm – something the Japanese would often do in comparing their smaller, lighter hands with my grosser ones. Dana's hands were strong and sun-tanned, with long, spatulate fingers and firm, dry palms – the hands of an athlete, the fists of a boxer. I thought they were beautiful in their male hardness and power, so I told him: 'Dana, your hands are perfect, front and back.' He rewarded me with a puzzled smile, as if he wanted to show he did not quite believe me, then with a kiss from sun-blistered lips, dry and firm.

Dana once said that the real proof of love was the sharing of a single toothbrush by lovers. Like many of his pronouncements, I thought this was facile. But as always I was wary of contradicting him, not wanting to antagonize him by even the slightest show of disagreement in case he left me. He did not like to be contradicted. On the few occasions when I had ventured a criticism, he always picked on some word or expression I used to prove his point, claiming that it was a subconscious betrayal of my true nature and my real thought. I always found this kind of slick psychoanalytic one-upmanship irritating, but I never attempted to defend myself, because I am bored by argument and discussion of any kind. It was easier just to let him have his way. After all, he was fifteen years or so younger than I, and presumably still intellectually immature, despite all his literary and philosophical name-dropping. That I myself was hardly any more mature than he, was beside the point: I had no very high opinion of people who claimed to be mature adults.

But I went along with him, and from time to time we shared a toothbrush, either his or mine. I quite enjoyed using Dana's toothbrush. The thought that it had been inside his mouth, touching his tongue and gums and those rather small but perfect teeth, that it had been drenched in some of his most intimate fluids gave me an erotic thrill. I often wondered if he enjoyed using my toothbrush as much as I enjoyed using his. It was a new slant on the eternal problem of the one who kisses and the one who is kissed. I was usually the active partner, or rather it was usually I who initiated a kiss or an embrace. He was my Rimbaud, certainly: I was the Vierge Folle. But I could be both Verlaine and

Rimbaud. He was always Rimbaud.

Today, of course, the test of love between men would be their willingness to share not just a toothbrush but also a razor. Dana did not shave as often as I did. His blond stubble was silky and made his mouth as exciting as an adolescent boy's. And I envied his smooth, hairless chest, with its peachy tan. A hairless chest would have been a great advantage for a bisexual like myself. For bisexual Dana, it was something to be proud of, and he looked down upon my inferior condition. He always had to be number one.

The only person I ever felt I might fall in love with again in the same way was a Japanese, the poet Takahashi Mutsuo. I met him briefly in 1963 at a poetry reading given in Tokyo at the American Center by James Dickey. He was sitting on a sofa outside the lecture-room, smoking a cigarette. He was wearing chinos, and looked almost American, and there was something sexually magnetic about him that at once reminded me of Dana. I was introduced to him but did not linger to prolong our acquaintance. I was too afraid of falling hopelessly in love with this protégé of Yukio Mishima, whose marvellous homoerotic poems I translated. Once when I was leaving for Europe, he came to see me off at the airport, bringing a parting gift. It was quite unexpected. But again I held myself warily at a certain distance, not daring to make contact with him for fear of falling into the kind of trap Dana had prepared for me. I often see his picture in literary magazines. Now that he is wearing a beard, he looks just like Dana – the square-shaped face, the mouth, the nose. Only the eyes are different, but they are a poet's eyes. Takahashi is one of those people I loved on sight, or with whom I just wanted to go to bed, but denied myself the opportunity, thus leaving them forever desirable in my memory.

Another Japanese who attracts me today is the unattainable sumo wrestler Kirishima, from Kagoshima in Kyushu, who is one of the most beautiful males I have ever seen. My Japanese friends wonder at my passion, because he is not very well known and not very successful, though when he visited Paris with his fellow *sumotori* he was at once called 'the Japanese Alain Delon' – to my mind, an insult to my hero, but for a while that kind of adulation seemed to give him a little of the confidence he needed, and on his return to Japan he delighted me by winning an unusually high number of contests. The success soon faded, but my adoration lives on. Kirishima is nothing like Dana, but he has that male charisma which makes me want to lie in his arms – I feel safer just gloating over his superb body on the television screen. No one will ever take Dana's place.

WINTER'S END

... the hounds of spring are on winter's traces ...

(*Algernon Charles Swinburne*, ATALANTA IN CALYDON)

Sing if you're Glad to be Gay –
Sing if you like it that way ...

Tom Robinson Band

I was utterly devastated by my father's death. But on my return to Salamanca Dana gave me strong support, a spiritual courage that entered our love and our poetry. I felt as if a huge gap had appeared in my existence, because one who had always been there was there no longer, and I should never see him again.

When I gave my first class, Manuela stood up as soon as I entered, and in beautiful English, then in Spanish, expressed the sympathies of the whole class. I was moved, and the tears fell on the pages of Jespersen. Everyone was so kind at the university. Professor Ruiperez told me I need not start my classes until I was quite recovered, and the women in the office and the library spoke friendly words to me for the first time. I had lost a father, 'someone to watch over me' who had done his best to do so, though he had failed. I did not hold that against him. Nor did I bear any ill-will against my poor mother, though she had brought me up in error, innocently ignorant of what she was doing to my psyche. I knew that she now expected me to live with her for the rest of her days. But I also knew I could not; it would have been the death of me. Yet I vowed to do as much as possible for her comfort and happiness, to write to her and see her regularly, too.

But could I live with Dana? Could I live with anyone? I was beginning to think that I was a person with whom no one could live. The trouble was, other people. They wanted me to be different from what I was. They wanted me to 'put down roots'. But all things in this impermanent world are essentially rootless. The desire to put down roots is a recognition of human rootlessness. I am like the leaves and flowers of *ikebana*, with roots cut off, stuck in a spiked metal holder (*kenzan*) instead of in the earth. Their ground is water, renewed every day, as the leaves and flowers are renewed in accordance with mood and season, even with the hour of the day. My hydroponic life was the only kind with which I was happy, a gypsy trait from my Viking ancestry. The true value of a lifetime's loneliness is then seen as Nothingness, Emptiness, perfectly expressed in the minimal art of traditional *ikebana*, and in the minimal, marginal existence of the person without ties, without permanent position, situation, family, roots. It is a transient death alive in art, in which all natural will-to-live has been severed. Such limitations are not deficiencies but modes of behaviour that are essences of reduction, to be valued for their essential selves.

This was how I valued other people, too – how I valued Dana, as someone who did not need to be improved but allowed to flourish in his own right, with all the confusions and contradictions of which he was capable. I gave myself to him completely, both as a human being and as an artist. But I began to see limitations in the amount I could give. I wanted to get back to myself and to my own work, to all that he had robbed me of – even my own name. Yet I could not let him go: his love was too precious to me, and I knew I would never find its like again. It could be kept only by giving my entire self, roots and all.

I knew that I should have to make a decision. I must choose between Dana's love and my own identity as a person and as a poet. Perhaps I knew already what the answer would be – that I must cut myself free from him. It would be painful for both of us, but more for me than for him, for he was young and beautiful and gifted, with the whole world before him. I was neither young nor beautiful, and now I doubted my gifts. Would they survive the surgical cut I was contemplating? It must come. The only question for me was, when? I began to see one way out of our dilemma. Joe had written to me suggesting that there was a post for me in Japan (available through the good offices of Stephen Spender, who had just returned from there with a commission from the Dean of the Faculty of Letters at Tohoku University) to go and teach English, in the poet-teacher tradition for which it was famous. The last poet they had had, had been Ralph Hodgson, before the war. George Barker had taken his place in 1940 but had escaped to the United States before Pearl Harbor, for he had been followed everywhere by the 'thought police', the sinister *kempeitai*, who suspected him of being a communist spy. But I knew nothing at all about Tohoku University, or about the city of Sendai. I pushed Joe's letter into the back of my mind.

One evening, towards midnight, I was walking back to my hotel from Dana's place along a deserted street. Suddenly, out of a dark doorway, a figure stepped and stood in front of me with open arms. It was Jordi! We embraced. I was bewildered. Where had he been? Why hadn't he

written to me? He had been in prison for three months. When he was
released, he sold up his home and moved to Barcelona, where he now
had a job in a printing press. We entered a café for a drink. Why had he
been imprisoned? He would not tell me, or could not explain. But I
gathered that it was because of some kind of political dissent, his being a
member of an unauthorized group that had held secret meetings. He
had aged: his hair was touched with grey, and his face was haggard.

Jordi had been in Salamanca only one day but he had found out
where I was living. And he had seen me walking from my hotel
apartment with Dana – *Americano*, he said disdainfully. Who was he? I
told him he was a student. 'Is he your lover?' Remembering the knife he
had displayed on our last night in Valladolid, I took fright and denied it.
Jordi gave a bitter smile. Not only his face had changed; imprisonment
and hardship had changed his sweet good nature, too. He had been
brutalized in prison and become cynical.

He was leaving on the early morning train for Zaragoza, then on to
Barcelona. He could not take more time off. I knew he could not stay at
my hotel. It was all right for Dana, because he was just another
foreigner, but for Jordi it was impossible. Again we were confronted by
that vengeful force which stood in the way of same-sex lovers in Spain –
especially if one was a foreigner, and one a Spaniard. We wandered
round the streets until dawn. There was no love left in Jordi. But he had
remembered me and come to say goodbye to me. It was the only way he
could let me know what had happened to him.

As we were sitting in the station waiting-room, waiting for the train
to Zaragoza, he took my hand and wept. He would not give me his
address in Barcelona – it would be too dangerous for us to meet again. I
thought of the refugees whose turmoil was invading the whole of
Europe. We, too, were refugees – the refugees of a forbidden love. I felt
this was a rehearsal for my parting from Dana.

The train entered the station. As he was getting into the train, Jordi
smiled and shrugged as he had done that night in Valladolid when the
secret police had led him away. But this time he drew out his knife and
showed it to me with a meaningful glance. My blood froze. 'No, Jordi,
no!' was all I could say as the train slowly carried him away into the
dawn. He was standing at the window of an empty compartment,
laughing, as he made the gesture of slitting his throat. I never saw him
again, never heard from him.

Whenever I am in Barcelona I expect to run into Jordi, even today,
thirty years later, in a totally different, freer, happier Spain. But
something tells me he is no longer alive. I carry with me the memory of
that knife's sharp flash in the rising sun.

I never told Dana of this encounter.

*   *   *

The first step was to leave Salamanca. I told Dana I could no longer bear the atmosphere of the city, the right-wing bullies, the Falangists, the deadening work of teaching mostly bored and resentful students. He said he would stay on until the vacation. Then what? Probably return to the United States. . . .

It was Easter again. I left for Bath. As soon as the train started, I drew a long breath of relief. I was not running away from anything – I was running towards something, my old self, my old talent, and – for a while – my own home.

Of course my mother thought I had returned in order to live with her. She was very lonely, though she had some friends and visits from relatives from time to time. But her whole life had been my father and myself; without us, she was lost. She had no other interests in life, nothing to fall back on. And her eyesight was getting worse. I had arranged for her to see a specialist, and he told me the condition was irreversible, that she would never lose her sight completely but that she would be almost totally blind within a year.

It was around this time that 'queer-bashing' began in Bath, as in the rest of Britain. Down by the bus station I was followed by a gang of youths chanting 'Puff, the Magic Dragon'. I escaped only by jumping on a bus to Warminster. If Dana had been with me, they would never have dared.

Without Dana I was suffering the agonies of hell. Perhaps sex had become for me a habit-forming drug. I was suffering severe and painful withdrawal symptoms, and my mother was alarmed by my fits of weeping, my chronic insomnia, my thinness. She had started attending classes at the Blind Club, and was being prepared for her further loss of sight. She now had a collapsible white metal stick she used quite defensively when out walking. In later years she would hit the shins of passers-by with it if they got in her way.

We went for walks in the enchanting gardens of Bath. In particular the special garden for the blind was her favourite, where she would gently rub the sweet-scented leaves and herbs and flowers between her fingers and recall their names – the names she knew so well from the allotment we had had in South Shields. Those daily walks with her helped to calm my mind a little, but I could not bear the thought of writing poems again, not without Dana. I was so sure I would fail.

My mother went on an outing for a few days with the Blind Club.

Left all alone, I was in despair. I wrote to Dana but got no reply. I did not really expect one. Yet his presence was everywhere in the house, like my father's, and in all the places we had known in London and Bath and Bristol.

While my mother was away I decided to take a trip myself, and took refuge in my old home town, South Shields, now changed almost unrecognizably. But the old market square was still there, the ferry to North Shields; Ocean Road, the Town Hall, the Library, Trow Rocks, the sands, the pier. . . . It was on the pier that I made my first stumbling attempts to start writing poetry on my own again; my very own poetry:

> I walk the long dark pier that bends
> Out of the seaport's lonely streets into
> The unlit centre of the northern seas.
> Slowly I leave the land's hard lights behind,
> And turn to the deadly power of the stars,
> The full moon's malignance racked in clouds.
>
> The sea runs on each side of me,
> Banging the stone defences of an endless sleep
> With bitter tons that die in fits of spray.
> Only the lighthouse at the end is true.
> To touch its burning tip will give love life.
> I shall not reach it if the gates are shut
> Against the storm that hoists the lunging sea.
> – But though the gates are shut, it reaches me.

In my utter loneliness I had only one resource: several times I took the ferry to North Shields, and walked up the steep bank to a certain public lavatory beside a roaring pub. The lavatory was below ground, and in the white brick walls between the two cubicles a hole had been hacked, one of the best glory-holes in existence at that time. There was usually some man waiting on the other side of the hole, like some sea creature waiting to grab its prey, and after I had settled on the seat, there would be a significant pause. We would start to make movements that suggested masturbation. Then a horny pit-lad's hand, coal-dust under the fingernails, would insinuate itself through the hole, just wide enough for his big, warm, tender hand. Already I would be in what Nabokov calls 'a manly condition', and the release was sharp and sweet. Then it was the turn for my own hand to explore the anonymous member beyond the missing brick. It was a pleasure of the utmost, basic simplicity, convenient and hidden, yet profoundly human and tender in its mutual concern. We never tried to see one another's faces: that would perhaps have spoiled the purity of the experience.

Yet when I emerged from that heaven-haven of sexual absolution, I would feel guilty, frightened, torn between happiness at being liberated from overwhelming sexual tension and the scared wonder of the events, as if they had been rituals in a half-remembered primitive religion. At night the place was jumping, the whistling urinals were all occupied, and then the smell of piss and semen was the smell of ecstatic terror, for we never knew when the place would be raided by the cops, and the person standing at the next stall playing with himself might be a copper's nark, an informer or an *agent provocateur*. How on earth I came through all those perils unscathed, unarrested, is one of the miracles of my early life. There was an angel watching over me, as someone had once predicted·in my childhood when she read my fortune in the tea-leaves, in my cup of white china with the gilt shamrock on the rim and in the centre of the saucer.

No one knew me now in South Shields. Occasionally I felt that a policeman or a plain-clothes dick was looking rather too intently into my face. But as usual I affected a supreme unconcern, and floated past them with a sway of the hips that was a touch exaggerated. Wolfenden had come and gone, but persecution was still abroad in the streets and back lanes of Tyneside.

I paid surreptitious trips to our old homes in Ada Street and West Avenue, where the fences my father had put up for Granny Kirkup before the war – in 1934, I believe – were still standing round the long garden of 'Mundesley', named after my grandmother's birthplace. I felt so proud of my father for having been such a fine craftsman. I had a letter about him from the Amalgamated Society of Joiners and Carpenters, of which he had been a prominent member. It said they all stood with bowed heads at the start of the meeting after they had heard of his death, 'and there was a silence that could be felt. . . .' Who would not be proud of such a father? And yet I had failed him, and he had failed me. Those psychic scars would never heal. Now I could not even write my own poems to my satisfaction: I felt crippled. Furtive but fulfilling sex was the only consolation.

*   *   *

I was back home before my mother returned from her little holiday. She seemed much more cheerful and was full of chatter about her new friends and about the wonderful workers at the Blind Club, where she was learning to write using a metal board with black elastic stretched across it for lines. She practised writing letters to me, though I was still at home. She must have sensed that one day I would be leaving her again, and that nearly broke my heart, knowing the sadness she must feel all too well in my experiences with lovers who never stayed long but left me feeling as if part of me had been torn from my body.

Aunt Lyallie must have been needling my mother while I was away, because one day she suddenly asked me, with tremulous anxiety: 'Why don't you get married, Jim? Don't you want to get married?' Unconsciously she put a note of hope into those half-scandalized questionings, because she knew I knew she would never be happy if I married. She wanted me to stay as I was, the way she had created me. All I could say in reply was: 'What for?' And she gave a faint smile, reassured. A few years later, when a Japanese professor on holiday in England visited her in our other house in Bath, Hill House in Sion Road, he said to her, in the usual Japanese joky way: 'I'm sure your son will be marrying some nice Japanese lady, Mrs Kirkup.' She at once sent me a terrified letter, accusing me of concealing my marriage plans from her. I had to send her a greetings telegram, so that she would not be alarmed at the sight of the envelope, saying: DARLING MUM I AM MARRIED TO MY MUSE AND HAVE NO INTENTION OF SEEKING A DIVORCE SO DON'T WORRY I'LL BE A BACHELOR GAY FOR THE REST OF MY LIFE LOVE JIM. Her reply was an almost audible sigh of relief.

Occasionally I spent a day in London, always returning at night to keep my mother company. I saw Joe, of course, and remember laughing at his description of how Morgan Forster had been interviewed by Alfred C. Kinsey for his researches into *Sexual Behaviour in the Human Male*. Joe had once taken Rose Macaulay to a Billy Graham revivalist, fundamentalist mass meeting and been utterly revolted by all the rabid emotionalism and the militant Christianity, and he reminded me what Graham had said about Kinsey: 'It is impossible to estimate the damage this book will do to the already deteriorating morals of America.' On May Day I got a shock that was half pleasant, half sad: Joe had printed, over our pseudonym, one of the last poems Dana and I had composed, 'Winter's End':

> We shall not watch the long delay
> Of snow, nor feel its sudden flight
> Alarm our sleeping eyes, and play
> Its rosy waterfalls across the white
> Suspensions of the rising day.
>
> Nor shall we hear its airy flakes

Feather the quiet as they fall
Their massive winds upon the lakes,
Nor shiver through their leaning wall
That always mends what nothing breaks.

– If winter wreathes our breath again
Upon a branch where summer blew,
Will it recall the season when
We made one weather out of two,
And snow its secrets on us then?

I was on the bus from the centre of Bath to the end of our street,
Avondale Buildings (we lived at No. 5), when I casually opened *The
Listener* and saw this May Day poem. My heart always jumped with
fright whenever I saw one of my poems in print, because I was sure it
would contain one of the misprints whose steady drizzle has haunted my
work all my life. But this was all-correct. My heart kept jumping as I
read it, remembering Dana and our many days and nights together.
When I had left him for Bath, he had said, sadly, seeing me off at
Salamanca station: 'I should have come with you when your father died.
I'm sorry. Then this parting need never have happened.' I had felt his
absence keenly at my father's funeral, among the little group of family
mourners at the Bristol Crematorium. I wanted to have Dana beside me
as his coffin slid so smoothly into the flames and my mother clutched my
arm, not daring to watch something she felt was horrible – and was to
happen to her one day, at the new crematorium in Bath, high up in
those verdant hills. Now, as I read our poem over and over again, I
longed to see him, to share it with him, to show him I still loved him,
however impossible my love might be. I remembered our last days in my
hotel room, their fevered, unhappy intensity, with the already-hot
Spanish sun blazing down outside the shutters.

I remembered also the time we finally accepted that British Council
invitation and went to give a poetry reading in Madrid. Dana read a
group of modern Americans, which must have annoyed the British,
starting with Elizabeth Bishop's 'The Fish' – I can still hear his voice, the
faint American accent and the hushed astonishment he put into the first
line: 'I caught a tremendous fish. . . .' Then I think I read some of my
favourite English poems – Hardy, Hopkins, Housman, Blake, Yeats,
Edward Thomas, Wilfred Owen, and I think one each by Ted Hughes
and Thom Gunn, the only contemporaries I could stand at that time.
We ended with a group of our own poems. In Salamanca we had taken
to living by candlelight in my shuttered hotel room, and those candles

crept into two or three of our last poems written there. We finished our
reading with all the lights in the hall turned out, and candles burning on
our reading-desk. The poem was about hypnotism, and contained verses
like:

> The room is growing darker with my voice.
> You see the candle shine and slowly weep
> Into the dark that listens to my voice.
> Look at the light that sends your eyes asleep. . . .

At the end of each of the five verses, one of us blew out a candle, and it
was very effective, dramatically. We could feel the tension among the
large audience of Spaniards and British and Americans, a tension that
relaxed into applause as I blew the last candle out and the room lamps
came on. People came up to us to congratulate us on the reading. We
were exhausted.

There was to be a reception, and later we were invited to dinner at
the house of the British Council representative. But we refused both
invitations. The representative seemed stunned. He sent his young
daughter over to try to persuade us to stay. 'People always do, you
know,' she told us, as if that were incontrovertible proof that we had to
conform. We rushed out of the building and started running along the
street, hardly knowing where we were or where we were going, until we
felt we had put enough distance between us and the reception. I had our
fee in my pocket – enough for us to have a magnificent seafood dinner at
a place just off the Gran Via, with a couple of bottles of wine. The
enormous relief at being released from that obligation made us light-
headed with happiness. I used to like giving poetry readings, but in the
end I had to give up, for I could not stand the socializing afterwards, as
if my poetry had just been the excuse for a drinking spree *à la* Dylan
Thomas. I could not stand the ridiculous questions people came and
posed about my work: 'But how do you find such interesting subjects for
your poems, Mr Kirkup?' Or: 'I don't understand all this modern poetry
at all, but I know what I like, and for some reason your poems manage
to penetrate even my thick head. How do you do it?' Or the many awful
questions beginning: 'Did you ever read. . . .' Or the dismaying prospect of endless explanations of my unusual background in reply to: 'Nice
to meet you. I really enjoyed your reading. Where you from?' Our
escape from that hellish occasion was an act of liberation. The agonies
of reading one's most intimate feelings and thoughts aloud to a roomful
of strangers, and then being expected to talk about them and explain
them in an acceptably relaxed and humorous manner were more than I

could bear. It would not be so bad if I could just stand up, read my poems and leave, but that was apparently unthinkable. It was as if poets owed an explanation to the audience for being what they were, to bring creatures apart down to the level of ordinary folks; as if the poet might be indulged his little failings and eccentricities as long as he allowed himself to be democratically mauled in public by thoughtless questioners or – even worse, much worse – by fellow-poets or by those who had poetic pretensions and who found in 'question time' an opportunity to assuage their jealousy or seek revenge for their own incompetence and mediocrity. Thanks, but – no thanks! Poets will do anything to put one another down. I remember the pleasant surprise I had when Olivia Manning, sitting next to me on some poetry-reading platform (the ICA?) turned to her husband after my reading and remarked to him – a BBC radio producer – 'Now *there's* a poet who knows how to read poetry. Why don't you . . .?' But before she could finish, he retorted: 'He's not a member of Equity.' As if that had anything to do with the ability of a poet to read his own poems! That is the sort of thing poets either have to learn to put up with, or retire from the scene in order to retain their sanity. And that is precisely what we had done in Madrid.

* * *

One morning the unbelievable happened: there was a letter from Dana. It informed us that he was leaving Salamanca for England on his motor bike, via Cherbourg, and that we could expect him in Bath on a certain day. My heart leapt, then sank, then leapt. My mother was guarded, but she said how nice it would be to have Dana stay with us again.

Day after day we waited for his arrival. Then late one night, around eleven o'clock, there was a ring at the doorbell. My mother had already gone to bed. I went to open it, and there was Dana, travel-stained and weary but with a beaming smile on his sun-tanned face. I looked past him and saw the old motor bike, which he parked in our front garden.

I made him some tea and supper while he bathed and changed and unpacked his things in my bedroom. There was much to talk about, and we were awake until after four. Incredibly, he had taken up with those student thugs, and they had taken him out drinking until they were all blind drunk – 'So drunk, nobody remembered what had happened next day.' I could guess what that standard excuse for sexual orgies might mean. So, after that, he had decided to leave Salamanca for good and return to the United States by way of England, to say a final goodbye to me and my mother in the house where we had all been so happy at Christmas. 'There's someone missing,' he said. 'You can feel his absence. I liked your father so much.'

We slept together, in one another's arms. Next morning I let him sleep until midday. He had left some notebooks on my study table. I picked one of them up and was struck to the heart, for it was obvious that he had been writing a lot of poetry, all of it, so it seemed to me, very good. And I had been dumb so long! I felt a furious jealousy. I felt our situation had been reversed: now I was the halting beginner, he was the fluent expert. Now I needed his help in order to get started again, and we took up once more our old collaborative writing habits. I realized that all I wanted was to stop him from writing on his own, and that this was possibly his own motive for working with me in Salamanca – to keep my true poetic self silent, subservient to his. It was a slow and painful realization, as when he had told me that he had been deliberately tempting me to have sex with him all along. . . . But our poetry started to flow again, though now it was he who distributed the favours: there was no call for him now to bribe me with sex, so this aspect of our relationship was something he kept under tight control, allowing sexual contact only when he felt like it and not just when I wanted it, as in the past. Nevertheless, I was quite happy. Bath was more beautiful than ever in the early summer. We took my mother to some of the events and concerts of the Bath Festival, among them a wonderful performance by Hepzibah and Yehudi Menuhin. One day as we were going to a choral concert in Bath Abbey, we were all three walking along the Parade when my mother stopped Dana and said, pointing across the road: 'That's the police station. So you had better be careful.' It was said as a joke, and Dana and I laughed, but it left me frightened. Perhaps my mother had received another anonymous letter which she had successfully concealed from me?

On the motor bike we rode all over the countryside, to Bathampton, Bradford-on-Avon to see the old tithe barn, to Bristol to visit the Llandoger Trow, and as far as Cheltenham Spa, Leamington and Gloucester. We even paid a surprise visit to Corsham, where Rosemary and Clifford Ellis welcomed us warmly and invited me to give a series of lectures and classes. We were broke, so I accepted, and Dana took me on his bike to and fro from Bath to Corsham throughout the next six weeks. But I was thankful when the summer holiday started and I could be released from duties I was finding it harder and harder to cope with.

In Salamanca, as a parting present, Dana had given me two of his most beloved treasures, two books of Chinese prints and ink drawings. They now inspired us to write a poem, 'Chinese Print':

He lies on rocks
As though they were a bank of clouds,
And reads a book.

He lifts the leaves
In one small hand to fan the light
Under his lids.

He reads the air:
Its empty pages are the wings
Of painted birds.

They fly with him
Across another turning page –
Clean out of sight.

How far will he
Go floating in his robe of mist
With lifted wrist?

This poem helped me to find a way back into my own poetry. Unknown to Dana, I began writing a series of free-verse poems about the pictures. They later appeared in *The Prodigal Son* as 'Seven Pictures from China', and have since proved popular with anthologists. Unwisely, I let Dana see my drafts of these poems, and at once I could sense his disapproval, his jealousy even, that I had written the poems myself. (When he finally left us for the United States, he took these gifts back from me, with the excuse that as he had bought them in Berlin he wanted to show them to the dancer. But the true reason was that he wanted to prevent me from writing any more good poems about them.)

He could see that I was slowly but surely getting back to my old self, and to my own poetry. A number of tentative poems took shape, and five of them form the first section of *The Prodigal Son*. I could not finish them until after Dana had left for the States, when I would sit day after day beside my desk, trying to write, while on the other side of Avondale Buildings the children screamed and shrieked in the playground. I wrote lines like this: 'I wait with a pencil in my hand/ Beside the morning's empty page . . .', 'The dumb words are fastened in my throat, / And will not come. . . .' And, in 'The Lost Poem':

Will what I now begin to write
Become the poem I have lost
So long, and did not wish
To find again? . . .

This period of inarticulate waiting began to end with 'After Pentecost':

> The wonder is that I write
> This, when I cannot find a word.
> Once, everything came to my hand,
> The farthest phrases, and the closest calls,
> And I drew my meaning lightly
> From the waters of a page . . .
>
> Yet for the first time now,
> As if I learned to speak
> Again, after a long dumbness,
> I seek the wind of a word.
> The wonder is that I write
> This, upon the waters of a page.

In the weeks before he left, Dana and I sometimes quarrelled bitterly. I think we were both wanting to be free, to write our own work, yet we were afraid to relinquish the relationship that had kept us writing together so long. I had gained a poet but was losing a lover, perhaps the last I would ever know. We had our little mock boxing-matches, in my study, circling round the table as if it were a ring. Sometimes the slaps and punches were for real now, and my mother would cry up the stairs in alarm whenever she heard a sudden thump as I fell on the floor or bumped into the furniture. Then I had to reassure her that we were 'just having fun'. She did not believe me. 'Queer sort of fun,' she would comment, her eyes, so gentle, so nearly sightless, filling with fear. She sensed the tensions we were suffering before we finally parted.

I stood at the front door of No. 5, watching Dana straddle his bike, adjust his backpack and wave cheerily to me as he roared off down the road. I watched him until he turned the corner. He never looked back. That was something I could understand, and approve of – to make a clean cut. I got on the bus at the terminus at the bottom of Avondale Buildings and rode it back and forth to the other end of the line, sitting on the top deck, not knowing where I was or what I was doing, until the conductor came up to me at the other terminus, after my fifth trip, and asked: 'You all right, mate?' So I got off and walked around for an hour or so, unseeing, my mind a total blank. I kept weeping. Trying to compose myself, I got back home in time to make tea, but could do nothing except collapse sobbing in my mother's arms. She held me tenderly and stroked my hair, and said nothing until I was calm again. Then we switched on the TV and had a cup of tea. 'Don't worry,' she

told me as she went to bed that night. 'It's all over now.'
But it was not.

*   *   *

Our love affair was over. But it lives on in the poems we wrote together,
and in the poems I wrote myself in Salamanca and Bath. Though we had
parted for ever, I did not believe our love was lost. Mine, at any rate,
after the initial angers and resentments, has lingered on to this day, and
I think there has never been a time when I did not remember that love
and think of Dana. I sometimes dream of him: at times he enters my
dreams with loving smiles, at times he is cold and indifferent, but we are
always friends.

One of the last poems we wrote together in Bath expresses perfectly
the state of our love at that time. It was about two skeletons discovered
in a stone coffin in Bath. We called it 'The Anatomy of Love':

> How comfortable they look,
> Laid out together in a bed of stone
> Whose rocky coverlet was rolled
> Away, stripping these sweethearts to the bone.
>
> No chance encounter has composed
> Their double genders in a single birth;
> Nor is it accident completes
> Their pleasure in the lively earth.
>
> Two skulls repose upon the same
> Worn pillow in their dusty mine.
> Their tangled joints are slung upon
> The cable of one common spine.
>
> Now those two contracted hearts
> Have wept each other's dust away,
> Their cages' interlocking ribs
> Do there embrace till judgment day.
>
> Among the innocent exchange of limbs
> The knees are capped with skipping stones.
> The fists have rattled down the shins
> To shake the footloose fans of bones.
>
> These chalky relics of the flesh
> Have danced beyond, and clean above

Boneless tongue, and melting eye,
And parts that want the whole of love.

The coffin is displayed in the museum attached to the Roman Baths.
Today, since my mother's death in that beautiful city, I cannot bear to
return. There are too many memories, all sad, in Bath and its environs.
But one day I must take my courage in both hands and go back to visit
all the places we knew – to Beckford's Tower on Lansdowne Hill, to
Corsham Court, to Brunel's great suspension bridge at Clifton, to the
ancient tithe barn at Bradford-on-Avon.

Perhaps the best poem about the ending of our love was one we
wrote in my apartment at the Hotel España in Salamanca, just before I
returned to England. We called it 'The Last of Love', and it commemo-
rates the last time we made love in Salamanca:

Behind the shutters' bended shafts
That slake our bodies with the lime of light,
We take our last of love; then float
The battens open to the ends of night.

Calming bewildered flesh, we coax
The spirit back into the haunts of breath
And catch the drift of loneliness
Whose wide confusions flank desire with death.

Here, in each other's arms, we end
A love that left no gentle wish to true
The compass of a common star,
No I to take the strangeness out of you.

What double weathers in our hands
Cause them to flutter in the air, and sneak
A flame through which to drag the time?
The morning is a wound that will not speak.

As time bends out before us through
A window that turns in upon the pane,
We draw unending parallels
Of light through eyes that cannot meet again.

The parallels with that coffin poem are evident. If we had gone on, our
love would have brought us the death we secretly called up every time
we embraced. We were like those skeletons still embracing in the dust of
their vanished flesh and dead desires. The flame of the cigarette we used

to light and share after making love was the last symbol of warmth we had when the fires of passion were quenched.

And even after Dana had left, there was something of him that remained in Bath, as we were to find out. A presence lived on in his absence.

Dana had wanted to take his old bike with him on the ship back to the States. We had gone to the Council Offices to obtain permission for him to take it with him. But for some reason I cannot remember, it was impossible to get permission to ship the motor bike. He said he might sell it in Southampton if he could not get it on board.

I had been away in London for the day, about three or four days after Dana's departure. When I got home, my mother's face was white with shock. A policeman had come while I was out and had asked her to tell me to call at his house as soon as I got back. 'What have you done now, Jim?' she whispered in a shaking voice.

I did not know what it could be, but I tried to reassure her and went up the road to where the policeman lived. I was quite calm. If I was to be arrested, I would be arrested with dignity. But the tall policeman who came to the door was quite amiable. It turned out that Dana had simply left his old motor bike on the quayside before embarking on the ship. The police at Southampton had got in touch with Bath, asking what was to be done with the bike, as it had apparently been abandoned. I explained everything to the policeman. He asked if it would be all right if the Southampton police were to sell the bike and give the proceeds to one of their charities, and I readily agreed. And that was that. I returned home for a late tea and carefully explained to my mother what Dana had done, and tried to excuse the thoughtlessness that had caused her such a shock. 'I thought he had come to take you away, Jim,' she said, breaking into tears. Then we both had a good cry together, and felt a lot better after a good strong cup of tea.

*   *   *

About fifteen years later I saw Dana again. It was when I was living in New York, in Greenwich Village, in 1974, after completing a semester of 'creative writing workshops' at Ohio University, where I had been very happy.

I found a directory of poets in a famous West Side bookstore, the Gotham Book Mart, and idly turned the pages of American names. Suddenly one name seemed to leap off the page from among the hundreds of unknowns – it was Dana's, and it was followed by his address and telephone number.

So he was now living in Washington, DC! The entry specified that he had Spanish as a foreign language, which made me smile, for his Spanish had never been more than rudimentary, though of course it might have improved since he was in Salamanca. He had vaguely mentioned that he was hoping to join the Peace Corps.

I knew Washington quite well, having visited it two or three times while I was at Amherst in 1969. I had been intending to return there to visit again the marvellous art galleries, in particular to see the Whistlers and the oriental art in the Freer Gallery. So I got on the Greyhound Bus for a six-hour ride to Washington and checked in at a cheap hotel opposite the bus depot. It was quite a respectable place, occupied mainly by blacks, and transients, and there was the unmistakable sweet smell of marijuana in the elevator. I looked up Dana's name in the telephone book, and, with wildly beating heart called the number. Almost immediately a woman's rather rough voice answered, and I said: 'Could I speak to Dana, please?' She put down the receiver and roared 'Dana!' I had the impression that she was shouting upstairs, and I seemed to hear footsteps tripping lightly down to the phone. Then was his voice, saying: 'Yes, hello? Who's this?' I could not answer. I put down the receiver, overcome by emotion at hearing that voice again, unchanged. But I felt I could not possibly meet him again.

The next day, after visiting the Freer, I went to inspect the brand-new modern art museum, the Hirshhorn Museum and Sculpture Garden. As I entered, I saw an unmistakable figure in front of me – Dana. He had his back to me, and he had grown a beard, but his hair was still thick and blond. He was with a group of friends whom he had apparently met in the gallery, and they were all standing around him admiringly, talking and laughing in that exaggeratedly animated way only Americans have, reacting and demanding reactions. One of Dana's reactions was very characteristic: he bent double with laughter at something he had said that made all the others laugh, too. He was wearing a dark suit. I was more casually dressed in corduroys and a black leather jacket. I did not want him to see me.

I managed to pass behind some tall screens on which those ridiculously huge contemporary paintings, works of the utmost nullity, were hung, and crept cautiously round a group of cranky statues. I looked carefully about me, hiding behind one of those contorted shapes, and glimpsed Dana in the distance, walking away from the group of friends and joining a young woman, tall, pale, dark, distinguished-looking – could it be that dancer of his? They walked slowly along one wall, laughing and talking and only incidentally looking at the eccentric pictures. They disappeared from sight, and I was about to advance into another part of the gallery from behind some screens when I stopped dead: Dana was there, alone, right in front of me. He looked at me as if he could not believe his eyes, and a faint, doubtful smile began to move his lips. I just stared back at him as if I did not recognize him, then moved away out of sight behind another screen. When I emerged on the other side, our little game of hide-and-seek was over: he had vanished, taking the girl with him. I got the impression that he was frightened, as if he had seen a ghost. The next day I took the first bus back to New York. But ever since then I have often wondered why he was in Washington. Was he, as I originally suspected in Salamanca, an FBI agent or working for the CIA? It was a mystery I had no longer any wish to clear up.

*   *   *

About ten years later, in 1980 I think, I revisited Salamanca, on my way back from Lisbon. I stayed at the Gran Hotel on the Plaza del Poeta Iglesias, more mortuary than El Escorial. What bothered me most after my long absence were the forests of TV aerials on even the humblest dwellings. The shallow, red-tile roofs of the Plaza Mayor, once so touching in their simple irregularities, now glitter with armies of metal rods, antennae. Trying to take pictures of the buildings without those intrusive TV aerials is almost impossible. And surely the Plaza was not the crowded car-park it is now? Perhaps it was just the effect of the tourist season, but Spain seemed very much more prosperous, and the construction companies and property developers had their giant cranes everywhere, their crude colours looming garishly over the old amber-rose stone of the city's most ancient monuments. People seem better dressed, and there are more cars in the streets, and fewer beggars and blind men selling lottery tickets. There are huge new blocks of flats, some of them with swimming-pools. The young people now seem much freer, and there are young girls drinking with their boy-friends in the bars of the Plaza Mayor.

I went to the university on the Plaza de Anaya and climbed the familiar stairway in the Palacio de Anaya. The bust of Unamuno is still there, and again it looks as if someone has attempted to defile it, perhaps in some would-be funny student jape. I stood in that upper gallery where I first saw Dana and he cast that look upon me which was to make me his slave. The beautiful old university buildings are un-changed – the Fray Luis de Leon lecture hall, with that scholar's statue outside, the ancient library, the delicately carved plateresque façades.

Next I went to the Clerecia, where I had been sitting with Dana watching that wall-clock's gilt pendulum busily wagging away on the wall in front of the great baroque gilt altar. The clock had been removed for repairs and only a small hook remained in the wall. I prayed a little and wept for my dear father, and for myself, my unhappy passion. I visited the Casa de las Conchas where that lonely schoolboy, so many centuries ago, had inscribed his sad and bitter thoughts. They are still there.

At the Hospedaje Lisboa where Dana stayed – 'Camas, Comidas' – I looked up at his window as I had so often done on those lonely days and nights he spent away from me. At night, sometimes the window was lighted, sometimes it was dark – either eventuality filled me with foreboding and sorrow. Then I ascended the narrow stairs to his doorway. There was a notice on the entrance: *No hay habitaciones. Gracias por su visita.* Down the twisting stone stairs again and out through the front door opposite the barber-shop where the barbers used to look so longingly at our flowing locks – later on, the regulation hair-style for most young men.

Summoning up all my courage, I entered San Esteban and its overpowering gilded Churriguera altar seemed to welcome me like a long-lost friend as I dipped my hand in the holy-water stoup at the door and knelt to pray in front of Claudio Coello's heavenly blue painting. The place where we had entered the crypt below the altar had been bricked up. I prayed for forgiveness. Again the tears flowed unchecked, and I was sobbing loudly in the empty church.

At San Martin the wall to the gallery had also been bricked in. Once we had sat together in that 'condemned' gallery until evening, and the sacristan, not knowing we were there, had nearly locked us in for the night. I prayed for us both before the altar, then lit two fat little night-light candles, one for Dana, one for myself, the larger one for him. As I prayed for the peace of our souls and for forgiveness for both of us, I was startled to see the wick on his candle fall over and almost go out, while mine remained upright and brightly shining. It was the sort of omen, one of the signatures of destiny, for which we were always watching. All my anger and envy and resentment were gone. It only remained for us to forgive one another, and for my part I gladly forgave him for anything that might still need forgiveness. It was a pilgrimage I had had to make, and I was glad I had made it.

I made no pilgrimage to Valladolid, where it had all begun.

But whenever I am in the United States, or near an American Center in Kyoto, Paris or Seoul, I always look at the Washington, DC telephone directory and seek out Dana's name, address and number. I gaze at the entry for a long time, torn between a longing to hear his voice again and the terror of becoming in thrall to even his disembodied form. But in my heart of hearts I know I cannot telephone him. My deep love for him still remains. But I cannot abandon my identity now as I did so freely in those days of my youth.

Yet I still dream about him, and write poems about him like the one that follows.

Photo Robot – Identikit Portrait

It was over thirty years ago. But
let me try again to get it right.

His face, front or profile,
how was it then – how exactly
was the hair? Am I making it
too thick, too wavy, too blond?

The nose, I'm almost certain, was –
No. Was it not rather more
flat, almost broken, a boxer's?
How sharp? The tip slightly tilted?

Was the mouth so full, that warm
memory of smiles and kisses, rough –
the tongue, rich hive of words,
the teeth even, white, rather small?

I'm sure the eyes were deep blue.
Or were they rather lighter, almost
grey, changing with his moods?
Were they so wide-spaced, in brows

so smooth, pale brown, and level
as the way he looked at me – that look
I now can barely remember, though
it has left its mark on me.

His body perfect, peach-sunned.
Its gold has rubbed off on me a little.
I loved it. Yet more than all
it was that face, that look I loved

and now lie long nights awake
trying vainly to recapture.

AFTERWORD

As for Dana, ever since we parted in Bath, over thirty years ago, there has not been one day in which I have not thought of him, sometimes in anger, sometimes in horror, but more often with love and forgiveness.

When I look back on my life, I am amazed at its variety and its endless changes. My multiple personality has now become more stable, and I am no longer so subject to sudden switches of mood and identity. Despite all the follies and foolishness of my youth, there is nothing I regret. As Edith Piaf sings: 'Je ne regrette rien. . . .' The same may be said of my middle age and now of my old age. I can now see it all in proper perspective, as I could never see it before. That is one of the great advantages of growing old. The past seems like a wonderful dream of trial and error, of risks and rashnesses, of madness and ecstasy. The one thing I am proud of is my writing, in particular my poetry, some of which I believe will endure. It is a comfort to know, as one approaches death, that one is leaving something permanent behind for others to remember one by.

But the dominant feeling in my old age is one of joyous release from the vagaries of passion, longing, love and lust:

> . . . he with new acquist
> Of true experience from this great event
> With peace and consolation hath dismiss'd,
> And calm of mind all passion spent.

Yet as I write those immortal words, I am reminded of a certain meaning in 'spent' and 'to spend' – its sexual connotation of reaching a climax. I am still in a state of perpetual climax, spending and spending, though rarely getting in the sense of Wordsworth's 'Getting and spending, we lay waste our powers. . . .' And never with any sense of waste, either. I still feel I am inexhaustible, in body, mind and spirit. But I'm glad that the past is past. I would not change the present for anything.

EPILOGUE

'To Someone Somewhere in the World'

This title is the dedication I gave to my novel, *The Love of Others* (1964), which I wrote during my first year in Sendai, Japan. It was a sort of desperate final cry for 'someone to watch over me'. Of course my father and mother had done the best they could with me, in their limited way. But they never tried to encourage me in any artistic activity, and indeed looked upon my writing of poetry with the Geordie's typical amused condescension. The only time I ever heard them spring to my defence was when the Duchess of Gloucester refused to 'receive' me when she congratulated the cast of my play *Upon This Rock* in Peterborough Cathedral, a comic incident described in *I, of All People*. My mother's indignant reaction to this 'insult' to the working classes, which I did not perceive as such, was: 'Who does *she* think she is – Lady Muck?' My father preserved as usual a grim silence in the face of another of my misadventures, but I could not help laughing at the seriousness with which my mother took this contretemps, which cast no honour on the House of Gloucester.

Many years later, my mother had occasion to make a prophetic remark when she happened to see Mrs Mary Whitehouse spouting her rubbish on the TV screen in our local pub in Bath. My mother sometimes came out with the most surprising statements: 'Mary! the same name as me! But I don't fancy those cold little lizard eyes behind her tarty harlequin specs. And that coarse tone of voice. . . . She's up to no good. And she's no lady.' It was as if my mother were warning me: she was Scots-Irish, with the second sight common on both sides of our family. My mother, usually so mild and gentle, could be savage when she took a dislike to someone. Now when someone writes that Mrs W 'is really a nice person', I remember my mother's judgement.

Another member of our family with the 'gift', my father's cousin, was an expert reader of fortunes in teacups, and I have always remembered her telling me what she had 'seen' in my cup on my twelfth birthday: 'There's a guardian angel watching over you – I can see him as plain as anything. . . .' I know now that she was right, because whenever someone hurts, or tries to hurt me, he or she without my wishing, intending or expecting it eventually suffers for it, even to the point of death. These frequent coincidences in my life I have ironically attributed to the 'evil eye', which I do not possess, but which I have encountered several times in my travels. I wrote a poem on the subject (about my first fatal meeting with Dana in Salamanca) in my collection *The Prodigal Son*. I have a peculiar sense of humour; but then, who doesn't?

I believe in my guardian angel. But I cannot believe in God, who has made such a mess of his Creation, like an incompetent father. He's a fairy-tale without the magic and without the charm. Rather, I put my trust in the gods. I prefer to believe in my guardian angel, and as I also believe in UFOs I feel sure he is truly a person from outer space. I have a very deep religious sense, and I think that is what upsets people. It is also a deeply personal religious sense, one which I cannot share with others except through my writing. All religions interest me – Christian, Jewish, Muslim, Buddhist, Hindu – but my interest is literary and historical. Some Christians have told me I cannot write poems and plays on religious themes if I am not a practising Christian, but that is nonsense. I have no wish to participate in Christian worship. From what I have seen of Christians, all I can say is: 'Save me from heaven!'

Clairvoyance has always been prominent in our family, ever since the days of the 'Barone' Seymour Kirkup, one of the Pisan Circle, friend of Keats, Shelley, Trelawney and, later, Swinburne. So I feel sure all these predictions are reliable, and that my guardian angel will always take care of me – and of my enemies. But I always wanted someone, man or woman or transsexual, of earthly flesh and blood to 'watch over me', a soul-sister or soul-brother. (One of the terrible disadvantages of being an only child is that one cannot have that longed-for elder brother.) That soul-companion did not enter my life until I went to Japan. But that's another country, and another story.